Playing with Math

Stories from Math Circles, Homeschoolers, and Passionate Teachers

Edited by
Sue VanHattum

Delta Stream Media,
an Imprint of Natural Math

This book is dedicated to
Seymour Papert,
author of *Mindstorms*,
creator of the Logo programming language for kids,
and advocate for environments where students can
take charge of their own learning.

Illustrations
Cover: Ever Salazar
Interior: Dahlia Evans, Gail Vinnacombe, Linda Palter,
Maurine Starkey, and Ray Droujkov

Editing
Sue VanHattum, Carol Cross, and Chris Evans

Page Design & Layout
Denise Gaskins
Howie Severson/Fortuitous

Publisher
Delta Stream Media, an imprint of Natural Math, 309 Silvercliff, Cary, NC 27513

Library of Congress Control Number: 2014954318
ISBN: 978-0-9776939-3-1

Contents

Homeschoolers: Doing Math

Passionate Teachers: Transforming Classroom Math

Community: Sharing Math

Conclusion   323

Resources

Preface

I love teaching math, yet throughout my twenty-some years of teaching I've struggled with the fact that what I *want* to teach is problem solving but what I *do* teach most of the time is how to follow recipes (here's how you find the slope or the vertex, here's how you factor, and so on). Until recently, I never felt that I had made much progress in resolving this dilemma. In early 2008, I started reading Living Math Forum, an email group where participants discuss how to help their children learn math. In the years since that discovery, my life has been full of math-play adventures. I'm still learning how to bring that spirit into my students' lives.

Living Math Forum has over five thousand members and generates about ten messages a day. The host of the group, Julie Brennan, has managed to create a community where people passionately discuss math and how to learn it, with mutual respect. Most of the list participants are homeschooling moms, but there are also a number of professional teachers like me. The vast ideological differences among group members don't interfere with some of the best discussions I've seen online about education issues.

That group pointed me to all sorts of online resources and to some marvelous books. I heard about *Out of the Labyrinth: Setting Mathematics Free*, by Robert and Ellen Kaplan, bought it online, and skimmed it within a day of its arrival in my mailbox. I immediately looked up the Kaplans online and registered for their first Math Circle Institute, held in July 2008. I have never learned so much math in one week, and what I learned there about teaching is taking years to incorporate into my practice.

While at the Institute, I met the inimitable Amanda Serenevy, who runs the Riverbend Community Math Center in South Bend, Indiana. One of my central concerns is social justice. I want to help change our culture, in which most children face schooling that does not encourage them to learn deeply, and in which people of color are so underrepresented among mathematicians. Amanda knows something important about solving these puzzles.

Many of the kids who participate in her math center come through the South Bend Boys and Girls Club, which is the main organization doing aftercare for public school students there. The kids from her center who joined us at the institute were mostly children of color. Amanda has helped them fall in love with math. Some day I hope to create something similar here in Richmond, California.

Meanwhile, back at the Living Math email group, I was starting to notice some intriguing posts by Maria Droujkova. When she started her Family Multiplication project in the fall of 2008, I eagerly joined in. Maria uses the web like it's her home, with a clearer vision of its potential than anyone else I've met. She's dedicated to using the web to promote a love of math in kids everywhere.

I also "met" Pam Sorooshian online and was impressed with what she had to say. She's an unschooler who loves math and hates what coercion does to people's capacity for joy in their learning. Unschoolers feel that we can depend on kids' natural desire to learn, and that the best way to keep their passion burning is to simply provide adventures and resources, letting the kids make their own decisions. Kids pour themselves into learning to walk and talk. If their parents are readers, curious about the world around them, and able to provide some resources for their kids, the learning will happen, on the child's own natural schedule. They don't need any push; they just need to be let loose and nurtured. I love that kind of radical respect for kids and for learning.

In my mind, these projects all had some common threads: playing with math, and learning it outside the constraints of the traditional classroom. But I was, and am, teaching in traditional classroom settings, and I wanted to find ways to use these insights in my work. That led me to one more exciting discovery online—the math teacher "blogosphere." I follow about two hundred math teacher blogs, and I write at my blog, Math Mama Writes.* The ideas I'm seeing and thinking about are helping me to transform my teaching.

I love the wisdom Julie, Maria, and Pam are offering up online, and I didn't want it to get lost in the hugeness of the internet; I wanted it all together, in a nice solid book I could read over and over. The only way that book was going to become a reality was if I put it together myself. So I did.

As a mathematician who loves teaching, a teacher who loves seeing people learn on their own, and a connoisseur of fine writing, being able to bring together these pieces has been an exciting and fulfilling journey for me.

---

* MathMamaWrites.blogspot.com

Now you have the book in front of you. We've all enjoyed writing it; we hope you'll enjoy reading it and using the ideas we've brought together. I have big hopes: that the homeschoolers among you will be reassured that you *can* be your child's math mentor, that the schoolteachers among you will see what you can do to teach math more deeply, that the parents among you will begin to play with math more often with your kids, and that you will all be activists in encouraging schools to become more playful.

And now, let the math play begin!

Sue VanHattum
Richmond, California

Introduction

Do You Like Math?

Some of you are nodding. You love math like the authors in this book do, and you were excited to see a book that comes at the ideas of math from a new direction.

But many of you don't like math. You almost didn't pick this book up, and you're not so comfortable reading it. But you'd like to change that. Or there are kids in your life and you'd like to help nurture their love of math, or help them rediscover an enthusiasm for it.

Maybe you're in between, and you'd like to have more fun with math. Perhaps you know a math enthusiast and you're curious about it.

Welcome to the party everyone! Whatever your starting point, I think you'll enjoy this. *Playing with Math* is nothing like a math textbook. It's a book about how people who love math are sharing that love with others. It's written in the hope that you'll use your favorite ideas from this book and create your own ways to get together and play with math. There is some math tucked in between the stories, of course, but you can sneak right by it the first time through, if you really want to.

What do mathematicians do? We play with math. What are little kids doing, when they're thinking about numbers, shapes, and patterns? They're playing with math. You may not believe it yet, but you can have fun playing with math, too.

Can you remember back to when you were very young, before you started school? Most kids that young love to count and they love big numbers—it's all a game. Some of them retain that love, but most lose it by the time they hit middle school. If you were convinced by sufficiently unpleasant experiences in school to believe that math was simply horrid,[*] it might be hard later to remember that delight, because the memory would clash with your belief. Our brains use stories to organize

> *"If you're not comfortable with math, try starting with the homeschooling section. A few of those chapters were written by self-proclaimed math haters, and all of them are especially accessible."*

---

[*] John Kellermeier, at Tacoma Community College, calls those unhappy experiences math abuse. See *TacomaCC.edu/home/jkellermeier/Papers/RiskableClassroom/mathabuse.htm*

what they keep, and a memory that clashes with the organizing stories won't have a place to fit in.

I loved math until college, but then I hit classes that were too hard and just didn't make enough sense to me. I got my degree, but lost my passion. For years, I thought I didn't like math that much. Luckily, I stumbled on some great teachers in my master's program and regained my love of math. My narrow escape allowed me to empathize with my students who hate and fear math. More than any other subject, math has to be approached by each student at their own pace, and in their own way, for it to make sense.

If you're not comfortable with math, try starting with the homeschooling section. A few of those chapters were written by self-proclaimed math haters, and all of them are especially accessible. If you're feeling more comfortable, you can read the chapters in any order you want. I put them in the order that made the most sense to me, but each reader will see the connections differently.

What Is Math?

Most people think math is adding, subtracting, multiplying, and dividing; knowing your times tables; knowing how to divide fractions; knowing how to follow the rules to find the answer. These bits are a tiny corner of the world of math. Math is seeing patterns, solving puzzles, using logic, finding ways to connect disparate ideas, and so much more. People who do math play with infinity, shapes, map coloring, tiling, and probability; they analyze how things change over time, or how one particular change will affect a whole system. Math is about concepts, connections, patterns. It can be a game, a language, an art form. Everything is connected, often in surprising and beautiful ways. The stories in this book are full of examples that show math from these angles.

"Math is seeing patterns, solving puzzles, using logic, finding ways to connect disparate ideas, and so much more."

And yet, the stories our culture tells about what math is may make you think "that's not math" when you see those examples. This sort of "cultural story" can be thought of as myth. A myth is a story that holds a lot of cultural weight, and that most people believe. Although myths may not be literally true, they often hold some deep truth—which is where they get their power. Math *is* hard, for instance. But it's hard like mountain climbing, with deep joy to be gained by the struggle.

The myths about math can lead you in some troublesome directions— thinking you don't have a "math mind" perhaps (it's much more about practice and persistence), or that mathematicians solve math problems quickly (they don't), or that men are better at math than women (social forces produce most, perhaps all, of the differences we see; check out the chapter on supporting girls in the resource section).

If you haven't enjoyed math, remember that you probably carry baggage from your schooling, where the teacher was spread too thin—with too many subjects to teach, to too many kids. What got in the way of that teacher helping you learn math with joy? Well, if we taught kids how to ride bikes with "objectives" for each age, and graded their progress, we might have lots of bike-phobic kids on our hands. And if you consider the fear most elementary teachers have of math,[*] it's easy to see how hard it would be for kids to make it through school with their love of number intact.

Math has lots of applications to the "real world," but this book isn't about that; it's about how glorious and delightful mathematical thinking can be—for anyone. Like dancing, swimming, or knowing the stories behind art and music, math is part of the richness of being human.

What about Memorizing?

Addressing the debate over whether kids should memorize their times tables, Maria Droujkova[†] says, "To memorize anything, you must love it first." If the teacher can find a way to help the student love it, then it will become no harder than learning to talk. (Think about all those thousands of words every one of us has memorized.) How can we help a child who's struggling with those tables to find more love for them? Waldorf schools have students draw and color in a beautiful star in a circle, in which the patterns of the multiples of a number become more visible.[‡] A similar technique is used in Vedic math. (You can read more about Vedic math in Tiffani Bearup's chapter about how the math haters came around.)

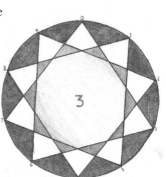

Before the multiplication facts come the addition facts, another memory task that can be kept pleasant (even exciting) through a focus on pattern. Many kids enjoy doubling. My son, DJ, who's not the huge math fan that I am, really enjoyed it. Here's a conversation we had when he was seven:

---

[*] There are many dedicated elementary teachers who would tell you themselves that math is their weak point. My intention is not to blame the teachers, but to point out systemic issues. One solution might be to have math specialists, like we do for music and art.

[†] See Maria's chapter, Rejoicing in Confusion, in the math circle section.

[‡] *DavidVanCouvering.blogspot.com/2007/12/now-that-is-way-to-learn-math.html*

DJ: Mom, what's 13 and 13?

MOM: 26.

DJ: How about 26 and 26?

MOM: Well, 25 is like a quarter, and 2 quarters are 50 cents, so 26 and 26 is...

DJ: 52. 52 and 52 is 104. 104 and 104 is ... 208. 208 and 208 is ... 316...

MOM: What's 200 and 200?

DJ: 400. Oh, so 208 and 208 is 416. What's 416 and 416?

MOM: 832.

Memorizing made painless, right? Another pleasant way to practice the addition facts is through dice games like Shut the Box and Yahtzee. Kids enjoy making up their own games, too, and will play games for hours that look boring to an adult. One day DJ made a racetrack for the numbers one to six, with ten spots for each number to race through. Then he rolled a die over and over, to watch the numbers race each other.

I have a terrible memory, and chose math over science so I wouldn't have to memorize long lists of bones, muscles, organs, chemicals, etc. My bad memory never slowed me down in math at all, because for me, everything was connected. If I wasn't remembering 7×8, I could do 7×7 and add one more 7, 49 plus 7 is 56. Got it. If I didn't remember the quadratic formula, I could derive it. I always hope that my bad memory confessions will get my students to re-think how to approach math.

Doing the Math...

A real math problem is something you don't know how to solve when you start, and that takes time. Only the practice exercises we do to internalize facts and procedures are quick. Real problems require lots of work, sleeping on it, going away from the problem to return later, discussion, doodling, and eventually writing out the steps in an organized way so you can find the holes in your reasoning.

Andrew Wiles spent seven years working on solving Fermat's Last Theorem. When he presented his solution to other mathematicians at an important conference after six years of work, he suddenly realized there was a gap in his reasoning. After another year, he managed to get it right.

There is a math problem I worked on for years, though not as diligently as Andrew Wiles. I first heard of this problem when I was a teenager, and finally solved it just a few years ago. I saw the solution once before I solved it, so I wasn't even doing it on my own, let alone creating new mathematics. But it's still been a satisfying experience to finally understand how all the pieces fit together, after years of thought.

Here's the problem:

> Draw a circle, put two dots (or points) on it, and connect them with a straight line. You've split the circle into two regions. Add a third point, and connect all the points. Now there are four regions. How many regions will there be for n points?*

You can read this book without doing any math yourself, but you'll know we've reached you when you decide to start trying the puzzles that looked crazy hard at first. And we've really succeeded if one of the problems in this book keeps you up at night or keeps you thinking for years on end.

If you're working at math, you'll make mistakes (just like Andrew Wiles did). Let go of the baggage you may have about that. Musicians make mistakes, even in performance, and learn how to flow past their mistakes so gracefully that only the most astute listeners notice. It's similar in almost any profession. We need to be willing to make mistakes in order to learn. So celebrate the hard work you're doing learning something new, and give yourself a break when you make mistakes. Notice what you did right.

We had a spirited debate about whether to provide answers to the puzzles and problems offered here. Some people said they wouldn't be able to use the problems with their students if they couldn't check the answers. Others wanted to give readers plenty of thinking time before making answers available. Our compromise: hints are available in the back of the book, and full solutions are available online (at *PlayingWithMath. org/solutions*). If you'd like, you can download and print them to keep with the book. If you can stand the suspense, we advise against looking up answers. The learning comes from the struggle.

---

* Hints for this and every puzzle in the book are located in back. Full answers are available at *PlayingWithMath.org/solutions*.

Our Stories

As you read this book, each author will tell their own story—each will share different facets of what math is and how it's learned. You'll develop a richer understanding of the breadth and depth of mathematics, while you read about how people are sharing their love of math with students.

Some of my favorite ideas:

- Math problems should be presented as "accessible mysteries." (Bob & Ellen Kaplan)

- It's important to provide kids with a "math-rich environment." (Maria Droujkova)

- "Living math," approaching math through stories and history, is a powerful way to make math come alive. (Julie Brennan)

I met almost all of these authors through the Internet, and many of the chapters will point you to online resources—to learn more about their projects, to play with math yourself, and to find community online. If you have questions, or you want to talk about what you've read here, join the conversations at *PlayingWithMath.org*.

Changes in education cannot come from above. We've tried that for the past decade, first with No Child Left Behind, and then with Race To the Top (which adds fuel to the fire of high-stakes testing), and we've seen that over-testing and under-funding don't work. Changes in math education must come from all of us—from every parent, child, and teacher trying to make sense of it all. As Alice Walker, June Jordan, President Obama, and the Hopi elders have said, "We are the ones we've been waiting for."

Math Circles and More: Celebrating Math

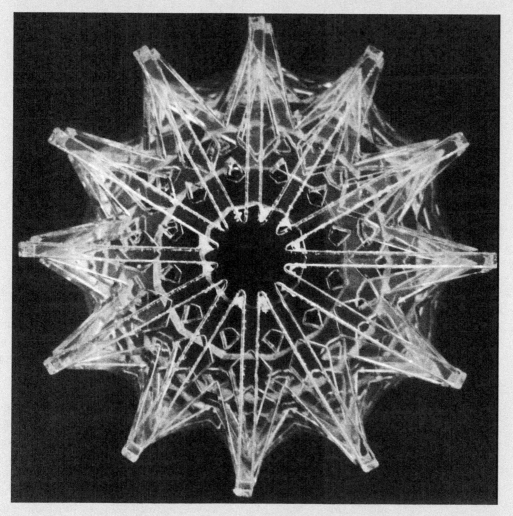

Stars of the Mind's Sky, by Paul Salomon

Art by Paul Salomon. Paul writes: "One of the ways I explore the world of mathematics is by creating art that showcases its beauty. This image was created as part of a study I call 'Stars of the Mind's Sky.' I used a computer-controlled laser-cutter to create all of the six possible 12-pointed stars from plastic, which I stacked and photographed to create this image." You can see more at LostInRecursion.wordpress.com /art/stars-of-the-minds-sky.

An amazing mathematical community has formed online among all sorts of math-loving people, many of whom have their work in *Playing with Math*. This artwork demonstrates how densely woven that community is. Paul's current work—starting Art of Math STL to share beautiful, playful, and creative mathematics with the children of Saint Louis—puts him squarely in the math circle crowd. But he's also a former teacher, and coauthors Math Munch, a weekly math blog written with middle-schoolers in mind. In his online wanderings he met up with Malke Rosenfeld, whose two chapters are in the homeschooler and teacher sections. Paul sent Malke a set of plastic stars, which she shared with her daughter. They played with them, drew new stars, and headed off on a mathematical journey all their own. This sort of cross-fertilization happens all the time.

Introduction

Twenty years ago, who could have imagined all the ways people today would be getting together to play with math? Math circles look much like classrooms at first glance, but the people up front are not teaching—at least it's not like the math teaching we're used to. They're doing something more like guiding a group on an adventure. Math festivals and math museums are full of people milling around, checking out the different offerings. Math centers and clubs take many forms, and are not just about tutoring. Sometimes there are toys, games, or puzzles involved. Other times it may look like a math test is going on, and yet the participants' body language and facial expressions show their eagerness to struggle through these tough problems and solve them.

Math Circles

Math circles are groups of people working on math problems together. The leaders do not "cover material," instead they offer up an intriguing mystery, record the participants' ideas, and give subtle nudges when needed. These leaders and students come together voluntarily to share their love of math. There are no exams or grades, no impositions from outside. The leaders are usually mathematicians: people who can see how one problem is connected to another, and how both are connected to powerful underlying mathematical structure.

There is a long history of math circles in Eastern Europe, and emigrants have been a driving force in the spread of math circles around the world.* Maria Droujkova and Julia Brodsky moved to the U.S. from Ukraine and Russia, respectively; their chapters describe the math circles they run for young children.

Math circles started out in the U.S. as two different things: some were mainly a way for talented young people to prepare for math competitions (see Mary O'Keeffe's chapter), and others were created as non-competitive communities bringing people together with challenging and enticing

---

* Read more about the history of math circles at MathCircles.org/content/history-american-math-circles-experience and TheMathCircle.org/history.

mathematics. The latter include a broader audience, both younger children and students who are intrigued by math but not quite so dedicated as those who compete. Steve Kennedy's chapter describes one of these. These two types have cross-fertilized each other, and now the line separating them is not so clear.

The Mathematical Sciences Research Institute (MSRI) sponsors many of the math circles in the Bay Area, along with conferences on math and math education. Until a few years ago, the only math circles in the Bay Area were the Berkeley and San Jose math circles, which were both geared toward students who would be competing in national math contests. Now there are math circles at multiple locations across the Bay Area, most of them focusing on a broader audience of students—the only requirement being interest. The two original math circles have also expanded to support a broader variety of students, both younger and less competitive students. The MSRI has supported this expansion and shift with funding, staffing, publicity, and the yearly Circle on the Road conference, where math circle leaders come together to exchange ideas, train new people to lead math circles, and inspire new communities to support mathematical engagement.[*]

The most exciting component of the MSRI's projects, for me, is their circles for teachers.[†] Math circles will never reach the majority of young people, but if they bring a new culture of mathematical exploration to teachers, the teachers can then bring it to the kids in their classes. Teacher math circles are a form of independent professional development, bringing in teachers who are eager to move themselves to a new level. So far, most teacher math circles have focused on middle and high school teachers. I'd like to see math circles form for elementary teachers, also.

And More

The ways people can get together and play with math go far beyond math circles. Many people run math clubs that have some of the features of a math circle but often cater to younger children and involve more hands-on activities. The audience for math clubs is often more diverse, with parents hoping to help their kids enjoy math, even when they themselves don't.

Some math centers just provide tutoring and homework help, but others are places where kids, and perhaps adults, get a chance to actually

---

[*] Much of the information about MSRI and other Bay Area math circle history comes from an interview with Brandy Wiegers.

[†] MSRI has worked together with American Institute of Mathematics (AIM) in creating and supporting the teacher math circles.

play with math. Colleen King and Amanda Serenevy both run innovative math centers; their chapters will give you a peek into two quite different ways this can take shape.

Math festivals are one-time or annual events that bring crowds of people together to do mathematics in a celebratory atmosphere. Nancy Blachman's chapter on the Julia Robinson Math Festival will give you a snapshot of one way that's done. Here's another, completely different: Paul Giganti runs the California Mathematics Council's Mathematics Festivals in school gymnasiums and cafeterias all over California. These festivals allow the hundreds of students in a school to play with math problem-solving activities for a day, and then draw in their whole families for more math play that evening. Imagine a few dozen long tables set up with math puzzles and math experiments. Imagine fifty to a hundred families excitedly trying out the offerings. If you live in California, you can work with your PTA to bring his festival to your school.*

The Math Midway (part of the Museum of Mathematics,† which opened in New York City at the end of 2012) is a traveling museum exhibit that is full of hands-on math experiences, like a bike with square wheels and the special surface it rides smoothly on.

Math trails are a way to get outside in the community, and notice mathematical relationships.‡ The leader makes a map of the route, and provides questions that can be answered by observing your surroundings.

The stories I've gathered together in this section barely scratch the surface. You can find more math circles, possibly one in your area, by checking online at *MathCircles.org*. (If there isn't one in your area, you might consider starting your own.) The other ways people can get together and play with math go far beyond the examples given in these stories. Once you start exploring math, the ways you can discover to do it in community are endless.

The people who create and lead these activities love math in a way most people don't. But the participants are mostly kids who just want to play, along with their parents and teachers, who want to move their families and students beyond the fear of math so common in our culture. Each math group is different, and each author tells a unique story. Join us as we celebrate mathematics.

---

* *cmc-math.org/activities/math_festival.htm*

† *MoMath.org*

‡ The website *PlayingWithMath.org* has links to all of these, and more.

I met Julia at a math circle conference in early 2009. I loved her presentation and invited her to contribute to the book I was just imagining at that point. —SV

The Art of Inquiry: A Very Young Math Circle

by Julia Brodsky

Why I Did It

I have three very inquisitive young kids. Before my daughter started school, she loved our discussions about math, science, and literature. When she started kindergarten, she went to a first grade class for reading and a second grade class for math. I don't know what caused the trouble, whether it was her teenage friends from our neighborhood, her second grade math classmates, her unusual schedule, or sitting still too much in school. One day I asked her what she had learned in school, and she told me that they were learning about circles. When I started to tell her about Mobius strips, she replied, "Mom, I don't need that, it's not going to be on the test."

I was stunned. She'd always been so eager to learn new things. I suddenly realized how much she was losing her enthusiasm at school. This called for immediate action. I started to look for classes that develop and sustain children's interest in thinking, especially in math and science. I made an extensive search for classes for elementary age children that teach any kind of out-of-the-box thinking, and found nothing useful. There are tons of "skill and drill" classes around, but none of them focus on developing inquiry skills and the joy of invention and discovery.

As I looked for a solution, I thought of my own childhood in Russia. My love of math actually came about quite accidentally. When I was a young child, math was never a big thing in my life. I enjoyed sports, poetry, and outdoor trips with my parents. Both of my parents were in science and engineering; when we hiked with them and their friends, my brother and I would often overhear funny math puzzles or profound scientific discussions. We would also ask all kinds of children's questions like "Why is the sky blue?" and get quite extended responses.

Later, in the seventh grade, my friend and I discovered Kvant,[*] a math journal for children, and spent some time solving math problems from it. What else can you do when it is raining for the third week in a row, and everything else is *so* boring? It was an accident that we found entrance exam problems for the math correspondence school in the first issue of the journal—but we solved them, and sent them to Moscow University, just for the fun of it. It did not take us that much time, not more than a couple of rainy evenings. We were accepted and spent the rest of the school year solving problems that arrived regularly by mail. No time pressure, no grades. Our parents had no idea, either—what a joy! Next year we were accepted into a magnet math school, and math eventually led me to my future career as an aerospace engineer, international space station crews' instructor, and, yes, math circle leader.

Getting Started

I would never have thought that I'd start a math circle, but no one else was offering what I wanted for my daughter. I decided to do it very differently from the school setting. My daughter is a social creature, so we invited some of her friends to join us. Our friends' daughter Daniela, a bright middle-schooler, offered to help. Instead of going into the standard math curriculum, I remembered some quiet evenings I spent with my brother reading the wonderful book by B. Kordemsky called *Math Intuition.*[†] I decided that solving intriguing math puzzles would be the best way to introduce problem-solving skills to the kids.

"I wanted them to make mistakes and enjoy it— the enjoyment is missing in our public education, but it is an important component in getting to love the process of thinking."

I wanted to provide the kids with an environment where they could play with a problem without the pressure to get a specific result by a specific time. I wanted them to make mistakes and enjoy it—the enjoyment is missing in our public education, but it is an important component in getting to love the process of thinking. I put a special emphasis on the problems that require students to distinguish between what is relevant and what is not—an important skill in both academics and daily life. In each class, I try to introduce a balanced set of problems that require the kids to analyze each problem from different angles, use multiple skills, and exercise logic and critical thinking. My other thought was that non-standard problems teach the kids to explore and adapt to new situations.

While I was planning, I was lucky to find an inspirational book by A.K. Zvonkin, a professor of mathematics in Moscow, about teaching

---

[*] Kvant is the Russian word for quantum.
[†] Available in English as *Moscow Puzzles*.

math to pre-schoolers.* One of the strategies I borrowed from the book is "never give kids a solution—wait until they figure it out themselves." For this approach to be successful, the problems need to be finely tailored to the kids' abilities and knowledge base—which is quite an art in itself. It is very difficult to find good non-standard math problems for kids this age, since they have very primitive math skills. Frequently, I modify Math Olympiad problems borrowed from the books for older kids. I also come up with some problems of my own.

Many of the parents who learned about our class wanted something for their older children, so I started another group for eight- to nine-year-olds. A wonderful high school student, Marina, volunteered to help me with that group. While my youngest group is mostly Russian-speaking children, my older group is much more diverse. Besides Russian kids, I have Asian, European, and some others. It seems that the only ones we do not have are Americans—with the exception of a few homeschoolers. I wonder if I just have skewed statistics, or if other cultures put more emphasis on logic and critical thinking skills for their kids than U.S. culture does.

I decided to call our math circle the Art of Inquiry because the art of asking questions is central to problem solving. Unfortunately, in school kids do not have much chance to ask questions. Teachers, too, are forced to cover the curriculum and do not have much chance to ask questions either. The art of asking questions: What are we looking for? Can I do it this way? What if …? Are there other ways? This is the only way I know of to analyze a problem and to reflect on the solution. It is said, "The right question is half of the answer."

"The art of asking questions is central to problem solving."

We started in October, to give the kids some time to settle their school schedules. I also made sure that they'd have enough time to eat and rest after school. I had developed a lesson plan for the first several sessions, so I knew what my objectives were and where we were heading. I was not sure what to expect from the kids at first, so I made a point of observing and writing down their reactions.

Peeking In

Soon, our sessions settled into a format that I am still using in my current math circles. Classes meet weekly for an hour. We start with a warm-up, a fun and unusual problem that is not very difficult, to help the kids concentrate and tune-in for the class. Warm-ups are followed by a few harder problems. Problems are presented in written format,

* *Math from Three to Seven*, now translated into English.

with pictures if possible. Kids are provided with various manipulatives (checkers, blocks, clay, toothpicks, mirrors, etc.), as needed. I take notes on students' approaches, frustrations, and mistakes; later I analyze those notes while preparing for the next class. We end the class with a game, like Blokus or Equate.

At first kids were very shy. They were waiting for the "right and only" answer, just as in school. I was pleased when they started coming up with all types of wrong answers. We never criticized them. Instead we invited them to "plug in" their solution, which often leads to very humorous results. In one logic problem, the students needed to sort kids versus their pets. There were different types of pets—dogs, birds and fish—and the information given concerned their legs. One boy, very eager to be first to answer, ended up with a four-legged fish. His friend immediately rushed to the board to draw this four-legged monster.*

Over time, kids have learned to enjoy both the process of problem solving and the value of their mistakes. While looking for the solutions, they joke and make fun of themselves and their solutions, and seem to be very relaxed. As they start enjoying themselves, they begin to associate those positive feelings with math. I'm often amused now to overhear conversations on math outside the class, on the playground, or during a birthday party.

While I am not concerned about covering specific math topics, I try to offer problems that require an array of problem-solving approaches, such as working backwards, generalization, approximation, elimination, making hypotheses, and so on. Kids enjoy open-ended problems with multiple solutions, and they equally enjoy problems with no solutions at all. Amazingly, kids of this age do very well with logic problems. I also noticed that the girls, in general, were more adept with number patterns, while the boys excelled at 3D geometry.

One of my objectives was to teach the kids to identify an ill-defined problem and turn it into a "good" problem. The first problem I gave them was: "Two kittens together weigh less than their cat mom. Do three kittens weigh more than their mom?" This problem caused a lot of discussion. Some kids said more, some said less. When one boy said they were equal, the kids realized that something was wrong, but they

---

* Here's the problem: Jenny, Benny, Kenny and Lenny are siblings, and each has a pet. Among them they have a dog, a cat, a fish, and a bird. We know that Jenny's pet has yellow feathers; Kenny dislikes furry animals; Lenny's pet climbs the trees well; and Benny's pet has four legs. Which child has what pet?

were not sure what. I asked them whether the kittens were well fed or not. Eventually, our discussion of all types of cats and kittens led us to conclude that some problems are ill-defined and cannot be solved the way they are stated. We also analyzed what basic information was missing from the problem statement. Finally, we wrapped it up by asking for all the ill-defined problems they could come up with, which was hilarious.

My Observations

Another strategy I borrowed from Zvonkin's book was to record my observations after the class. Here are a few of them:

Six-year-olds seem to have problems with mirror symmetry—we spent quite some time in front of the big mirror, raising hands, writing letters, and yes, making faces. It is interesting to note that this age group was pretty comfortable with rotational symmetry, but was easily confused with line symmetry. When I asked them to pretend that one of them was a mirror and to "reflect" the raised hand of the "object," most of them would raise the wrong hand. I observed the same problem while giving them the "mirror images" and asking them to reproduce the original. My older group seemed to have little difficulty with that.

Here is an example of a puzzle we did for mirror symmetry:

What shape comes next?

Kids spent a lot of time analyzing the pattern and arguing with each other, trying to persuade others of the rightness of their solution. The situation resolved when one of them put a pencil at the center of each shape and saw the reflection feature.*

Kids easily catch on to ideas. After solving a problem of building four triangles with six matchsticks, they now always remember to check for three-dimensional solutions. For example, that really helped them when solving the problem of connecting three castles with three guard

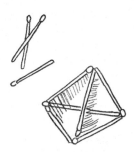

---

* If you don't see what the next shape would be, cover the left half of each shape with your finger, and draw each right half on a piece of paper.

huts by paths.* If you can use bridges, tunnels and other three-dimensional paths, then all the guards can visit all the castles, but no paths cross.

While introducing problems to the kids, I always try to give them some historic background. Kids are excited to learn that some of these problems were invented a thousand years ago, and many wise people have tried to solve them. It brings both excitement and a feeling of connection between them and "real" mathematicians. There are many math history books for kids to get you started.[†]

Out-of-the-box thinking is a great way to improve creative reasoning skills, so I always try to introduce problems that require an insightful solution. While I do not know how to systematically teach students to solve these problems, my observations show that if kids expect an insightful solution, they are much more likely to find one. It is amazing to observe that young kids tend to favor problems they do not know how to approach. They readily spend time exploring, and share their solutions with friends and parents. Insight problems also motivate kids to look for insightful ways of solving regular problems, approaching them from different angles, and recognizing and avoiding clichés.

My observations show that by middle or high school, kids partially lose the innate ability to solve non-standard problems that they have in childhood, when every problem comes across as non-standard. Hence, I believe it is very important to start early and continue solving complex multi-steps problems on a regular basis. Compared to older students, when the young kids are presented with non-standard problems and puzzles, they are very enthusiastic and have fewer mental blocks, which makes it exciting to work with them. Solving tough problems together creates a special atmosphere of friendship and support, which continues outside the classroom. Non-standard problems teach the kids to adapt to new situations and to explore on their own. And working as a team teaches kids to respect others' opinions and to reflect on their own solutions, which are great skills in themselves.

---

* Neither of these problems can be solved in two dimensions. The second is a variation on the classic three utilities puzzle: *MathForum.org/dr.math/faq/faq.3utilities.html*

† Editor's note: My son and I like *From Zero to Ten: The Story of Numbers*, by Vivian French and Ross Collins.

The Big Picture

My work has taught me the value of a systems approach. This is another thing I am trying to teach kids—seeing the big picture, finding the interconnections of the solutions, and making transitions among the topics. I show them how to use algorithms, decision trees, and diagrams—the tools of system analysis—to help them learn to see the big picture.

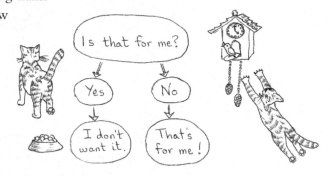

Both my helpers and I have noticed tremendous leaps made by the students over the year. Besides making great friends, they also feel very confident about their problem-solving abilities. They do not feel intimidated by a difficult problem, and they do not see themselves as dumb if they cannot solve it right away. They've tasted the joy of solving a complex problem, and now know that making mistakes is the "right and only" way to go. They may not have the subject mastery yet—but they've gotten some exposure to problem-solving approaches, and they've learned a great deal about themselves along the way.

As for my daughter and me, she is enjoying thinking once again, and I've learned something new about myself. I found out that conducting a math circle is a very fulfilling activity. It's exciting to observe and guide all this creative energy, all this amazing intellectual turbulence generated by kids. It pushes me to learn more, to research more, to think more, too. And I will tell you a secret—that's an effective anti-aging solution.

PUZZLE
Imbalance Abundance

by Paul Salomon

My fifth graders have been writing problems this week. Mostly things like "5 branches have 40 leaves, and 10 trees have 200 branches. How many leaves will 320 trees have?" Some of them have been writing problems with symbols that amount to systems of linear equations, and earlier this year we worked on balance problems to get at that sort of thing. On Thursday, while all this was going on, inspiration struck. What if the scales don't balance? What if one side weighs more? Behold, my imbalance puzzles below.

Friday was our last day before spring break, and I worked on them with every one of my classes. They liked the puzzles, but the examples I had were a bit too easy, so our real goal was creating good imbalance puzzles of our own, which is *way* harder than solving them. My students had the best ideas for tweaking the puzzles and making new ones. The last puzzle below comes from my student, Felix! It was cool for them to realize you couldn't draw just any picture, because sometimes they were impossible, and other times they didn't give enough information.

I've been working the last two days on my own puzzles, and I've never had a better time working with inequalities in my life. They have a sneaky way of revealing information that I'm really liking. The inequality $2x < y + z$ tells you some interesting stuff, for example. (Can you see why x cannot be the biggest number?) After you've solved the puzzles here, I hope you'll try making your own. If you do, let me know in the comments at *LostInRecursion.wordpress.com/resources/imbalance-problems*.

Here are twelve of our imbalance puzzles. You can assume the fulcrum is at the center, and if the shape is the same, the weight is the same.

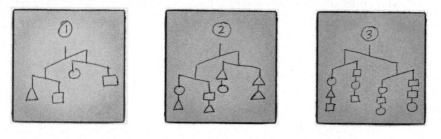

We're going to solve number one together to get you started. In the left scale we see the square side is lower, so square is heavier than triangle. Similarly, the right side of the picture tells us square is heavier than circle. Putting these together we can say that square is the heaviest, but who's heavier between triangle and circle? Looking at the large scale holding the two smaller ones we see that square and triangle together are heavier than square and circle. The squares' weight is equal on both sides, so the difference in weight must be due to the other shapes, and we can conclude that triangle is heavier than circle.

Finally we can summarize: circle < triangle < square.

Now it's your turn!

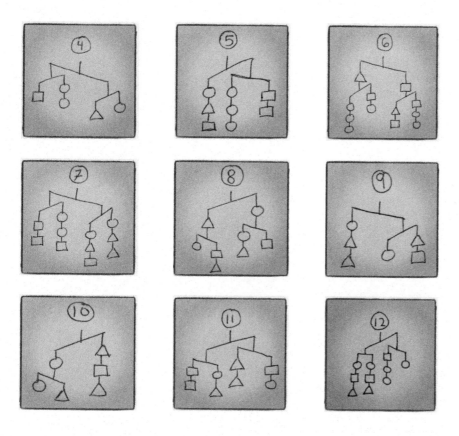

Number twelve is a bonus problem from my student, Felix Yancey. You'll like the surprise twist.

More imbalance puzzles and variations can be found at *LostInRecursion. wordpress.com/resources/imbalance-problems*.

Maria runs many math clubs in the Cary, North Carolina area. In each of the two math clubs described below, about ten seven- to nine-year-olds met each Thursday for six weeks to explore infinity. This started out as a report to the Natural Math email group; all of the club parents took turns writing a summary of each week's activities. —SV

Rejoicing in Confusion: One Day At the Math Club

by Maria Droujkova

The 1:00 Club

We took some time for a team building activity with LEGO bricks. I asked kids to model multiplication using my big box of bricks, and off they went!

A few kids built something symmetric to show multiplication by two; others arranged the bricks in rectangles where multiplication was represented by the rows and columns of little bumps on the bricks. One made a staircase with each level a multiple of the first: doubling, tripling and so on; others used sets of people or horses to count body parts (so 5×4 is shown by the twenty total legs on five horses).

I asked, "How many multiplications are there?" Their answer was, "Just one, the operation of multiplication; however, there are infinitely many multiplication examples." I am happy to see such careful language in kids: attention to word details, even minute ones, is a strong mathematical value! I am adding this to the Parent Bingo.[*]

We worked through a referential paradox next, role-playing it with two characters who each might lie or tell the truth. The kids picked G.W. for George Washington, for obvious reasons, and also chose Jarl, after one child's character from World of Warcraft.

G.W. said, "Jarl lied!" and Jarl said, "G.W. told the truth!" Which one told the truth, and which one lied?

---

[*] Parent Bingo is a way to help parents at the clubs observe mathematical behaviors in the kids; details follow this chapter.

This is a classic math enrichment activity, with many versions you can find online under "liar paradox." It's quite fun. The point I wanted to make with this activity is that infinity is paradoxical: it is "the last number" and at the same time, as one of the kids said, "You can always add one to it." I am not sure if they were able to relate this particular example to infinity, but they definitely understood that infinity is paradoxical.

We had a discussion at the end of the club on how we are all confused now, but pleasantly so, and how important it is to rejoice in confusion and to be comfortable with it. Adults often strive very hard to get rid of any and all possible traces of confusion for kids, making things dreadfully boring. That prevents kids from developing problem-solving skills, and other tools for mathematical decision-making. Dealing with chaos and ambiguity is an integral part of the Do-It-Yourself (or DIY) approach* to all areas of life, mathematics included!

We also progressed to the next stage in the Hotel Infinity story.† Last week, we ended with a cliffhanger, when infinitely many aliens had arrived at the door from Hotel Infinity Two, in the next galaxy over. What to do? This week, the owner's clever solution was revealed: he picked up his intercom and told everybody to move to the room with double their current room's number. So One moved to room 2, Two to room 4, Three to room 6, and so on. Every odd numbered room was empty, and there were infinitely many of them to accommodate infinitely many guests.

So is the number of aliens still the same? How about the number of rooms? Opinions vary, and kids are very aware by now that it's a paradox rather than something you can answer one way or the other. To resolve this paradox, we will have to move from the arithmetic idea of "equality" (the same number) to the set theory idea of "one-to-one correspondence," which is quite suitable for working with infinities. For example, there is one-to-one correspondence between all counting numbers (one, two, three...) and all even numbers, (two, four, six,...). And you can easily draw the

---

* Making up a math example is the DIY attitude on a small scale. Anyone can be a "maker": Write your own math poem, create your own math puzzle, draw your own repeating pattern.
† David Hilbert was the original creator of this story, but many people have retold it with their own details, including me. Ivar Ekeland's illustrated *The Cat in Numberland* is a very accessible version. The story goes that the numbers One, Two, Three ... live in a big hotel (infinitely big) called the Hotel Infinity. If a new number comes, can the numbers all move to different rooms to make a room available for the new number?

correspondence on paper if you write both sequences side to side, which we did during the club, or you can get it from the Hotel Infinity story.

We did another fun activity where several kids laid down head-to-foot to form a line. If we kept doing this, would we get an infinite line? Something interesting happened: in both clubs, kids answered, "Yes, the line will circle the Earth and meet itself and this ring will be infinite, because there is no end." The idea of a cycle (in this case, walking around a circle over and over) as an example of infinity is powerful with children. Apparently the image of the Earth being round goes with this infinity representation in their cosmologies. We will need to devote at least one club meeting to cycles.

Then I asked, "What if kids could go on and on like this in a *straight* line? Would the length of that line be infinite?" The question led to a nice discussion about running out of kids, running out of space in the Galaxy, and then distinguishing what exists in math and in our abstract imagination from what exists in the physical realm. This discussion has to happen again and again around every calculus idea!*

The 3:30 Club

We talked about a picture Macie brought for us, with a fraction chart with even denominators, and did Apple Math† instead of the multiplication modeling activity. Fractions with even denominators went so well with this next step in the Hotel Infinity story! Numbers and their doubles provide another example of a set with one-to-one correspondence to the counting numbers. Our example space is increasing.

For our Apple Math, this time I asked, "What is the maximum number of pieces you can make with one cut and a given number of starting pieces?" After a good number of tasty examples and discussions, the conclusion was that you can make four pieces out of two, six pieces out of three, eight pieces out of four, and in general, double the number of original pieces.

---

* For example, we can't take limits by hand, as Zeno explained so well, since each action takes time, but we can imagine their results.

† Apple Math is a snack time where we play with food. I invite kids to measure around fruits and veggies, predict how many pieces will result from cutting, and solve little puzzles about the curves and shapes of their edible, healthy manipulatives.

Generalizing patterns like this is extremely valuable mathematically. As Alan Kay has said, "similarities over differences" is a cultural non-universal, a rare and precious accomplishment of advanced cultures.[*]

Instead of the Liar Paradox role-play that we did in the morning, we did the Achilles and Turtle role-play, with a swift character chasing a slow character around a squarish spiral with each side half as long as the previous. Would the chase ever end, theoretically? What if we did not pause between each episode? Again, this is a classic activity with decent online descriptions.[†] However, most math enrichment lessons do not go into helping kids resolve the paradox (Achilles easily catching the Turtle in real life, but taking infinite time in the story), and this is where we are going with the clubs.

After doing the "infinite line of kids" activity, I asked the question, "Do infinitely *many* pieces always make an infinitely *long* line?" Everybody but Jasmine said, "Yes!" and we did a paper cutting activity next. Cut a strip of paper in two and lay down one piece. Cut the remainder in two and lay down that piece next. Cut the remainder in two again. We can imagine doing this indefinitely. Now put all the pieces back together again! They add up to the old, finite strip of paper. After yet another all-important discussion of distinguishing the physical paper from our mathematical ideals, kids could see how adding infinitely many pieces can result in a finite length. That was a big surprise! I will definitely do more of this in both clubs, with paper folding and cutting. The idea of a finite limit of an infinite sum is extremely powerful. It resolves several infinity paradoxes and provides important metaphors for understanding the world.

Both groups disengaged after the resolution of the Hotel Infinity's current episode, which was a big mathematical idea. The 3:30 group disengaged after the "infinite sum can be finite" revelation. Big math revelations and "ah-ha" moments require a lot of processing. Children intuitively switch to running around, playing non-math games, or otherwise distracting themselves. It is a very healthy reaction, helping memory and understanding. We should celebrate and support it.

---

[*] Alan Kay pointed out that all human cultures have some things in common (his "universals"), which include using language, telling stories, play, and noticing differences (over similarities). These things are easier to learn than the non-universals, which include reading and writing, abstract deductive mathematics, democracy, and noticing similarities over differences, or generalizing. See *LearningEvolves.wikispaces.com/nonUniversals*.

[†] See Zeno's Paradoxes on Wikipedia.

Snapshots

Here are three final scenes from the clubs I want to share with you:

I bring out a colorful blanket on which we sit for our storytelling session. The kids focus their attention on the blanket and play with it for ten full minutes, with such a strong flow I don't interfere.

Layla is taking a picture of the projector's lens, point blank. We chat about the wonderful self-reference of this scene. The refraction in the lenses causes the projector's light to split into rainbow stripes. Everyone is mesmerized by the resulting photos.

Macie is explaining that, since Darleen made a special nets picture last time, she decided to bring a chart of her own this time. Erin is referring to Darleen's work in her infinity examples. Everybody is more interested, because the works are connected to one another, and the connections enhance our topic. My math community dream come true!

GAME
Parent Bingo*

by Maria Droujkova

PARENT BINGO: Mark the square when you notice a kid ...				
A	B	C	D	E
1 Experiment with **examples** to find out if an idea is right	Find a **loophole** in questions, problems, or statements	Significantly change their **math behavior** when in a group	**Explain** an idea to someone, correctly or not	Notice and share mathematical **beauty**
2 Drop whatever they are doing and get totally distracted after a big **AHA! moment**	**Get lost** in weird places when **switching** from objects to pictures, or from pictures to symbols	**Bravely interact** with software or manipulatives, having no clue about the purpose	Answer questions in **math actions** or gestures, rather than words	Come up with **original ways** of doing math, right or wrong
3 **Question** whether **something believable** is in fact right	Participate in math-rich **dialogues**	**Evaluate** a task: "I like this problem" or "That's a lot of computations!"	**Anticipate** results before the work is all done	Find the **same idea** in two or more **different contexts**
4 "**Just play**" with new objects before paying any attention to suggested activities	Notice and **celebrate successes** in math, big or small: jump, high-five a friend, scream "YES!," or say "it was OK"	Switch **between representations**—words, gestures, objects, graphs, symbols, objects, and so on	Get fascinated by ideas **far above** their heads, or amused by ideas **far below**	Create a little **ritual**, repeating a phrase, a song, or a gesture in the same situation
5 Persevere, concentrate, and cope when the going is **tough**	Ask "**What if?...**"— however fanciful	Notice a **mistake** and try to fix it	Notice a **pattern** or any general rule, however strange and silly	Put a **wrong idea** to good use

---

* For more information, see: *NaturalMath.wikispaces.com/bingo*

This can be used during a math club or other open math activity that involves lots of kids. You may wish to observe your child. If you do, here are some cool things to look for. One objective of Parent Bingo is to let go of judgment and just notice, like with meditation.

Parents and Kids Together: Learning in Community

by Sue VanHattum

Classrooms

I've taught math for over twenty years, and have always been frustrated by the constraints of classroom teaching. I've been teaching my community college students a lot of "how to"—how to solve equations, how to factor, how to graph—and I've had very little opportunity to help them learn to think mathematically on their own. My goal is to get them solving real problems* with just a bit of guidance from me. But when I've tried that in the past, I've sometimes failed dramatically.

Students are so used to math classes being about learning to follow a set of steps that they're likely to rebel when a teacher changes that script. I had never seen a classroom that operated the way I wanted mine to, and so had no new "script" in mind to help me mentor my students. In the past five years the homeschoolers and teachers I've met online, along with the math circles I've participated in and led, have all given me new ways to look at math class, so I can help my students gradually move toward more independent thinking. They've also shown me some wonderful ways to learn math outside the constraints of a classroom.† Much of what I've learned is easier to apply in situations where the students come eagerly to play with math, but five years later I have finally completed the circle, and brought my new knowledge back into my classrooms.

---

* Exercises help you practice something you've learned how to do. Real problems have no obvious solution method. They require exploration.
† Each of the chapters in this book tells part of that story.

This all came about when I got the chance to teach at my son's freeschool, Wildcat.* I would be teaching kids who were mostly eight- to ten-years old. I could set up my small classes however I wanted. As I started researching all the ways people teach in small groups, including homeschoolers and math circles, I discovered a wealth of exciting ideas and learned a lot more than how to teach at Wildcat.

Discoveries

As a single parent, it's hard to get out of the house once I'm home from work, so of course I did my research online. I quickly stumbled upon Living Math Forum, a Yahoo group with thousands of members discussing homeschooling math. Along with the other riches I discovered there, I heard about the book *Out of the Labyrinth: Setting Mathematics Free*, by Robert and Ellen Kaplan. I ordered it immediately. When it came, I couldn't put it down—their vision of helping students create their own learning in math circles was utterly captivating. I attended their first Summer Institute, and loved every minute of it. The Institute was so refreshing, both intellectually and physically (with our long walks and the amazing pool), that another mom and I dubbed it the Math Spa. We talked math from early morning until bedtime, energized by the camaraderie. There were no tests, no grades, no obligations. We came because we wanted to learn about math circles, and we got math circles—from morning to night.

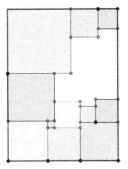

On the first day, we struggled with trying to find a way to fill a rectangle with squares, no two the same size. I felt sure it couldn't be done, and wasn't very interested in proving that, so I didn't engage much. A bunch of my new friends kept working on it all day, in between other activities. I did join them later in the day, to help out by drawing adjustable rectangles on my computer using Geometer's Sketchpad. This allowed us to visualize the possible combinations of sizes more easily. I was still convinced it couldn't be done, and was impressed with their persistence. My jaw dropped the next morning when the group that had kept working on it came up front and showed the solution they'd found. We struggled with similarly intriguing problems all week, loving the intellectual struggle the way rock climbers love the physical struggle of their climbs.

---

* Freeschools often have no required classtime. At Wildcat, the kids had lots of freedom to play, and attended classes in reading and math for less than two hours a day. The school also provided special classes at the kids' request.

We also each ran one session of a math circle for the kids who had volunteered a bit of their summer afternoon free time to come do math with us. I wasn't satisfied with what I did—the tasks I chose turned out to be way too hard for the kids to dig into. I left the Institute feeling both more excited than ever about the possibilities and just as far as ever from being ready to run my own math circle.

I knew I wanted to start something, though, and took my inspiration from Amanda Serenevy's Riverbend Community Math Center. The Center's kids volunteered for our Summer Institute circles. The kids hung out with us beforehand, in a big room with lots of math books, toys, and puzzles from Amanda's collection. The kids worked intently with Polydrons, origami projects, and puzzles on the whiteboard. This intense free play with math was what I wanted to support back at home. It seemed much easier to provide a space for math play than to lead math circles, since standing in front of a group brought out all my teacherly instincts, which I was trying to get away from. I thought maybe I could pull something like this off on a smaller scale in my home, and so began the Richmond Math Salon.

"This intense free play with math was what I wanted to support back at home."

My First Salon

I decided to start with puzzles and games. That would give me time to get to know the people who showed up. I knew I could introduce math circle-style problems later, when I felt ready. I put notices up on a number of email lists: for local homeschoolers, my neighborhood, and Wildcat. I also told my college students about it. Altogether, twenty-eight people were planning to come. I was excited to bring together so many people, but concerned about whether my tiny house would hold them all. I was relieved when only seventeen actually showed up.[*]

I asked people to bring snacks, and mentioned my trampoline—it would provide a good break from thinking hard to play hard. I moved the furniture around to create lots of spaces for two or three people to work together. And I went out and bought some of my favorite games—Mastermind, Battleships,[†] Quoridor, and Quixo—along with tangrams and origami paper. I already had Set, Blink, and Quarto.

---

[*] In later months, this unpredictability sometimes caused problems.
[†] I wish there were a similar game—with the grid and finding your opponent—but without the military theme. How about hide and seek, with crouching kids as the game pieces? How would *you* design a non-military Battleships alternative?

Photo by Kathy Kramer.

On the day of the salon, people arrived gradually, and my house filled up with kids, parents, and other adults, all playing with mathy games. It was very satisfying to see such enthusiasm for math, since I usually work with students who are in my class because it's a requirement.

Crossing the River

I was eager to come up with topics for the next few months. There was a broad range of ages, abilities, and interests, so I needed topics that could be approached from different levels.

A few months after we began, in my first attempt at getting all the participants working on a problem together, I used a problem called Crossing the River. It starts with a story that gently leads people into problem-solving and thinking algebraically—first they find a solution for a small number, then they generalize, finding a solution pattern that will work for any number.

I didn't want to start the group activity until everyone had arrived, so I found this simpler problem for people to play with until we were all together.

Crossing the River #1

A farmer is traveling with a chicken, grain, and a fox. She has to cross a river and can only take one across at a time. If she leaves the fox and chicken together, the fox will eat the chicken. If she leaves the chicken and grain together, the chicken will eat the grain. Can she get them all to the other side?

After everyone had settled in, I asked people to work in four groups. Each group had just kids or just adults. They used toy dinosaurs to help them solve this problem:

Crossing the River #2

Imagine:
A group of five adult dinosaurs and two young dinosaurs need to cross a river. A small boat that can hold either one adult or two youngsters is available. (If more get in, it will sink. If the boat is sent across the river empty, it will float away.) Everyone can row the boat. Can the whole group get across? If so, how many trips

---

are necessary to get everyone across the river? (Count a trip as just going from one side to the other.)

Harder:
What if there were still two young dinosaurs, but they were with a hundred adults? [Hint: Try groups that have two youngsters and one, two, three or more adults. Can you see a pattern?]

What if there were still two young dinosaurs, but they were with n adults?

Play with it:
What if there were more youngsters?
Can you modify the problem in other ways?

I didn't intend for the groups to split by gender, but they did. There was a girls' group and a boys' group, a women's group and a mostly men's group with one woman in it. The boys' group struggled with this problem and answered the first question. The girls' group preferred to invent ways to get across creatively, felling trees over the river and providing other adventurous non-mathematical solutions. The men's group solved the problem completely, finding the number of trips needed for n adults. The women's group started out talking about how intimidating it was, and we had a great discussion about how their previous experiences had made them uncomfortable with this sort of thinking. We eventually got back to the problem, and they answered the first question. Although the event was a success overall, it was a bit too intimidating for many of the participants. I knew I needed to start simpler, so participants could feel safer and revel in the joys of exploration.

Each month since then, I've tried new activities, puzzles, and problems, all exploring the terrain of math as a fun family endeavor. Most months, kids play with whatever games and puzzles they want, and parents play with their kids. Every once in a while, I've tried math circle formats again. One month we played with base three. There was a sign on my front door...

The people of Triplay have three fingers on each hand, and are usually holding onto a baby with one hand (making that hand unavailable for counting purposes). So their number system developed using three as its base. The kids really enjoyed inventing the money for Triplay—pennies, trickles, trimes,.... I'm used to being the one to pose problems, so it was delightful to see two of the adults solving problems I hadn't asked about, as they tried to figure out how to go from base ten to base three and back.

Each time that I've led the whole group through a topic, I have still found myself leading more than my mentors—Amanda Serenevy and the Kaplans—do. But I started to feel like I could do this, given a good starting point. I still have trouble finding good math circle topics,* and don't feel like there's any guarantee the next topic I try won't flop. And sometimes I can't resist the urge to tell people when they're on the right track. Or my body language will betray my concern when I think they're headed up a dead end. But that happens less and less.

What I'm learning at my math salon, besides how to run a math circle, is something about how to get families thinking about math together. I'm looking for topics that have even more going for them than being "accessible mysteries." I also want the topics to intrigue thinkers from age seven to seventy. The adults come to bring their kids, but I want to pull the parents in too, by providing a math-rich environment that gets everyone playing. If you'd like to see a few scenes from the math salon, Jeremy Stuart and Roy Robles produced a short segment on it for their film on homeschooling, Class Dismissed. You can watch it at my blog, Math Mama Writes.†

Families and Math

My math salon is pretty much parents and kids, and the parents come not because they want to do math but because they want their kids to. They are hoping to find a way to make math palatable.

*A spoonful of sugar helps the medicine go down,
in a most delightful way.*
—Mary Poppins‡

You can think of puzzles and games as the sugar that helps the medicine go down, and you're at least a bit healthier in your approach to math. But even better than sugar and nasty medicine is food that's delicious

---

* Math circle leaders generally agree that finding good problems is the hardest part of making a math circle work.

† *MathMamaWrites.blogspot.com/2010/08/richmond-math-salon-sweet-sampling_08.html*

‡ *Mary Poppins*, by Pamela Travers, was made into a Disney movie. This line was written by Roger Sherman for the movie.

enough to take away our craving for sugar and nutritious enough to take away any need for medicine. In the same way, good problems can help us fall in love with math and make a delicious meal of it, sinking our teeth into tough problems, tenderized by their intrigue.

Long ago, children used to see all the adults in a community working, so their play was typically in imitation of the work they saw around them. Play is a powerful way to learn, provided through the eons of evolution.* In the past century or two our work has become less visible to the children. They still see adults reading, so it's something they want to emulate—given enough time, most kids will learn to read without any prodding. Math, on the other hand, is not a leisure activity for many adults, and its use in work is invisible to kids. That creates a huge roadblock to the natural way of learning through imitative play.

Not only is math invisible to most young children, they also often get a sense that it's not valuable. Many parents will say, "I'm no good at math." If parents acknowledge being bad at math, their children don't feel math is necessary in the adult world. Kids are more likely to care about learning things they know their parents (or peers) value. For parents who've avoided math all their life, it's a hard thing to change. My goal is to give parents both the motivation and the resources to make that change.

I've come to realize that anything I do in our three hours a month together at the math salon is tiny compared to what parents can do every day, working with their own children who they know so well. So I want to do anything I can to help the parents change their *own* relationships to math.

Most people like games, so that's an easy place to begin. At first the games can be the sweetness that helps the math medicine go down. Over time perhaps you can find the sweetness in the math itself—in a problem that inspires you to work and struggle, until you finally get it, just for your own satisfaction.

A Parent Transformed

When I think about how parents can change to help kids, it takes me back to Wildcat, to a story about Sarah, another parent there. While I taught math to the older kids, Sarah was teaching the younger ones. But

"I've come to realize that anything I do in our three hours a month together at the math salon is tiny compared to what parents can do every day, working with their own children who they know so well."

---

* It's fascinating to think of this in relation to wolves and how they learn through play. But Peter Gray argues in his book, *Free to Learn: Why Unleashing the Instinct to Play Will Make Our Children Happier, More Self-Reliant, and Better Students for Life*, that our play is so much more complex that it's what makes us human.

before she could even imagine teaching math, the school's free-flowing community had to take her on a little journey.

Sarah's math story starts like that of many parents. She wasn't interested in math, and didn't see herself as good at it. But while she was hanging out at the school, and loving up the kids there, she started helping Tina. Tina was supposed to come to math class with me, but she really hated math. She'd had a bad experience with it at her previous school, and now avoided math class whenever she could. Sarah had a way of connecting with the kids—she'd sit in the middle of the chaos, reading to a couple of kids, and would quietly help other kids work out their conflicts, or offer small suggestions that helped kids in big ways. She reeled Tina in, and eventually Tina was hanging out with her, doing math problems joyfully. Sarah was so happy to have helped Tina that she began to think more about math herself, and to look for cool problems.

The next year she began teaching math classes for the younger kids, doing a great job at it. Her limited depth in math was no problem for this level. She enjoyed playing with the most basic ideas, and had a great rapport with the little ones. She's been transformed by her experiences there, and her youngest two will probably take to math much more easily than her older kids.

This sort of transformation is what I'm hoping for with the parents who come to my salon. I'm hoping their love and concern for their children will help them overcome a lifetime of bad math experiences. I'm hoping they'll become children again themselves and create a new relationship for themselves with math.

Completing the Circle

Always on the lookout for accessible problems, I recently discovered a great problem related to the game of Spot It. Spot It is a game of quick observation, with no obvious math connections. There are fifty-five cards in the deck, with eight pictures on each one. Everyone is looking for a match between their card and the card in the center—and there is always exactly one match. The first one to call out their match takes the card off the center pile. Whoever ends up with the most cards wins. My son loves this game (partly because he beats me at it). For a year—every time I played it—I kept asking myself, "How did they do that? How did they make sure that every single card matches every other card in just one picture?"

One day my friend Chris and I decided to try to figure it out. We made progress together, and then I worked on it diligently for the next few weeks, until I understood it fully. It doesn't look like a math problem. To really understand it requires no higher-level mathematics, not even algebra. And yet it has a deep mathematical structure. I've run a number of math circles using it, and am looking forward to posing this question to the families who come to math salon.

Teaching at Wildcat got me started on this journey. I hope I helped a few kids find a bit more joy in math. We made our own Set cards, figured out lengths, areas, and volumes, played a wide variety of math games, and did some Singapore lessons. I also got them making their own simple programs in Scratch.* My favorite time with the kids was reading them math stories and playing chess with them. (It made my day each time one of the kids was able to beat me at chess.) What I did there never felt very significant to me—perhaps because I wasn't nearly as skilled with a group of kids as I am with my adult classes.

Back at the college, I'm finally finding ways to incorporate what I've learned from math circles into my classrooms. Taking a cue from Bob Kaplan's list of ways to become invisible,† I'm finally able to hold back my enthusiastic explanations a bit more, so the students can explain to each other. I've also managed to move away from the textbook in my classes. More and more often, I bring them problems like Fawn Nguyen's Area of a Circle.‡ Getting students to think more—after they've experienced so many years of just learning to follow the steps—is an ongoing project. I'm bringing in better activities for it, and I'm conducting this orchestra of learning better too. My desire to help students learn to think mathematically is gradually coming to fruition.

---

* Available for free at: *scratch.mit.edu*
† Read How to Become Invisible in the Community section.
‡ Read about Fawn's adventures in her chapter in the Passionate Teachers section.

Here is a meadow.
In this meadow some foxes and rabbits are hiding.
Each has very good eyes, and can see all the others.
Each fox can see twice as many rabbits as foxes. (Yum!)
Each rabbit can see an equal number of foxes and rabbits. (Yikes!)
How many are in the meadow?

---

* I made my own version of the puzzle I saw at *Math-Frolic.blogspot.com/2011/07/friday-puzzle-on-farm.html*. My cousin said, "This is a word problem. Word problems give me head-aches." If you feel that way, skip this one. Or, instead of trying to solve it, draw your own picture for it. (Maybe that will make it more fun, and you'll solve it by accident!)

Rodi is the best observer of math circles I know, perhaps because of her mindfulness practice. Those observational skills, along with the historical vignettes she shares with her students, enrich her circles and her writing. She runs math circles in Philadelphia and blogs at TalkingStickLearningCenter.org. —SV

On Noticing and Fairness: A Mindful Math Circle

by Rodi Steinig

Ogres, Noticing, and Voting

We began today's math circle, the first of six sessions, sitting in an "ogre." Not a circle, not an oval, but an ogre, the kids' way of precisely describing the shape we made. Once situated, we played a version of the shell game using three origami shapes: a blue triangle, a pink square, and a yellow pentagon. This game helps develop mindfulness—the longer attention span and eye for detail needed for extended mathematical inquiry. The kids closed their eyes while I rearranged the shapes; then I asked what had changed. They noticed changes in position and, eventually, orientation. We then moved to our task at hand: to create a scenario that would involve land plots and voting so that we could explore the topic of our course—Maps, Voting, and Counting.*

I told the story of Zooman, who collected animals and asked his neighbors to vote on a new animal to add to his zoo. The children greatly improved the story, thereby making the problem their own. The problem was this: how to set up a fair voting system, and then how to count the votes fairly. Lily wondered aloud whether this was a math problem with only one answer. She posited that I knew this answer and was coaching her to figure it out. "We don't know whether there is a single answer to our problem," I replied, hoping to keep all control in the hands of the kids.

We discussed that in some places and times only certain classes of people, such as whites, males, and landowners, were allowed to vote,

---

* Many thanks to Amanda Sereveny for providing me with some of the mathematical background for the voting activity.

an idea that shocked most of the participants. "That's like saying that you can't vote if you're wearing a purple jacket!" Arthur said. Lily added, "It's not fair to people who live in hotels!" I told them about the Marquis de Condorcet and Madame Sophie de Condorcet, figures from the French Revolution. He was a mathematician who worked on fairness criteria in voting and was also a feminist. Sophie was a highly-educated woman who stood up to Napoleon on behalf of a woman's right to an education. Only Shane had heard of Napoleon. He informed the group, "Napoleon thought he owned the world."

Then the group came up with its animal voting plan for Zooman's neighbors: all the neighbors would secretly write on slips of paper which animal they preferred, and then on a board a check would go under each animal's name for each vote. The plan was to count the checks. Whichever animal had the most votes would win. Since the group, not the individual participants, came up with this one plan together, I could tell that the group was already moving nicely into a practice of collective inquiry. One child had come into the class saying, "I am the best at math here because I know my times tables up to twelve," but that kind of competitiveness, that so often mars math classrooms for students, was totally absent once we got to work.

I reported to the group that Zooman's neighbors had used this exact system, with the following results: six votes for the tamandua (anteater), five votes for the clouded leopard, and four votes for the emperor tamarin (monkey).* There was excitement that the tamandua won. But then I broke the news that all of those who voted for the leopard or the tamarin were totally opposed to the tamandua because of the possibility of unpleasant odors. The excitement immediately evaporated. Shane suggested combining the votes of the defeated animals. Lily reported that nine were against the tamandua. Arthur called out, "Then the leopard should win!" Most cheered this suggestion until Candy wondered whether the tamandua's supporters might actually prefer the tamarin over the leopard, which would generate ten votes combined. (Sighs.)

Candy and Savannah pointed out that this occurred because "we only counted the likes, not the dislikes." Excitement filled the room as students suggested several alternative voting methods. I listed these on the board, and our group voted on which voting method should be used to be fair. (Ironic, isn't it?) I mentioned that I was bothered that we ended up with eight votes from seven voters. "Someone voted twice.

---

* These are real animals that can be found in the London Zoo.

Who was it?" asked Shane. But since most of the votes were for the same option, this incongruity was dismissed.

I told the group that they had invented something on their own that is actually used in real life: approval voting, which allows voters to indicate both likes and dislikes. I asked whether they thought there was any one system of voting and counting that would always be fair. No one was sure.* Circle ended as kids raced up to the chalkboard to vote for their own personal preferences.

Voting Alternatives and Focus

Since we had a few visitors when we came back together the following week, we started with a collective recap of our voting scenario. Kids immediately started suggesting even more voting and counting methods. Damian suggested multiplying votes in different positions (first, second, etc.) by different numbers. I briefly explained Borda Counts, which do count votes in that way. Arthur suggested some sort of competition among the candidates to determine who should win.

Some of the kids were getting distractingly physical with the math manipulatives on the table, so we engaged in an attention-focusing activity: watching the bobble-head doll. This doll ("who is a distant relative of Zooman") sat in the middle of the table. I tapped his head, which is on a spring, and told the kids that they had to watch until his head stopped moving, and then put their own heads down. The doll never stopped; every fidget (and possibly every truck passing outside) intensified the bobbling. At this point, however, attentions were sharpened, so we decided to put him away. We made a plan to use him on the floor instead of the table next time. I hinted that the doll was related to math somehow, and with that we were ready to return to our story.†

The kids were curious to hear what Zooman decided to do. I told them that he did just what the kids had invented the week before ("approval voting"): he held a second election where people indicated their likes and dislikes. I showed the results on the board. The kids immediately called out, "The monkey did win! Hooray!" I told them that the anteater's supporters were pretty mad about this, and had extracted a

---

* Kenneth Arrow proved in 1950 that it is impossible to design a voting system that will always be fair, given some reasonable criteria of fairness. This branch of mathematics is accessible, and vital to our understanding of how democracy works. See *tech.mit.edu/V123/N8/8voting.8n.html* for more.

† This led to an amazing math circle subplot. For the next *two years*, the kids would ask about random objects, "Is *this* related to math?" We almost always found a connection. One mathematical aspect of the bobble-head is the rate at which the head bobbles.

promise from the man to explore other voting methods before choosing a new animal the next time one died (my way of keeping the door open for more play with voting).

You never know which idea in a math circle will take root in someone's imagination. Hours later that same day Savannah was playing with an old-fashioned whirligig, and said to me, "This has something to do with math, doesn't it?" "Yes; how could you tell?" "It just seems like it would."

More Mindfulness Snippets[*]

Week Four

The children sat on the rug around a green tape square which enclosed some toy cars, office supplies, a plastic dog, a book, and other sundry items. I explained that in our continuing story, Zooman had four children—Ginny, Ron, Fred, and Percy—who needed to be brave in order to feed some of the animals. These four, I explained further, played games to enhance their bravery, and this set-up on the rug was one of those games.

I asked the kids to look at the assortment for ten seconds, and to then close their eyes while I removed something. They were then to open their eyes and try to discern what was missing. The game went quickly until debate emerged over whether the book was "green with three men on it" or "green with four women on it." The book was *Women in Mathematics*, by Lynn M. Osen. I called on the children who were not shouting out answers and found that, as usual, the people not volunteering were actually quite engaged. We played a few more rounds of the "Take-Away Game" before I asked them what this might have to do with math.

"We talked about how math requires the bravery of Neville Longbottom of Harry Potter fame: the courage to make attempts without certainty of success."

We recalled the feelings of frustration encountered the previous week when we attempted to solve a complicated problem. Our group realized quickly that the Take-Away Game helps with noticing, which helps increase attention, which helps increase frustration tolerance, which hopefully increases bravery. We talked about how math requires the bravery of Neville Longbottom of Harry Potter fame: the courage to make attempts without certainty of success.

We then addressed our mathematical task at hand: an investigation of a classic math problem based on rates.[†]

---

[*] I want to thank Susan Kaiser Greenland (*SusanKaiserGreenland.com*) for her work on teaching mindfulness to children.

[†] *TalkingStickLearningCenter.org/there-is-a-unicorn-dying-at-the-end-of-a-bridge*

Week Five

To start our session I pulled out a small musical instrument in the shape of a triangle and said, "When I strike this and you think the sound has ended, you'll be wrong. Listen harder. Then put your head down when it's really done." I struck it. Heads went partially down, back up, and then down again.

Candy asked whether eyes should be open or closed, and I said, "Whatever you think; you could even try both ways." Damian asked, "You mean like this?" and closed one eye. Sophia said, "I can't do that," so I suggested covering an eye with a hand like a pirate's eye patch. We focused our attention with three triangle chimes before I asked them to recall what had been happening in our zoo story the previous week.

Week Six

I had hoped that we could quickly focus attention by starting with a game of "How Are They Different?"* I had thought that we could eliminate the distraction of inequitable turn-taking by saying, "We'll go from youngest to oldest." I was wrong. It was easy to know that Sophie goes first and Shane second, but then came the seven-year-olds. All five of them compared birthdates and expressed surprise about their places in the age ranking.

While it wasn't a quiet game of "How Are They Different?," some useful mathematical concepts emerged: a method to rank ages by month and date, and also the fairness criteria that no one should point out more than one difference, so that Damian, the oldest (by a few weeks), would have a fighting chance as the person who goes last. Everyone had come to class simmering with physical energy this day after Halloween, but all were silent, focused, and ready to do math by the time that Damian made the final observation.

---

* Participants study two similar but non-identical drawings and point out differences in them.

Can you cut and fold one regular piece of paper, so it ends up looking like this?

---

* Avery Pickford took this photograph so he could share this classic puzzle with a math teacher circle. He also shared it at his blog: *MathTeacherOrStudent.blogspot.com/2010/07/paper-puzzle.html*

Colleen is the cofounder and director of Math Advantage Learning Center in Wellesley, Massachusetts, where kids come for after-school math enrichment. —SV

Bionic Algebra Adventures

by Colleen King

The captain of the Blue Lamborghinis was the first to arrive. He claimed the seat in front of the prime numbers poster, pulled a crumpled stack of paper from his pocket, then vanished down a quiet hallway without saying a word. When he returned, all the other seats in the room were filled. Representatives from the Wheelies, the Denominators, and the Brainiacs swapped stories and laughed as only good friends do. The top of the hour, however, was fast approaching. These carefree classmates would soon become fierce opponents in a world of numbers, equations, trust, and betrayal. Another round of Bionic Algebra Adventures was about to begin.

Making It a Game

The year was 2002 and Math Advantage had just launched its fourth year of enrichment programs. This group of students from different schools, towns, and backgrounds came together each week in a small, nondescript classroom to learn algebra. The first few meetings were less than spectacular. The students did not know one another. It was Saturday morning and it always seemed much too early for this sleepy group of adolescents. This was clearly going to be a challenge. I made it my mission each week to develop engaging content, guiding each class through a careful mix of puzzles, problems, and activities. Students soon began to participate, asking questions and volunteering answers. I was pleased with our progress and thought it couldn't possibly get any better than this. But I couldn't have been more wrong.

Eventually this group began to socialize before class. They discovered they shared a common bond. They were all zealous gamers. One student wrote cheat sheets with his friends; another made her own computer games. The students brought in their electronic games to play before class (long before that was common). While I was thrilled this group was bonding, I was apprehensive about all the gaming that was taking place. It was difficult to get students to put them away and nearly impossible to end game discussions. My puzzles and problems were no match for the lure of Nintendo.

And then something completely unexpected happened. Denay raised his hand and asked, "Can we make this a game?"

In the seconds that followed, a dozen thoughts raced through my mind while quiet anticipation blanketed the room.

Wow, that's a really interesting idea! Could this be a game?

Algebra does have its own set of rules just like games do. Maybe we could make it a game.

How would parents respond? They're expecting a traditional algebra course.

What if a game setting made the material more engaging and students were solving relevant problems?

But there's so much material to cover. Would it even be possible?

I broke the silence, postponing my answer while posing a question, "What would an algebra game look like?"

The responses came quickly.

"We could use graphs to predict things," said the soon-to-be commander of the Wheelies, "and use patterns to make codes." A future Brainiac added, "We can solve equations for all sorts of stuff."

It was a start.

What began as a very traditional classroom setting slowly evolved into a real world simulation of a video game. The captain of the Blue Lamborghinis took the lead in story development and rules creation. The class came in early and stayed late each week to fine-tune the details. The story was set in the future. Teams of space travelers participating in an intergalactic race had been set off-course by a shift in a magnetic force field, and had landed on an unknown planet. The object of the game was to get back to Earth.

The mathematics that drove this sci-fi adventure was to be my contribution. I had to find a way to bring the concepts I wanted my students to learn into the game environment they were continually creating. Topics such as functions, graphs, systems of equations, ratio, and proportion would be relatively easy to integrate into the story. Factoring, properties of exponents, and polynomial operations would pose a challenge. While some students were taking algebra in school, others were studying pre-algebra. That meant that the class could not consist entirely of applications and that some direct instruction would be necessary. I opted initially for a fifty/fifty split, using the first half of our class time to introduce new concepts and to review assignments. The second half was reserved for the game.

The students assembled themselves into teams of two. Each week they were presented with a challenge related to the story. While traveling through space, the teams learn of an impending asteroid storm that threatens their safety. Mission control sends data to the teams that details the location of the asteroids. The teams must fire a laser along a linear path that will bring the beam of light in contact with as many asteroids as possible. Later in the story, the space teams encounter an invisible boundary on Planet Alpha. They must graph inequalities to determine areas to avoid. Throughout the game, the mathematical concept of function continually evolved. Students learned to identify and transform both linear and quadratic functions. Soon they could see the graph of a function and determine its equation with ease (quite high-level skills for Algebra I students).

And so it went for twenty-four electrifying weeks. It was a bold step but one that established a paradigm for future math classes and transformed our center into an innovative learning environment.

The Results

The results were impressive. I began and ended the course with an assessment covering both conceptual knowledge and personal views toward math. There was significant improvement in both areas. Although previous groups had made similar gains on the conceptual knowledge test, this group clearly showed deeper understanding. Interestingly, the topics that I was unable to integrate into the game were not as well understood as those that were important to game play.

Assessment questions that sought an explanation from students received higher-quality responses than any past assessments. Students demonstrated a profound understanding of functions and graphs, which had been revisited many times throughout the game. Problem solving was another area where the students demonstrated exceptional skill. This came about because the course was taught as a series of connected problems to solve. To move through the game, students had to work simultaneously with several different concepts, analyze and respond to data, and create models to communicate ideas.

In the initial assessment, most of the students expressed disinterest in math. Many indicated that they saw no connection between math and their own lives. Tom very candidly shared that he did not want to be in this class and was forced to be there by his parents. Not one of the eight students admitted liking math or being good at it. In contrast, the end-of-course assessment revealed more positive attitudes. All of the students stated that the course made math more meaningful for them. I found this interesting since all the math applications had occurred in a fantasy setting.

From that point on, games of imagination and competition became an important part of the center's approach to math instruction. A group of fifth-grade students, learning to identify coordinates on a graph, imagined they were adventurers on a mission to find a sacred scroll. In the spirit of the game Battleship, each team was given a first quadrant section of a Cartesian graph. They drew five keys in various positions for the opposing team to locate. The game evolved to include negative coordinates and transformations. Encapsulating an inherently dull topic in a compelling storyline enabled us to cover concepts in greater depth and made it possible to reveal connections to other math topics. Students expressed a greater appreciation for the role of coordinates in the real world and were free of the usual confusion students have when plotting or identifying points on a graph.

Further Adventures

A group of sixth-grade girls who were struggling with percents came to the math center for extra help. They were discouraged and had given up any hope of understanding or ever enjoying math. Kate was a promising artist. She liked to sketch models dressed in trendy clothing. The other girls were impressed and tried to emulate her talent. I asked the girls if they would want to run their own fashion boutique. Their eyes grew wide and they all nodded an enthusiastic yes. The girls formed groups of two and named their stores. Each team was given $1000 in play money to start. We decided that the object of the game, much like that of any business, would be to make the most money possible in a specific period of time. The game ran over the course of eight class meetings. During the first two classes, students made decisions about what to sell and how to price their products. These decisions were based on data I had made up about business trends at a fictional mall. The success of each team's store depended on how the students interpreted the data.

A group of fourth-grade students in an adjacent classroom volunteered to be customers. Prior to their shopping excursion, the fourth graders had learned about unit cost and how to determine the best buy. They were given $50 in play money and told to buy the greatest number of products possible. To meet this goal, the students had to be thrifty shoppers. In turn, storeowners who had priced their products too high would not have many sales. After the shopping spree, the storeowners calculated their profits and determined how much money was needed to restock inventory. Teams had to compare the terms of local bank loans and decide which offered the best option. The teams were also asked to run a sale on certain items. Our fourth graders reprised their roles as customers two more times during the game. At the final meeting, students determined their profit or loss and analyzed their decisions.

Throughout the game, the students created graphs, studied data, determined unit rates, and calculated sales price, percent increase, tax, and more. By the end of the game, the girls not only were able to accurately compute percentages, they had developed an understanding of terms associated with percent that would have been difficult to attain through worksheets alone. Commission, tax, and interest are foreign concepts for most sixth-grade students. Yet they are expected to solve word problems related to these ideas. By immersing students in an environment that naturally incorporated these terms, they were able to attain computational fluency and relate these ideas to a real world application that was meaningful to them.

Stirring Their Passions

We began to see that there was a way to reach students for whom math was both tedious and boring, the students who had come to the conclusion that math was simply not for them. The key was to find something that stirred their passions, captured their collective imagination, and placed learning in their control. Math became something my students wanted to learn, *had* to learn. How could our algebra students get back to Earth without knowing which linear equation passed through the intergalactic doorway? How could our fifth graders win Treasure Hunters without being able to identify coordinates or reflect an image across the y-axis? How could our sixth graders run a successful clothing boutique without knowing everything possible about percentages and data?

Motivating students through games has long been a successful classroom strategy. Commonly, games have been used to reinforce knowledge rather than teach new concepts. Certainly, that was how we had always used games before at the math center. We often held Math Olympiads and similar contests to foster the spirit of academic competition and give students a chance to showcase their math skills. Math Jeopardy was a game we frequently used to strengthen and assess skills. Our categories would relate to concepts students had learned in class and had intriguing names such as Shape Up, Half and Half, What's the Point?, Divide and Conquer, and X Marks the Spot. Students could

"The key was to find something that stirred their passions, captured their collective imagination, and placed learning in their control."

choose a category with which they were comfortable and an amount that corresponded to easy, medium, hard, challenging, and genius levels. Teams that gave the correct answer were rewarded with play money equal to the value of the question. And that, naturally, led to even more math. Games and competitions were perfectly suited for review but hadn't seemed to be the right tool for instruction. What made a game like Bionic Algebra Adventures unique is that it both introduced new concepts and provided an engaging context with which to apply these new ideas. The game itself was the vehicle of instruction.

This creative approach to teaching was making a difference for a population of students that had never been able to connect with math in a positive way in the classroom. Students who had struggled for years with math facts and pencil and paper computation found a way to enter a world of math that had not been accessible to them in the past. Our learning center became a lively mix of creative problem solving and animated discussion. Kids were engaged in a way that none of us could have imagined. We became convinced that any student could find success with math if the concepts were presented in meaningful contexts.

"I no longer teach classes. I teach students. And that seems to be making all the difference."

A number of years have passed since the Bionic Algebra Adventure transformed math for a group of inspired students. Today, role-playing games continue to be an essential teaching tool at the center. But they're not the only one. One thing I've learned is that my math teaching must be fluid and adapt to the unique needs of each group of students. There is no single textbook, curriculum, or teaching method that works for everyone. That knowledge has made me a better teacher. I no longer teach classes. I teach students. And that seems to be making all the difference.

Meet Alexandria Jones, Mathematical Sleuth

by Denise Gaskins

It began with some fourth- to eighth-grade friends who met in my dining room to work math puzzles and play games. At first, a few of the kids wondered how anyone could have fun with math. But we did enjoy ourselves, and Math Club grew until we couldn't fit anyone else around the table.

When one girl had to move away, I thought, "Why not send Math Club with her?" Thus was born *Math Club by Mail* newsletter (which was later renamed *Mathematical Adventures*), a four-year enterprise that brought puzzles, strategy games, art projects, historical tidbits, and more to readers as far away as Hawaii. Never very many readers, I admit, but it was a blast while it lasted.

The newsletter followed the fictional adventures of homeschooler Alexandria Jones, her archaeologist father, and the rest of their family, as they discovered a triangular treasure from ancient Egypt, puzzled over patterns in Pythagorean pebbles, and explored the applications of math in daily life. We learned about hieroglyphic math, fractals and chaos theory, logarithms, geometric algebra, and how to multiply any numbers using only the two-times table.

Here's Alexandria's first adventure. You can find more on my blog, Let's Play Math.*

The Story: Alexandria Jones and the Secret of the Pharaoh's Treasure

Alexandria Jones stood outside her father's tent. The glare of the sun on the rocky desert hurt her eyes. Holding up a hand to shield her gaze,

---

* *LetsPlayMath.net/alexandria-jones/*

she spotted her dad, the world-famous archaeologist, arguing with the foreman.

Poor Dad, she thought. He was sure this was the right site, but so far he's found nothing.

She looked down at her feet, where her faithful dog Ramus panted as he waited. "Well, Rammy, it looks like Dad will be busy for while. What do you say? Shall we go exploring?"

Alexandria ducked into the tent for her backpack and canteen.

Thump! Something bounced against the side of the tent. Ramus barked.

Alex stepped outside and looked quickly around. No one was in sight. Next to the tent she saw a fist-sized rock with a note tied to it. She picked it up and read:

Ha! The real Pharaoh's Treasure lies under a pyramid of stones, and it's mine. You can't stop me this time!

—Simon Skulk

"Find him, Rammy. Which way did he go?"

Growling, the dog ran down the trail to the valley. Alex followed him, but pulled up short when Ramus bounded into a dark cave. She swung her backpack off her shoulder and drew out a flashlight.

"The treasure must have been buried in a cave, as some of the later pharaohs were," she mused. "Okay, Rammy. Lead on."

The trail ended at the foot of a head-high pyramid of small, rough-cut stones. Her father's enemy was just setting his lantern on the ground.

"To keep their pyramids, temples, and other buildings squared up properly, Egyptian surveyors (called "rope stretchers") used a powerful design tool—the right triangle."

"You creep!" Alex shouted. "That treasure belongs in a museum."

The man laughed and reached for a stone. "Not if I find it first. The Pharaoh's Treasure should bring me a pretty profit!"

Alexandria Jones ran to grab a stone from the pyramid. If she could just uncover the treasure before he did…

…

"I can't believe it!" Simon Skulk shook his head at what he saw. Then he threw down the last stone in disgust and walked away. At the mouth of the cave, he turned back and shook his fist. "You haven't seen the last of me, Alexandria Jones."

Her muscles aching, Alex sank to the ground and hugged her dog. Then she gave him a little push toward the front of the cave. "Rammy, go get Dad."

Ramus barked once and took off running.

Alex turned back to look at the Pharaoh's Treasure. Where the last stone had stood was a hole. In the hole lay three wooden sticks, like tent pegs, and a long loop of rope with twelve evenly-spaced knots.

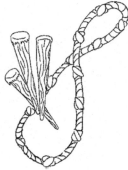

What could it be?

It seemed as though Alex sat there forever, shivering as the desert sun went down, her muscles growing stiff. Then Ramus came bounding into the cave and licked her face.

Her father gave her a hug that chased the stiffness away. Then, Fibonacci Jones* reached into the hole and tenderly lifted out the pegs and rope.

"You found it," he said. "The Pharaoh's Treasure! Isn't it beautiful?"

Alexandria frowned. "But what is it?"

The ancient Egyptians were careful builders, her father explained. To keep their pyramids, temples, and other buildings squared up properly, Egyptian surveyors (called "rope stretchers") used a powerful design tool—the right triangle.

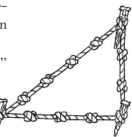

"It works because the loop has exactly twelve evenly-spaced knots," he said. "Look, you hold this knot, and I'll hold it four knots away on one side, and three knots away on the other. See how the rope makes a right angle?"

After notifying his foreman and making sure the cave site was secured, Professor Jones led the tired Alex back to their camp. He stacked multi-layer sandwiches while she poured milk and set the table for supper.

"Geometry," Fibonacci said.

"What?"

"*Geo* means earth, and *metry* means to measure. So geometry means to measure the earth. That is what the Egyptian rope stretches did."

Alex thought for a moment. "So in the beginning, math was just surveying?"

"And taxes…"

As he sliced a sandwich diagonally into two triangles, Professor Jones explained, "Every farmer in Egypt had to pay a property tax to the Pharaoh each year, based on the size of his land, so the rope stretchers spent most of their time measuring farmland. The scribes could easily calculate the area of a rectangular plot of land: Area equals length times width."

He waved the knife as he talked, drawing imaginary diagrams in the air.

---

* Author's note: What? You were expecting a different name? Do you think I want a lawsuit?

"Dad, would you please put the knife down?" Alex said. "You're making Rammy nervous."

"Oh, yes, of course. And since a right triangle made exactly half of a rectangle, the area of a right triangle was simple, too."

"I know that one," Alex said. "Area equals one half times base times height, where the base and height are the two legs of the triangle—the two sides that form the right angle." Then she frowned, "But what if the farmer's property had some really weird shape?"

Her father began to lay the pieces of sandwiches on the tabletop in an asymmetrical design. "The Egyptians discovered that they could divide any piece of property with straight borders into right triangles."

"They could cut any property into triangles?"

"If it had straight sides." Fibonacci picked up the last sandwich and took a big bite.

Alex grabbed a sandwich half and held it up, tracing its edges with her finger. "Then when they measured the sides of each triangle, they could calculate its area. What a neat system!"

Her father nodded, "Adding the areas of all the triangles together gave them the area of the entire property—"

"And the proper amount for the farmer's taxes!" Alex laughed.

GAME
Pharaoh's Pyramid

Can you find the Pharaoh's treasure? Whoever takes the last stone wins.

Two players use the game board below.

Each needs a pencil.

On your turn, draw an X on one or two stones. You can choose any stone you wish, but if you want to mark two stones, they must be touching each other.

Take turns marking stones until they're all gone. Whoever marks the last stone uncovers the Pharaoh's Treasure.

From Ancient Egypt

Pythagorean Triple Puzzle

The rope with twelve knots makes a right triangle with sides of lengths 3, 4, and 5. Can you come up with a longer rope that would make a different shape of right triangle?

When the three sides of a right triangle all have whole number lengths, we call the numbers a Pythagorean triple, because Pythagoras was the first European to prove that the sum of the squares on the legs is the same as the square on the hypotenuse. But many cultures knew about these special triples, and Chinese mathematicians proved this relationship long before Pythagoras. Exploring Pythagorean triples can take you in many directions.

An Egyptian Farm Puzzle

Can you find the area of this farmer's property, so that he will know how much tax money to send to Pharaoh? (If an angle looks like a right angle, you may assume that it is one.) Use a ruler to measure the property lines. The short line at the upper left of the farm on the map below is equivalent to 100 cubits (about 150 feet) of farmland. How many square cubits must the farmer pay taxes on?

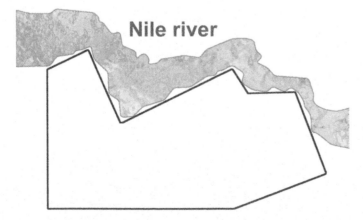

Nile river

Jamylle is one of the few authors I connected with in person instead of online. I'm honored to share her work here. —SV

The Oakland Math Circle: A First Iteration

by Jamylle Carter, Ph.D.

On March 19, 2008, I arrived at the Museum of African-American Technology (MAAT) Science Village just fifteen minutes before the Oakland Math Circle was scheduled to start. I still had to park, unload, get keys from next door, set up the snacks and activities, and greet parents.

I was scrambling to get everything together when I looked up and saw Astiney Green, a brown-skinned sixth grader with long hair and a bright smile. She was standing outside the MAAT, waiting for me with her hand on her hip. She glared at me, then smiled and gave me a hug. I exclaimed, "Astiney! I'm so happy to see you. Where have you been? I didn't think you were coming back."

She said, "My mom had car trouble, so I took the bus to get here."

Students like Astiney were the reason I started the Oakland Math Circle, an after-school mathematics enrichment program that used hands-on activities to make advanced mathematics accessible and enjoyable for African-American middle school students.

To supplement my postdoctoral fellowship at the Mathematical Sciences Research Institute in 2005 and 2006, I taught in the San Francisco Math Circle, which targets "unenriched" students and their teachers in San Francisco. I was disappointed that so few of the students were Black. As an African-American mathematician, I know firsthand how underrepresented African Americans are in mathematics and science, and I wanted to share my talents with my own community. So in 2007, I founded the Oakland Math Circle. (Oakland is about 30% Black, while San Francisco's Black population is under 10%.)

With the support of three partner organizations, I pulled together engaging activities that would provoke students' interest in higher-level mathematics.* We would work our way into the conceptual challenges through their delight, passion, and engagement. We met for an hour and fifteen minutes a week for twenty weeks, to explore concepts in geometry, trigonometry, music, and statistics.

Geometry Unfolds

I led the students in cutting, folding, and coloring tessellating shapes.

Tessellation refers to covering the plane with repetitions of the same shape; some shapes will tessellate the plane and others won't. They used the three plane symmetries—rotations (twisting), reflections (flipping), and translations (sliding) of their shapes—to create a piece of tessellation artwork.

They also made tessellations with pattern blocks and copied their tessellations onto triangular grid paper, enlarged to the scale of the pattern blocks. By physically manipulating the tessellating shapes, students became more adept at identifying the symmetries.

The classroom later became an art gallery with at least fifteen M. C. Escher prints on display. Students studied the mathematical prints and determined which, if any, contained plane symmetries. None of the students had heard of Escher, and most were surprised that they were doing "art, not math." The mathematics of pattern recognition was so well buried in the activities that one parent commented, "They don't even realize they're doing math."

In the final week of this session, we did some of what the students would call "real math." We played Fantastic Four, a card game designed to sharpen basic math skills and problem-solving.

I knew I was on the right track when I read the students' evaluations of this first five-week session. They had written: "It is fun here," "It rocked," "I loved it all," and "It was amazing!" We were off to a great start.

Sneaking up on Trigonometry

Rockets were the theme of the second session. In order to measure how high a rocket goes, students need to be able to measure both distances and angles. Students estimated distances using their own two feet. After measuring distances with a few different foot sizes, we decided to switch

---

* The Exploratorium, the MAAT, and The Institute for the Advanced Study of Black Family Life and Culture. Most of the activities described below came from the Exploratorium, where I held a National Science Foundation internship to bridge research and public education.

over to something standard; we chose the metric system. Our aim was to figure out how high the light was. We measured the distance along the floor from us to a spot on the floor below the light. Then we measured the angle we had to look upward to see it, with inclinometers the students had made themselves.*

They then made scale drawings on graph paper showing the horizontal distance and angle, and were able to calculate the height from that. Each graph paper box counted for a meter, so they just had to count boxes to find the height. When they compared their estimated heights to the actual heights of the distant objects, they realized their estimates were a little bit off, discovering how the uncertainty in their measurements of distance and angle affected their height calculations.

Now they were ready to make and launch some paper rockets. The rockets are made by simply rolling paper, taping one end, and adding fins using card stock. The launcher is a soda bottle with a bit of plastic tubing added. You can find more details in *The Math Explorer*.† The kids were so enthusiastic about launching those rockets that their enthusiasm overwhelmed my ability to direct them. We didn't make the final measurements, but they really could have done it, given a bit more time.

Ray Gilstrap, a network engineer with NASA's Research and Engineering Network group, gave a guest lecture on satellite Internet connections that complemented the rocket theme nicely. Gilstrap spoke about satellite Internet connections from remote field experiments, and showed photos of the satellite dishes and the desert environment. The kids loved him and peppered him with questions like, "How long does it take to make a satellite?" and "How do you replace a shuttle?"

Music as Math

This was my favorite topic. A new group of students arrived at the Oakland Math Circle expecting conventional math, and the music surprised them. Students rediscovered the least common multiple by playing polyrhythms. What's a polyrhythm? Imagine half the students clapping twice a second and the other half of the group clapping three times a second. The two groups will only clap together at the end of each second. The diagram below shows that it takes six boxes to cycle

---

* An inclinometer, made from a straw, a protractor, and a weight on a string, measures the "angle of inclination", the angle above horizontal. The drawing above shows a boy using an inclinometer.

† *The Math Explorer: Games and Activities for Middle School Youth Groups*, by Pat Murphy, Lori Lambertson, Pearl Tesler, and the Exploratorium, page 149. Used with permission. See *Exploratorium.edu* for more information.

through this rhythm, and 6 is the smallest multiple of both 2 and 3 (or their 'least common multiple').

The students made a diagram like the one below—a musical notation called the Time Unit Box System—in order to notate their polyrhythm. It helped them to focus solely on the rhythm by showing only the timing and not the notes. Our first experiment was one example of a polyrhythm, which involves playing multiple rhythms simultaneously. We played with a few others, notating each one.

Beat	1	2	3	4	5	6	1	2	3	4	5	6
group1		X		X		X		X		X		X
group2			X			X			X			X

The musical, physical, and visual representations of the least common multiple challenged the students who thought they already knew it. Sixth-grader Astiney said, "The least common multiple is so fifth grade." However, when she counted two beats per measure against three beats per measure, she was surprised that she needed to count a total of six beats to return to the simultaneous downbeats. She exclaimed, "That is so weird. And you knew that was gonna happen!"

Sound travels in waves, so understanding waves helps us to understand sound. Students played with phone cords and Slinkies to distinguish between the two types of waves: longitudinal and transverse. They were excited to see how many transverse waves they could make in the phone cord. They got six whole waves, quite an accomplishment. The Slinky moved differently. We started with the Slinky slightly stretched on a tabletop. The students pushed one end toward the other and watched a longitudinal wave of compression travel through the Slinky. Astiney was excited to relate these new terms to the P-waves and S-waves that she had learned about in earth science.[*]

Statistics from Candy and Dice

Students graphed M&Ms by color to discover differences between data from a population (the whole bag) and data from a sample (a scoop out of that bag, which is used to represent the whole bag). They computed their average height and noticed which of their shoe colors occurred the

---

[*] The P and S stand for primary and secondary—a primary wave is a wave of compression, also referred to as a longitudinal wave, whereas a secondary wave, also referred to as a transverse wave, moves particles in a direction perpendicular to the wave's motion. Watching an online demonstration may make this clearer: *YouTube.com/watch?v=yd-G6KYwzvA*

most frequently (the mode of the shoe color). They also rolled dice to explore probability.

After they were through figuring out the probability distribution for the sum and difference of two dice, they decided on their own to investigate the distribution for the product.

Our group also enjoyed a guest lecture on biostatistics from Tanya Moore, Ph.D., senior health management analyst in the City of Berkeley Division of Public Health. Moore discussed how researchers use statistics to determine the best medicines for people who are sick.

Summing Up

The Oakland Math Circle served a total of twenty-three African-American students (seven girls and sixteen boys) over the academic year. Although students ranged from the second grade through the eighth grade, the fifth- and sixth-grade students (like Astiney) attended the most consistently and seemed to enjoy the activities the most. Students came from private and public schools in a seventeen-mile radius of Oakland.

Through the hands-on approach, students learned mathematics in a new way. They wrote (in their own words): "I learned to measure my distance from a object using a inclonimeter," "I learned that you can never count how many of each color are in a M&M's bag," "I learned how to figure out the height of my eye," "I learned about probabilities."

On the last day, the kids received gift bags with calculators, math activities, and certificates of completion. In turn, they gave me hugs and a signed card with a song they'd made up!

The Oakland Math Circle provided a secure and collegial atmosphere where students gently corrected each other's mistakes, bragged about good grades on math tests, and recommended math books to each other. More important, it provided a social atmosphere for African-American students to do math together. African Americans are glaringly underrepresented in math and science professions. Even when Black students are motivated to learn, academically prepared, and encouraged by mentors and professionals, they tend to work alone.* This isolation not only heightens the often-experienced dichotomy between racial identity and academic interest, but it also contributes to students'

---

* Uri Treisman conducted research at University of California, Berkeley, on the study habits of students from a variety of cultures. He found that African-American students traditionally studied alone, which interfered with their success. He got them working in groups on challenging problems and their success rate soared. See: *bfc.sfsu.edu/cgi-bin/prob .pl?Uri_Treismans_Dolciani_Lecture*

"demoralization, disorientation, and ultimately, their decision to leave the sciences,"[*] if not higher education overall.

The Oakland Math Circle introduced Black students to their mathematically-minded peers and encouraged them to work together. It fostered social and intellectual connections among Black students and buffered them from the academic isolation that many Black students experience. This was crucial for students studying unfamiliar mathematics; they got the unequivocal message: "It's okay to be Black and like math."

I enjoyed the students immensely, but I ended the Oakland Math Circle in 2008 due to administrative difficulties that came with an ambitious partnership with several community organizations. Unfortunately, my relationship with each institution was new and fragile before the program started. This led to issues with communication and the overall vision that weakened the collective commitment to the project.

Exploratorium director Dennis Bartels spoke eloquently about working with partner organizations: "You've got to work with people you already know. You start in your own backyard, form the relationship, and then the funding opportunity naturally arises." I look forward to resurrecting the Oakland Math Circle in the future when I have strong partners who are committed to a clear vision of what it can be. In this first iteration, I learned how much time and dedication are needed to form the partner relationships, create the curriculum, publicize the program, and recruit students and staff.

The greatest success of this first iteration was the establishment of a fun place for African-American kids to enjoy doing math together. Kelly Robinson, the mother of a fifth grader, summarized it well, "You are helping me and my husband raise our son by showing him that it is okay to love math. You can look like 'this' and walk in the world as a mathematician."

> *"The Oakland Math Circle fostered social and intellectual connections among Black students and buffered them from the academic isolation that many Black students experience."*

---

[*] Author unknown. Source: *vccslitonline.cc.va.us/mrcte/treisman.htm*

GAME
Fantastic Four

*from The Math Explorer**

What you need

Two to five players
Deck of cards (face cards removed)
Timer
Paper and pens or pencils

How to play

Dealer puts out four (helper) cards up , one (goal) card down.
Everyone writes the four numbers (Ace = 1) on their paper.
Set the timer for five minutes.
When everyone is ready, start the timer and flip the goal card.
Now use the four helper numbers to make an expression that equals the goal number. Write as many different expressions as you can, using two, three, or all four of the helper numbers.

Scoring

Each expression using two cards scores 4 points
Each expression using three cards scores 9 points
Each expression using all four cards scores 16 points
Everyone checks all the expressions. If someone made a mistake, you get 7 points for finding it. (They get 0 points for that expression.)

Example:
The helper cards dealt are 4, 9, 1 (the Ace), and 2. The goal card is a 7.
Here are three ways to make 7: $9 - \frac{1}{2}$, $4 + 2 + 1$, $9 - (4 - 2)$

---

* *The Math Explorer: Games and Activities for Middle School Youth Groups*, by Pat Murphy, Lori Lambertson, Pearl Tesler, and the Exploratorium. Reprinted with permission. See *Exploratorium.edu* for more information.

Variations

If your group prefers cooperating, you don't have to use points; the group can hunt together for solutions.

You can use dice instead. The numbers will be smaller, which may work better for younger kids.

Another game like this is called Make Ten: Roll five dice; use all five of them to make a total of 10 points.

Amanda Serenevy founded and runs the Riverbend Community Math Center in South Bend, Indiana. This is just one of many projects they sponsor. —SV

A Culture of Enthusiasm for Math

by Amanda Serenevy

The Math Studio program was an informal program meeting in many of the places children gather after school—Boys and Girls Clubs, churches, and schools. This one met in the common area of one Boys and Girls Club during their after-school program. Students were free to come and go as they chose and spent as much time as they liked at the Math Studio table.[*]

With polyhedra and polygons as my chosen theme for the semester, I broke the ice by encouraging students to build polyhedra using origami Sonobe units[†] and plastic Polydron pieces. For the first few weeks we just built polyhedra, occasionally naming shapes built or discussing properties of those shapes informally. During the third week, the students asked if they could have a point system for building and learning about the shapes so that they could earn some of the origami objects that I make that require more skill.[‡]

Students began recording the things they built along with their observations. I awarded 1 point for recording the number of faces, edges, and vertices of each new polyhedron they built. Students could earn more points by learning to use a protractor to measure angles, by verifying experimentally that the angles in any triangle they made added up to 180 degrees, or by learning to name the five Platonic solids. Students

---

[*] Some after-school programs require students to stay with one activity for a set time. It's impossible to get the same level of engagement in that situation.

[†] Sometimes origami is done with a single sheet of paper; other times shapes are made using many copies of a standard unit. The Sonobe unit, top picture above, is made from a small square of paper and works very well for making polyhedra. See *RiverbendMath.org/modules /Origami/Sonobe_Polyhedra/* for more information.

[‡] Although point systems are not normally useful for deep intellectual engagement, this one worked because the kids themselves invented it.

earned still more points by proving that there really are 180 degrees in a triangle, or by proving there are exactly five Platonic solids. But the students soon decided that the fastest way to earn points was to discover formulas. I would frequently overhear students explaining to each other what a formula is and how to go about discovering formulas for the various challenge questions.

Felicity was the Queen of Formulas. She found formulas for the family of pyramids by first recording the number of faces, edges, and vertices for the triangular, square, pentagonal, and hexagonal pyramids and then extrapolating from there.

She also found formulas for the families of bi-pyramids, prisms, and anti-prisms. She noticed the pattern embodied by Euler's formula[*] and derived the formula for the number of degrees in each angle of a regular polygon.

Felicity's friend Amari preferred to build things. She folded Sonobe polyhedra, discovered all of the Platonic solids after hearing only the definition, and built a large menagerie of irregular polyhedra. In November, Amari built a shape using Polydrons that she called a pentagonal jewel box. The jewel box consisted of two identical halves. Each half was built by attaching equilateral triangles to a pentagon and then joining the equilateral triangles together with right triangles. The two halves then snapped together to make the finished box. Felicity saw the box Amari made and asked if she could make a similar shape using hexagons. When Amari succeeded, Felicity encouraged her to make the same shape using squares and triangles.

---

[*] The number of faces + the number of vertices − the number of edges = 2, for any convex (no indentations) polyhedron.

Felicity realized that Amari had succeeded in inventing her own family of shapes. The two girls had to leave after the polyhedra were built, so they asked me to save them for the next session. During the next session, the two girls asked me for their shapes and sat together to work out the formulas for the number of faces, edges, and vertices in Amari's jewel box family.

I was excited by the response of the students at the Boys and Girls Club. That fall, they began to create a culture of enthusiasm for mathematics that deepened during the course of the next several years. Because they spent several hours each day in the after school program, there was plenty of time for them to become intrigued, first by the fun trappings of a mathematical activity and later by the underlying patterns and ideas. The fact that so many students choose to devote so much time took me very much by surprise. Students commonly spent up to *three hours at a time* building new shapes, working on formulas, and answering challenge questions. Many students who usually exhibited very short attention spans learned to focus on complex tasks for long stretches of time as they constructed their own origami stellated icosahedra or other projects.

"...there was plenty of time for them to become intrigued, first by the fun trappings of a mathematical activity and later by the underlying patterns and ideas."

Some students who commonly resisted formal instruction in school chose to pour all of the exercises they refused to do in school into their journals as a sort of furious private declaration that they could do math if they wanted to. Other students began gathering together by the whiteboard in the corner to challenge each other to a game of Function Machines* or to work on challenge questions together. After we completed a semester on digital electronics (building binary adding machines using integrated circuits with AND, OR, and XOR logic gates†), several students begged their parents for electronics components that they could use to continue explorations at home.

Many of the students in the Math Studio went on to join other science, technology, engineering, or mathematics programs in later years. I see the amazing results we achieved and grieve that I can't offer this to every child I meet. I hope to eventually find ways to spread this work far and wide.

---

* See the Function Machine game on page 162.
† A XOR B means "A *or* B but *not* both."

ACTIVITY
Faces, Edges, and Vertices

by Amanda Serenevy

Play with Polydrons, or some other shape-building set. After a while, you will find that you've built lots of different shapes. If you'd like to think about similarities and differences between your shapes, there are a few ways to do that.

You might notice a number of different *pyramid* shapes, all starting with a base at the bottom, and coming up to a point. You might notice a number of different shapes that are the same on the top and bottom (and stay the same as you go from the top to the bottom). Those are called *prisms*. Do you have any shapes that are neither pyramids nor prisms? Perhaps you can find a name for those online.

Name, description, or drawing	# of vertices	# of edges	# of faces	Observations
Cube	8	12	6	

Here's another way to think about your collection of shapes. Count the number of faces (flat sides), edges (where faces come together), and vertices (corners—where edges come together) on each shape you built.

Give each shape a name, description, or drawing to identify it, and record all your information in a chart like the one below. Do you see any patterns in your data?

On Platonic solids, all faces are the same shape, all edges are the same length, all angles are the same size, and all vertices have the same number of edges coming into them. How many Platonic solids can you find?

Bob and Ellen Kaplan have written about their math circle work in the book Out of the Labyrinth: Setting Mathematics Free. I wanted an overview of their work for this book, and they pointed me to Stephen's piece. —SV

Seized by a Good Idea*

by Stephen Kennedy

Peter Panov and David Plotkin can barely stay in their seats. They're firing questions and comments and conjectures and quips at their instructor, Jim Tanton, as fast as he can respond. The whole class of thirteen-year-olds was giggling when I walked in. On the board is a list of some Pythagorean triples[†] and a procedure for generating more. Tanton had just generated the triple $(-1,0,1)$,[‡] and a general hilarity about the idea of a triangle with a negative side-length erupted. Now it's as if he were dangling strings in front of a pack of puppies. They're all worrying at the problem, tossing out ideas, wiggling in their seats. It's the most rambunctious, joyous math classroom I've ever been in, but it's not just fun and games; they're working on real mathematical problems. These kids are not just being lectured to—they're dictating the approach and the ideas.

I'm visiting The Math Circle in Boston, Massachusetts, and I'm amazed at what I'm witnessing. There are three classes going on simultaneously so I wander down the hall to Bob Kaplan's class on knot theory just in time to hear him tell the students that there are enough open problems left in that field to keep them "happy forever." It's the first day of the new session and they're working on the problem of defining what it means for two knots to be the same. Eventually someone says, "If you can wiggle one around so that it looks like the other." Exactly right. But almost immediately another student notices the difficulty, "That's a fine definition, but I still have a problem. How do you *know* when you can

> *"It's the most rambunctious, joyous math classroom I've ever been in, but it's not just fun and games; they're working on real mathematical problems."*

---

* Originally published in *Math Horizons*, April 2003 as The Math Circle. Reprinted with permission. Copyright the Mathematical Association of America. All rights reserved.

† A Pythagorean triple is three whole numbers that satisfy $a^2 + b^2 = c^2$; this equation gives the relationship between the three sides of a right triangle. The simplest Pythagorean triple is $(3,4,5)$ because $3^2 + 4^2 = 5^2$.

‡ This triple of numbers satisfies the Pythagorean Theorem, since $(-1)^2 + 0^2 = 1^2$, but it's nonsensical for a triangle.

do it?" Exactly right and still the essential problem of knot theory; how do you find a computable way to tell whether two knots are different?

They kick this around for a little while and Bob tries to subtly push the class in productive directions, but they don't really need him now and they ignore him. They've framed the problem and now they just want to attack it. Brute force is the order of the day and Bob, wisely, lets the students take the lead. The guy in the front row has an idea that I am sure can develop into what mathematicians call a parametrization.* He wants to describe the path of each knot with some sort of equation, and compare the knots that way. Of course, he's a fifteen-year-old high school kid and he doesn't know quite how to say that; he just knows that he'd like to get his hands on some numbers that describe the knot. I leave as he tries to articulate his thought, "Suppose we imagine that the x-axis is curved...."

I've been so engaged by Bob's and Jim's classes that I've barely left myself time to watch Ellen Kaplan lead the third group. As I enter she's just started telling them the history of Renaissance banking. Banks were first founded as safe places to store your excess cash and depositors paid a fee for the security. Eventually the original bankers (the Medici in Florence) realized that most of the money bags in their vaults were never opened, so they could get into the money-lending business using the same sum of money as both debit and credit. This was so fantastically profitable that the Medici started paying their depositors rather than charging them, so they could attract more deposits to loan out. Thus the birth of banking (and, soon after, Christmas Clubs, checking accounts, and bank robbers). All this is by way of explaining how negative numbers came to be accepted as more or less natural during the Renaissance. The course is about number systems, and its development was motivated by a former student of Ellen's who pleaded with her one day, "Please tell me, I just *have* to know, what's i to the i power?"†

---

* A parametrization (especially of a one-dimensional object like a knot) carries with it an explicit sense of motion that most equations do not. For example, the equation of the unit circle, $x^2 + y^2 = 1$, describes a static object. A parametrization of that object, for example $<\cos t, \sin t>$, with t going from 0 to 2π, carries with it the explicit invocation of a dot traveling around the curve, in a sense creating the curve in time t.

† i is the square root of negative one, the basis for imaginary numbers. These were invented to solve one set of mathematical problems, but created others. If you've gotten comfortable with the arithmetic of imaginary numbers, your next question, much harder, might be the one this student asked.

Reaching For Your Passion

Creating that kind of need to know is what every good teacher tries to do. The folks at The Math Circle have a simple recipe: take a bunch of kids, add a heaping handful of exciting problems, mix well, then get out of the way. It doesn't sound like it could possibly work, but I'm seeing it. It's nine o'clock on Sunday morning and these kids, who could be home in bed, are sitting in these classrooms working on math problems.

The Kaplans, back in the early nineties, asked themselves why so many people are frightened of mathematics when, as Bob put it, "its beauties are so many and its pleasures so great." They decided that the problem lay in the way that mathematics is taught. More specifically, they believe the problem is our assumption that mathematics *can* be taught. They are convinced that mathematics must be experienced to be appreciated. Of course, the problem then becomes how to entice the students into opening themselves to the experience. Ellen explains, "By the classic technique of intellectual seduction: trailing attractive questions in front of them."

One favorite class, for eight-to eleven-year-olds, is about infinite sets. (Bob observes that kids of that age are fascinated by the idea of infinity, much in the same way that younger kids are fascinated by dinosaurs, and for pretty much the same reasons: infinity is big and powerful, inaccessible, mysterious, and a little scary.) The class starts by asking the kids to explain to Martians (who count 1, 2, 3, many) how to tell a pile of eight objects from a pile of thirteen. Eventually they get to one-to-one correspondence, the countability of the rationals,* and the uncountability of the reals. These results are not handed to them; the students work out the answers themselves.

The Kaplans are not the first to try teaching by asking questions; the idea has a history dating back to Socrates. They've taken the basic insight that people learn mathematics best when they construct their own knowledge instead of being handed it, and built that insight into a method that bears the hallmarks of their personalities: creativity, playfulness, wonder, and a boundless curiosity. Their students are inspired and their classes are joyful.

The Kaplans believe that everyone has the capacity to appreciate and enjoy mathematics—in fact, that everyone has the ability to *create* mathematics. Ellen says all it takes to do mathematics is opportunity, a

---

* A fun way to get to an understanding of 'the countability of the rationals' is to read *The Cat in Numberland*, by Ivar Ekeland.

frustrating problem, and a bit of stubbornness. When I argue for inborn talent, Bob tells me the story of his son and the bassoon. As a kid, Bob and Ellen's son desperately wanted to learn to play the bassoon. They took him for lessons but the teacher told them he could never be successful; there is on the bassoon a particular lever called the whisper key that must be operated with the little finger and is quite difficult to reach. Michael's hands simply weren't ever going to be big enough. But he was stubborn and he was determined and he managed to find a way to reach that key; two weeks later he went to the teacher for another lesson and the impossibility of the whisper key was never mentioned again.

Constructing the Circle

They're missionaries, the Kaplans—they're excitable and exciting and zealous about spreading the good news of mathematics. They're both from New York, he upstate, she New York City. About forty years ago he left New York for the University of Chicago. In those days at Chicago one could get credit for a course by passing an examination. Bob passed a lot of examinations and in one year earned his BA. Feeling a bit of a fraud, he made his way to Boston and began, as he puts it, studying illegally at Harvard. That is, he was never registered or admitted to the University; he just hung around and attended classes. Ellen took a more traditional, and legal, approach; she actually applied and was admitted to Radcliffe. They met and married during their college years.

After Ellen's graduation, the Kaplans started teaching at The Commonwealth School, a progressive private school in Boston. Bob eventually became chair of the mathematics department and Ellen taught history, mathematics, and Latin. They both look and talk like well-educated college humanities professors. Their conversation is full of literary and historical references; they seem to have read every great book, studied every great philosopher, and know enough about every science to sound competent. They must have been captivating teachers at the Commonwealth School. But, one day in 1994, Bob said, "There must be a better way to teach math." The Math Circle idea was born out of their ensuing conversation.

Bob and Ellen are apparently susceptible to being seized by a good idea. They left the Commonwealth School, rented space in a church basement, and spread the word that they were open for business. That first semester, in 1994, they had 29 students, several from Boston's Russian émigré community, from whom they learned of the Russian tradition of *matematicheskiy kruzhok*. These are gatherings—the word "kruzhok" means "little circle" in Russian—outside the educational establishment, to discuss math and solve problems. It seemed perfect to borrow the name for their venture. They moved to Northeastern University and added sessions at Harvard. Demand kept growing; they now have sessions at Northeastern, Harvard, and in two Boston suburbs, and serve over 200 students. In 2001 they convinced Jim Tanton to give up college teaching and take on The Math Circle as a full-time job.

Jim grew up in Australia and majored in physics as an undergraduate. Near the end of college he had an epiphany about the difference between math and physics, and he decided that his brain was "wired for math." He came to the U.S. for graduate school at Princeton. After earning his Ph.D., he taught at New College in Florida, St. Mary's College in Maryland, and Merrimack College in Massachusetts. His website, Thinking Mathematics!,* showcases his playful, appealing, problem-centered approach to mathematics.

Tanton is, in style and philosophy, a perfect fit for The Math Circle. This was very clear at the opening organizational meeting of The Math Circle this morning. Since my visit is the first day of a new session, all the participants and teachers and some parents (no doubt a little nervous about what exactly they're committing their children to) have gathered in a small auditorium for Jim to welcome us to the new session and give us some idea of what's on the program. He set the tone immediately by presenting us with three problems:

1. A honeybee living on the hexagonal comb pictured wishes to move, but is constrained to always have an eastward (left to right) component to her motion, as shown by the arrows. Given this constraint how many different paths are there from cell B to cell E?

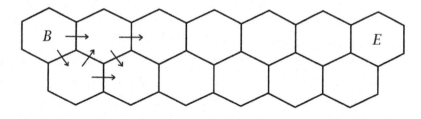

2. How many ways are there to write the number 3 as a sum of 1's and 2's if order matters (that is, $1 + 2$ is different from $2 + 1$) and you have two different kinds of 1s (say, thick and thin)? By way of example, there are 5 such ways to write the number 2: $1 + 1, 1 + \mathbf{1}, \mathbf{1} + 1, \mathbf{1} + \mathbf{1}, 2$.

---

* *James Tanton.com*

3.   There is a language called ABEEBA which has only three let-
     ters, A, B, and E. Words are formed in the usual way, by con-
     catenating letters, with the exception that "AE" is not allowed
     to appear. So, for example, AA, AB, BA, BB, BE, EA, EB, EE,
     is a complete list of the two letter words of ABEEBA. How
     many five-letter words are there?

There was banter and byplay aplenty as Jim explained the problems. Kids shouted out ideas and suggestions and jokes. The energy
and excitement in the room was doing more to wake me up than
the Starbucks coffee in my hand. Jim told us all which classes were in
which rooms and where we should all go. He promised we'd get back
to these problems when we reassembled after class with our mystery
guest speaker.

Students in the Sunday sessions of The Math Circle have two hour-
long classes (classes are organized roughly by age) back to back, separated
by a cookie break. After classes are over, the entire group gathers in the
auditorium for a guest lecture. As it turned out today's mystery guest
was Jim Tanton and we started by discussing the honeycomb problem
above. Several of the students had already solved it and Jim did his best
to organize the chaotic free-for-all of student solutions that ensued. We
moved on to the other problems, the students again pushing the discussion forward. Jim rode herd on the crowd and kept the discussion
moving; he frequently pointed to the connections between the problems and was occasionally able to slow the mob down by suggesting new
problems and generalizations.

By the end of the hour we'd pretty much solved the three problems,
but we had, in the best mathematical tradition, uncovered several more
mysteries that needed explaining. As the students noisily and happily
gathered up their belongings and chattered to each other, sharing their
ideas about these problems, Jim shouted above the chaos and got the last
word, "I don't really know why the answer to the ABEEBA question
is the bottom row of the honeycomb—you folks should figure that out.
See you next week."*

---

* Hints available in the Resources Section; full solutions online at: *PlayingWithMath.org
/solutions*

For Further Reading

You can read more about The Math Circle at the website *TheMathCircle.org*. To really get the flavor of The Math Circle at home, your best strategy is to buy Jim Tanton's *Solve This! Mathematical Activities for Students and Clubs*, and gather ten or twelve of your friends to read and work your way through it. It would amplify the experience if some of them had the energy of nine-year-olds.

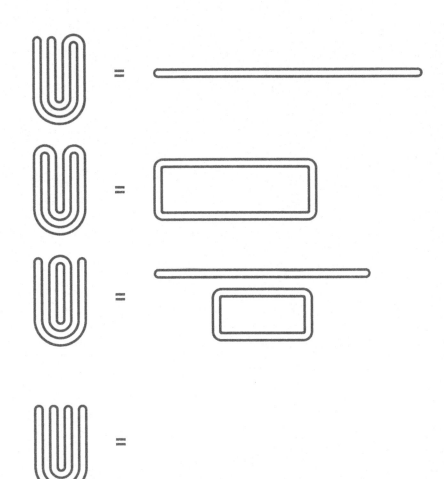

* From James Tanton's book, *Math Without Words*, in which this is #4.

=

=

=

I once asked the Kaplans if math circles required participants who already enjoy math. "Oh no, definitely not," they said…—SV

A Prison Math Circle

by Bob & Ellen Kaplan

We were once coaxed into doing a Math Circle in a state prison. Just going into it confirmed our worst fears: the ultraviolet stamp on our hands, dumping our pockets into locked trays; the crew-cut guards in their A stances, hands on hips by their holsters; the prisoners in their color-coded jump-suits, yellow for novice, blue for veteran, red for danger; the swiveling ceiling cameras, the doors on punched-in codes—and then we were in a very small room with a lot of very big people, who seemed to have spent their time on body-building.

We'd rehearsed our opening lines again and again, but they came out in whispers: "Math—is there anything worse?"

"Right on!" came the thunderous answer.

"Gee—they ask you to add 1 and 2…" we paused, as planned.

"Three," said a helpful voice.

"Three, of course, and then they ask you to add 1 and 2 and 3…"

A longer pause, and from another corner of the room, in a less friendly tone, "Six, what the hell do you take us for?"

"Sure, sure, six, we all know that," said one of us, while the other began writing on the blackboard: $1 + 2 + 3 + 4 + \ldots$ all the way up to 20, in a single line. "And then, you know, they ask you, what do all those add up to, 1 and 2 and 3 and 4, all the way up to 20…"

"That's it! That's it! That's why I hate it!" from a very large fellow in the front row. "They ask you some damn fool question nobody could answer, and you get it wrong and you get it wrong, and they tell you the answer, and what is it, just some stupid number!"

We managed to say, "Right on, you're bound to make mistakes along the way…"

We didn't feel and didn't want to sound patronizing, but wanted somehow or other to get us all on the same side, looking at this problem: the situation everyone's in, confronting the unknown. "And yet—there must be a better way than just adding up, $1 + 2$ is 3, and 3 more is 6, and 4 makes 10… you're going to get it wrong pretty soon—there must be a simpler way…"

A new voice: "You could make ten-bonds."

We'd never heard of ten-bonds. "What are they?"

"You know, 3 and 7 is 10, and 6 and 5…"

"No, you asshole! 6 and 4!"

"So 6 and 4." We drew slanted down lines from 3 and 7 to a 10, and now from 6 and 4 to another 10, and at their dictation, a few more ten bonds, the lines crossing in a tangled spider-web. We soon ran out of ten-bonds, but at least had become their secretaries, with them doing the math.

After a strained silence: "You could make twenty-bonds."

"You mean …"

"1 plus 19 is 20…"

The angry voice we'd heard before: "No, stupid! We've already used 1!"

"Oh, O. K., 11 and …" But there were no smaller numbers left to make twenty-bonds with.

"We'd had enough experience to recognize that 'I know this is wrong, but …' is usually the preface to an insight."

We'd fallen into those depths there never seems a way out of, when the impersonal world weighs you in the balance and finds you wanting. We were desperately thinking how to get out of there, when from the back a crouching little fellow said quietly, "I know this is wrong, but…" We'd had enough experience to recognize that "I know this is wrong, but …" is usually the preface to an insight. "I know this is wrong, but 1 and 20 is 21…"

We erased the spider web and drew a line connecting 1 and 20, and labeled it 21. "And 2 and 19 is also 21." Another connecting loop, labeled 21.

"Sheer luck," one of us said.

"No! They're all 21!"

"What all?"

"You know, all twenty of them! They're all 21!"

"Idiot!" (a new bass voice) "Not twenty, the watchama callems, those things!"

"Pairs," said the croucher.

"How many pairs?" we asked.

"All of them!"

"Yes, but…"

"All ten! Ten 21s! 210!"

High fives around the room! "Can we do another?"

"Sure," we said, "what would you like—adding 1 up to 100?"

"Do it!" They did it.

At the end of the hour, intense exhilaration.

"What do you call what we did?" one of them asked.

"Math."

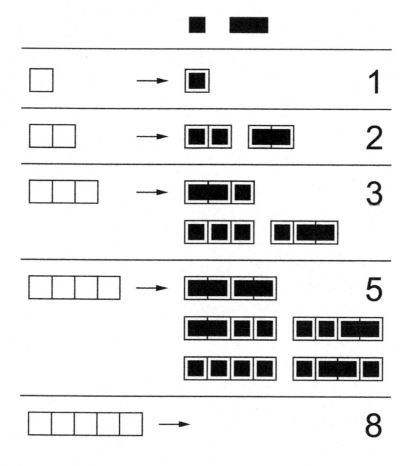

* From James Tanton's book, *Math Without Words*, in which this is #27.

89

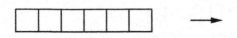

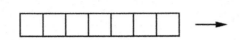

This chapter comes from a talk given by Mary O'Keeffe at the Great Circles Conference at the Mathematical Sciences Research Institute in March, 2009. —SV

Agents of Math Circles

by Mary O'Keeffe

Last October the New York Times printed a series of pictures. You see three girls who are supposed to be good at math—they all look quite unhappy, and they're each isolated. This connects with the stereotypes of mathematicians being really isolated and unhappy people. What's missing in those pictures, and what I've tried—out of desperation, really—to create, is a sense of belonging to a community, shared 'Eureka!' experiences with kindred spirits, and joy and laughter. I know the young women in the pictures, and I can attest that they actually have all those things in their lives. I'm not happy that the New York Times chose to paint a misleading picture by printing those particular photos. I've tried to address that on the website for our math circles; I have engaging photos there, showing the joy in our community.*

A Community for My Daughter

There was a workshop in 2008 about how to make graduate school a more positive experience for young women. Abbe Herzig, from State University of New York at Albany, talked about the notion of developing a mathematical identity and a sense of belonging. That's what motivated me, an unqualified economist, to start the Albany Area Math Circle. When my daughter was eight, in a very good school district, their solution to having noticed that she was ready for more advanced math was to send her down the hall to a supply closet. By herself. With a computer. If the rest of the third grade was working on two-digit addition with regrouping, then she was on the computer and got to

---

* *AlbanyAreaMathCircle.blogspot.com*

work—by herself in the supply closet—on three-digit addition with regrouping. I said there had to be a better way.

After Christmas, we pulled her out and began homeschooling. But I didn't want her to do it alone. We started volunteering in schools—inner city schools, actually. I said to the teachers, "Just give me your troublemakers, five or six of them. Alison and I will come in, and we'll do math games with them." Over time this grew into something that became the Albany Area Math Circle.

I'd bring in a pan of brownies and ask, "How can we make these brownies last forever?" Before cutting them, I would hand out markers and squares of graph paper with sixty-four squares on them, and I'd say, "Suppose we ate half of them the first day," and then the kids would color in the thirty two squares that had been eaten. I'd continue, "And then we'd eat half of that (sixteen squares or a quarter of the pan) the next day, and then half of *that* (eight squares or an eighth of the pan) the next." We continued down to one last brownie in the picture, and they proceeded to color half of that. They saw that, with a sharp enough knife, the brownies could last forever. And then we'd eat the brownies, the new idea filling our minds and our bellies.

I had lots more games like that. However, I was very encouraged to hear a distinguished mathematician like Harold Reiter say he could do things for Lenny Ng when Lenny was ten, but not when Lenny was twelve.[*] The same thing was true for me with my daughter, and for some of the other people who ultimately joined the math circle. So I had to find ways, as she and her friends got older, to engage them.

The main reason I felt the need to create the Albany Area Math Circle was that when my daughter went to the Math Olympiad Summer Program (MOSP) for the first time, she discovered a sense of community and belonging with kindred spirits that she'd never felt before. I think that's an amazing thing, and it doesn't automatically happen. When she went, she was lucky; Melanie Wood[†] was on the staff, and Melanie knows how to cheerlead. That probably made all the difference. It can't just be math; there has to be something to inspire the confidence you need to do the math. Melanie brought that spirit to MOSP.

---

[*] Harold Reiter mentored Lenny Ng (*math.duke.edu/~ng*), a very talented mathematician, when Lenny was a young child.

[†] Melanie Wood was the first young woman to make the U.S. team for the International Mathematical Olympiad, and has since won a prestigious prize in mathematics, the Morgan Prize.

Heart and Soul

Preparing students to participate in national mathematical competitions is one part of what the math circle does. But I consider it the frosting on the cake. I'm really trying to reach a much broader and more inclusive audience. So I created awards for the Heart and Soul of math circle. I try to create a sense of shared ownership of all the accomplishments of the math circle by encouraging students to help younger students, and even to help more advanced students—by asking good questions, and by pushing each other to think more deeply.

We have a big room that we work in. There's room for sixty students; we typically have about thirty. Students work in flexible groups among themselves. For the first hour and fifteen minutes, they are working by themselves. I hand out a wide variety of problems when they come in the door. They sit down, and they work for seventy-five minutes on their own. There are too many problems for any one person to do them all, so everyone is choosing the problems that feel most accessible to them.

People say, "Gee, this is stupid. They could be doing this at home." The fact is, they have very crowded lives. If I assigned it as homework, they wouldn't show up. Nobody knows what anybody else is doing during those seventy-five minutes. Everybody is in their own separate sphere.

Then we have pizza, which is very important. After that the students assemble into groups to talk over the problems. They choose groups themselves. But an important part of my role is cross-fertilizing the groups, connecting them. I look for who is feeling disconnected, who is feeling left out, and I try to find a role for that person that's empowering to them.

We have a continuous stream of new students coming in. It's been very effective to take a veteran student who's looking a little disengaged, a little lost, who's thinking, "Everybody's better at it than I am" (which may or may not be true, but they're feeling that anyway) and put them together with a brand new student who's also feeling lost. Suddenly the veteran student becomes the expert—that's very empowering. I think that is one of the things that has made our math circle so successful.

It is an incredibly diverse group. Anybody in high school who wants to come can come. This year we have about thirty students who come regularly; five of them qualified for the USA Math Olympiad (USAMO). We have other students who aren't even interested in math competitions, which is perfectly fine. We also have students who try them, and

"The key thing I tell new students is to come with an enthusiasm for making mistakes."

haven't made the AIME* yet. That's fine too. We have a community—in which girls are very well represented—where they all feel a sense of ownership; they all feel a sense of identification and belonging.

A lot of that is because of the way I've structured things. If you go to our Hall of Fame,† you'll notice that the first thing I've listed is the captains, who are not always the most mathematically able, but they're the ones who inspire, and help, and encourage. Then we have our Heart and Soul Award winners, who were two especially wonderful co-captains. They retired a few years ago and never made it to the USAMO themselves, but they were incredibly encouraging to other students. I consider them proximate causes of several of this year's USAMO winners. Then I list all the students who've helped younger students. Finally, underneath all this, are our USAMO qualifiers and our AIME perfect scorers. It sends a message, a message about belonging. You belong not just because you made the USAMO, not just because you helped us with a whole lot of points on the New York state math league. You belong because you ask questions, because you're brave enough to ask those questions, because you're willing to make mistakes.

Enthusiasm for Mistakes

The key thing I tell new students is to come with an enthusiasm for making mistakes.‡ I tell a lot of stories about that. I love how Richard Feynman, a world-class physicist, talks about making mistakes. And Einstein talks about needing a big trash can for his office at Princeton. I also talk about Andrew Wiles working for all those years, and then discovering a mistake.§

I want our strongest students and the rookies to all see that everybody makes mistakes. I especially want the grown ups advising our math circle to show this. I talk a lot about the mistakes I make. Mukkai Krishnamoorthy, a computer science professor at Rensselaer Polytechnic Institute and my co-advisor, will often say, "Great minds think alike, not necessarily correctly, but alike. A student comes up with a wrong answer, but it's the same wrong answer I got."

When I first created the math circle, before I even dared to call it that, I was afraid to admit that I couldn't do a lot of the problems we

---

* American Invitational Mathematics Examination

† *sites.google.com/site/mathcircle/albany-area-math-circle-hall-of-fame-2*

‡ See *Surely You're Joking, Mr. Feynman!* and *What Do You Care What Other People Think?*

§ See *Fermat's Last Theorem*, by Andrew Singh, or the PBS NOVA video 'The Proof'. After many years of quietly trying to prove Fermat's Last Theorem, Wiles announced his proof, only to realize it had a mistake. A year later, he was able to clear up his mistake.

offer these amazing students. I used to spend hours cutting and pasting until I could find a set of problems I could explain how to do. Finally I decided it was better to be honest—to admit that I couldn't do many of these problems. So a lot of what I do is cheerlead. I think that's a really important role.

I sometimes see negative interactions even in my math circle—thoughtless remarks students make that leave other students feeling bad. That's why I celebrate the students who encourage other students with the Heart and Soul award. Especially as your math circle scales up, you can't personally encourage everybody. What you can do is empower students to do it. I have seen transformations in students who were feeling bad about themselves, once they had someone else to encourage.

Three of our original math circle members have graduated from college now, and when they come home on vacation, they still come back to solve problems with our students. I think that is the ultimate measure of our success. They're not eligible for math contests any longer, but they love the community and the fun of coming back to solve problems.

Maybe because the math isn't my specialty, I became good at finding what works organizationally. This is what I did to create this community, and you can do it too. You get together some charismatic high school students, both male and female. You break them up into groups; you have a big room where they can spread out. You lead the students; you work with that chemistry.

Here's another suggestion for giving that sense of belonging. Recently I made cards with our web site address on it, which my students love handing out. The students hand them out at math contests; they give them to younger students who express an interest. It really makes them feel like agents of math circles.

PUZZLE
Food for Thought[*]

by Jan Nordgreen

ANABEL: I'm thinking of four numbers.

BESSY: I'm thinking of when we're going to eat.

ANABEL: The second of them is a positive integer.

BESSY: If there are five cows staring at you, are two cows staring at you?

ANABEL: The sum of the first two equals the third. The sum of the second and the third equals the fourth.

BESSY: Hmm… What is the sum of the third and the fourth?

ANABEL: The first number.

BESSY: Bummer!

ANABEL: No, 'number.'

BESSY: What are the four numbers?

ANABEL: Who cares? What I would like to know is how big can their sum be?

BESSY: Can we eat now?

---

* From Jan's blog, Think Again, *EasyQuestion.net/thinkagain/2010/05/18/rhetorical-food-for-thought*. Jan modified a question from The Bay Area Mathematical Olympiad to create this puzzle.

The Julia Robinson Mathematics Festival

by Nancy Blachman

It was March, 1972. My tenth-grade math teacher, Mr. Forthoffer, was handing out another problem set from Saint Mary's College. We didn't have to do them, so some kids just left them on their desks. I had so much fun with the ones we'd gotten earlier in the year that I couldn't wait to start working on these. The first few problems were usually pretty straightforward, and solving them would boost my confidence for tackling others. I never could solve all of them, but I enjoyed trying.

I liked experimenting—cutting a 10x10 square into two pieces to make a rectangle, plugging values into equations, learning more about the problems as I worked. Even after I solved a problem, I liked thinking about whether there was an easier way to solve it.

Students who scored high on that year's qualifying problems would be invited to the Saint Mary's Math Contest at the end of the school year. Schools all over the San Francisco Bay Area sent busloads of students. I didn't actually care much about going. For me, the fun was in the problems I was doing at home.

I went to the contest that year and the next two, but it was a disappointment. Sitting alone in that room all day, without being able to discuss my ideas with my father—it wasn't nearly as much fun as the problems I got from school. To this day I remember them with deep fondness.

When I teamed up with Josh Zucker and the Mathematical Sciences Research Institute (MSRI) in 2006 to create something new, I was determined to bring back the best of the now-defunct Saint Mary's Math Contest, and leave behind what didn't work. We decided to emphasize fun, creating a mathematics festival instead of another competition. The festival would have dozens of tables with mathematical problems,

"We decided to emphasize fun, creating a mathematics festival instead of another competition."

puzzles, games, and activities, each with a facilitator to help students stay connected with the math.

We wanted the festival to nurture students, so we let them work individually or in groups. We hoped to attract students at a wide range of abilities with math at all levels, so we chose problems and activities that would connect to one another. We started each set with simple problems everyone could work out, leading to progressively more difficult questions (we even included unsolved research problems). We hoped to have so many problems that not even a mathematical genius could solve all of them during the festival.

The festival needed a name to match its spirit. Julia Robinson was a great mathematician who, along with two other mathematicians, was renowned for solving Hilbert's tenth problem. She lived not far from us in the San Francisco Bay area, and was a distinguished mathematics professor at the University of California at Berkeley for many years, until her death in 1985. It felt perfect to honor her legacy with this festival.

In March 2007, the first year we ran the festival, we were concerned that we might not get many students to sign up, but within a few weeks the festival was oversubscribed. With more registrants than space, we asked our sponsor, Google, for a tent to accommodate more students. They came through, and the day of the festival started out sunny and chaotic.

It all fell into place, with hundreds of students eagerly approaching the problems we'd devised. There were thirty tables with activities, puzzles, games, and problems. When we announced that sandwiches were available for lunch, many of the kids would not stop working. We may not have managed to feed their bodies, but we surely fed their minds! The prizes from Google were icing on the cake.

The response was so enthusiastic that we've been able to make the festival an annual tradition. And we've grown, offering festivals in over a dozen locations—California (eight different locations), Connecticut, Washington D.C., Michigan, Texas, North Carolina, Arizona, Virginia, Washington (state), and Wyoming.

My goal was to inspire, delight, and challenge children, as the Saint Mary's Math Contest did for me, but with more collaboration and less competition. Thanks to its many sponsors and volunteers, the Julia Robinson Mathematics Festival is a success, and I've seen my dream come true.*

---

* You can find more information at: *JuliaRobinsonMathFestival.org*

1. A company named JULIA has an advertising display with just the five letters of its name, lit up in various colors. On a certain day the colors might be red, green, green, blue, red. The company wishes to have a different color scheme for each of the 365 days of the year. What is the minimum number of colors that can be used for this purpose?

2. How would you decide whether a number in base 7 is even, based on its digits?

3. Given the sequence 1, 2, 4, 5, 7, 8, 10, ... where every third integer is missing, find the sum of the first hundred terms in the sequence.

4. Find the sum of the cubes of the numbers from 1 to 13. Now find the sum of the cubes of the numbers from 1 to n.

5. Using exactly five 5's, and the operations $+$, $-$, $\times$, $\div$, and factorial (!), represent each of the numbers up to 30.

EXPLORATIONS
Candy Conundrum*

by Joshua Zucker

Julia Robinson
Mathematics Festival

Colors

Some years ago, a candy company advertised the large number of flavors that could be made by mixing their candies in your mouth. How many are there really?

1. You have 5 red apple candies. How many different nonempty sets of candies could you put in your mouth?

2. You have 5 red apple and 4 green lime candies. How many different nonempty sets of candies could you put in your mouth?

3. You have 5 red apple, 4 green lime, and 3 yellow pineapple candies. How many different nonempty sets of candies could you put in your mouth?

Flavors

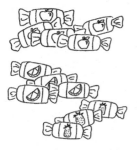

We'll consider two sets of candies to be the same flavor if the ratio of candies of each color in one set is the same as the ratio in the other. For instance, 2 green and 1 yellow is the same flavor as 4 green and 2 yellow; it's 2/3 green, or a 2:1 green:yellow ratio. Similarly 3 red is the same flavor as 2 red: pure red!

4. You have 5 red candies. How many flavors could you make?

5. You have 5 red and 4 green candies. How many flavors could you make?

6. You have 5 red, 4 green, and 3 yellow candies. How many flavors could you make?

---

* Find more problems at: *JuliaRobinsonMathFestival.org*

Geometry

There's a geometric interpretation of all of the above. For instance, with 5 red and 4 green candies, the possible combinations are ordered pairs. (2,1) and (4,2) are the same flavor, for example.

7. Expressed geometrically, what does it mean for two different sets of candies to be the same flavor? Assume for now that there are only two colors.

8. Describe a geometric way of understanding how many different flavors there are. Compare it to the numeric approach.

9. What does symmetry tell you about the number of flavors with k red candies and k green candies?

Generalizing

Now let's try for some bigger patterns.

10. If you have 1 candy of each of n colors, how many different flavors are possible? If you have k candies of 1 color, how many different flavors are possible? OK, sorry, that was too easy.

11. If you have 2 candies of each of n colors, how many different flavors are possible? If you have k candies of each of 2 colors, how many different flavors are possible?

12. Generalize as much as you can!

13. How do the previous answers change if the candies are large, with an upper limit to how many fit in your mouth at once?

14. What can you say about the relative probability of various flavors if you pick a random handful of size n out of a set of candies? Start by considering some easy cases, where n is small, and there aren't too many different flavors, and plenty of candies of each flavor (since n will limit you, it gets more complicated if you also have limits due to running out of candies).

15. What other questions can you think of about how to count combinations of candies?

Amanda draws a wide variety of young people into the math circles we do at the Institute each summer. Elisa's story is a powerful one. —SV

A Young Voice:
Consider the Circle,
A Space Without Corners

by Elisa R. Vanett

The clock on the wall is a daily reminder to the little girl that her peers have intellects that are far superior to hers. She sits silently in the quiet of the small, nearly-empty classroom. There are three round tables; she's been ordered to sit at the one in the corner to finish the textbook she's been neglecting for weeks. The ticking circle talks softly in the corner, rehearsing its never-ending speech about time and how much of it is being wasted away. She listens, watches as the jolting hand on the clock winds around, documenting the wasted time.

Counting up the seconds, the minutes, the hours, and the days, she begins a silent protest, going as slowly as possible to fight the teacher's desire to drag her through the pages of meaningless symbols. She resists teachers who don't teach, classmates who taunt her for going to the "resource" room, this corner for the mentally impaired. Handicapped kids are placed here—the ones too slow to keep up with the group, brought here to become someone else's problem. Shoved into a corner and forgotten.

She wishes someone would take her as she is and teach her. Teach her what she doesn't know. But she remains in the corner, and the teaching she craves will never happen in that room.

This silently protesting girl was me.

By the time I met Amanda Serenevy, I was hungry for knowledge. Ironically, as much as I hated and despised mathematics at that point in my life, I was so ready, so open to discovering what I was missing. I wanted to get math. My hatred and my eagerness were two sides of a chasm I was terrified of crossing. But the reward of comprehension kept calling to me from the other side. I knew that there had to be something beautiful and creative about mathematics.

Dr. Amanda Serenevy, a mathematician, professor, scholar, and teacher, is the one who has guided and directed me to new levels of understanding. Her insights and intelligence were a revelation to me. I could not believe it; someone was willing to take the time and effort to teach me, listen to me, answer my questions, and most importantly, mentor me. No one was forcing me to learn anything I did not want to, motivating me to pursue my academic career.

In the summer of 2008 I had the honor of attending my first math circle, held at the University of Notre Dame. My mentor, Amanda, invited me to come, promising that it wouldn't be like anything I had ever experienced before. The math circle more than fulfilled her promise. Besides meeting a collection of amazing and peculiar people, I participated in actual mathematical collaboration for the first time. There I met Bob and Ellen Kaplan. I will never forget the time when Bob was giving his usual morning lecture, rambling on about both students and math, when he said something that struck me very oddly because I had never heard anyone say anything like it before. "Either they get the answer right, or they get it interestingly wrong," he said with a chuckle. Was he actually suggesting that it was okay for students to get the wrong answer? ... that getting the wrong answer could be a good and positive thing?

Bob and Ellen convinced me that math does not have to be a terrifying and horrible experience, and my point of view turned around 180 degrees because they had such open minds. They were funny, open to suggestions and questions, and made note of everyone's input. Everyone in the room was willing to learn from each other. It was collaboration, a group effort, a situation that I had never been in before.

"It was the corner where things would always be dumbed-down just enough for the teachers to simply pass me on."

Looking back on my experiences in the resource room, one of the largest issues was that the teacher did not approach math creatively or effectively. I felt as if I were being treated like a number rather than a person who could actually think for herself. I was cheated out of my education; I was shoved into a small corner by adults who didn't care about me, my intelligence, or my education. It was the corner where things would always be dumbed-down just enough for the teachers to simply pass me on.

When I met Amanda, all of that changed. At the Math Circle Institute, all of that changed. The grades that I had received suddenly didn't matter anymore. The teachers who abandoned me didn't matter anymore. I found a set of wonderful people who loved math and teaching. I was surprised to hear one of the teachers say that he was afraid of losing his students forever to a system that unjustly puts people in categories, where the worth of a child's mind can suddenly be weighed based on a test score. This statement surprised me because I realized that there were teachers who actually cared about their students' progress.

Perhaps the truth is that teachers can't save all of their students. But it would certainly mean the world to that struggling, particular student if one teacher would take the time to show them that they have a voice that deserves to be heard. As a student who struggled, I needed something more than just hard work; I needed someone to listen. I needed someone to accept that, yes, I was slower than everyone else, but even so, I wasn't going to quit as long as someone was willing to teach me.

Math circle is awesome because it inspires me to think of my own creative math ideas. The style of instruction differs from a traditional math class because there is a feeling of freedom to make mistakes. Another important aspect is that there are people in the room who have enough math background to know where your ideas could end up or to answer your questions. A participant may not be able to understand every detail of the discussion, but the open nature of the collaboration can still lead everyone to interesting insights.

During my third summer at the Math Circle Institute in 2010, I had the joy of discovering a few advanced math concepts for myself. On one occasion, the discussion touched briefly on the concept of infinity and triggered me to think of slicing three-dimensional shapes into infinitely thin slices. I wondered whether there were any mathematical expressions that correlated with this idea. I was excited to discover that this idea forms a major component of second semester calculus. Another time, I was inspired to draw a series of pictures of a cube morphing into a sphere. It turns out that this idea is involved in homotopy theory, a branch of topology. These were ground-breaking experiences for me because I realized that not only could I think critically, but that I could discover advanced mathematical concepts on my own without being taught. I learned that I was just as capable of doing math as anyone else, in spite of those who thought I belonged in the corner of the resource room.

Homeschoolers:
Doing Math

Kentucky flame, by Erik and Martin Demaine

Kentucky Flame, by Erik and Martin Demaine (photo by the artists), is a curved crease origami piece, made with Mi-Teintes watercolor paper in 2013. The original is 7"×9"×16" tall. Erik writes, "When folded along curved creases, paper shapes itself into a natural equilibrium form. These equilibria are poorly understood, especially for curved creases. We are exploring what shapes are possible in this genre of self-folding origami, whose many applications include structures that can be deployed in space." See *ErikDemaine.org/curved* for more of their beautiful and ground-breaking work.

Martin homeschooled Erik until he entered college at the age of twelve. Erik is now a professor at MIT, where Martin is an artist-in-residence.

Introduction

Homeschoolers come in many flavors. They are conservative Christians, progressive pagans, folks who don't think much about religion, and all the rest; urban, suburban, and rural; families whose particular kids would not be well-served by the local schools; parents who want to protect their kids from people who are wildly different than them, parents who want to protect their kids from the pressures to consume and conform, and parents who simply want to share the joy of learning with their kids.

People who don't know any homeschoolers often have stereotypes in their minds. Even when true on the surface, those stereotypes can hide deeper truths. From what I've seen, homeschoolers can be better at connecting across differences than most folks. In the time I've spent on Living Math Forum, an online list for discussing how to help kids learn math, I've met many people with world views and politics quite different from mine, and had great conversations with them about how we can best help our kids learn. That is where we most easily agree. We all love our children, and want the best for them. I have learned something there about letting go of my own perspective, and approaching questions from each parent's own point of view.

My own personal leaning is toward unschooling. Unschoolers believe that children have a "rage to learn," and that "they can and should be trusted with their own education" (see the chapters by Holly Graff, Tiffani Bearup, and Pam Sorooshian).* But I want this book to be accessible to all parents, whatever their beliefs and whatever values they hold, so I've tried to provide a balance. Julie Brennan made math study a daily part of her children's lives and then thought deeply about how to work with each child's learning style. Her insight inspired me to start collecting the pieces in this book.

---

* If you'd like to learn more about unschooling, you might want to read John Holt's books, especially *How Children Learn*. The site HoltGWS.com may also lead you to useful information.

I've provided a diverse palette of ideas because this is not about the right way to raise your kids; it's about how kids learn. The common thread is that the parents, however they originally felt about math, are finding ways to approach it enthusiastically and playfully.

As you read these chapters, you may feel like you'll never have the depth that Julie has. Or that your child isn't as comfortable as Holly's daughter. That's ok. Jimmie shows you her path forward from fear. And Tiff shows you how even a math hater can have fun with math. To me, the deepest theme in this section is trust. Each child learns differently, and trusting your child will mean following different paths in different circumstances. Trusting your own ability to learn the math you never really learned before may be vital too!

Julie hosts discussions of homeschoolers' math education issues on a Yahoo group called Living Math Forum. She's learned a lot over the years, and often shares stories of what she's learning as she teaches her four children. —SV

Tying It All Together: Reflections on Homeschooling Math

by Julie Brennan

It felt so rewarding to be a part of my daughter Hannah's learning process today, and I'd like to share it. Here's our story...

It's one thing to philosophically grasp and agree with an idea or principle. It's another to actually see it displayed in the learning of your children. And, even when you theoretically believed it to be true, it can be amazing to see it play out in some wonderful ways as you had hoped.

Each One Is Different

With my first son, Michael, I spent many years trying to traditionally educate him in math. When he was around eight, we made the gradual change to a living math approach. So I had "attitude damage control" to do for years. But still, I recall being absolutely floored at how quickly he could learn mathematical ideas at age eleven that were difficult even six months prior, and how in mathematical areas that motivated him (geometry at the time), he could advance way beyond "grade level." He only fully mastered most of his elementary math, beyond basic number sense and arithmetic, in the year after he turned eleven.

With my next son, Nick, I thought I had learned my lesson, but unfortunately I gave in to the temptation to "recognize his ability," and tried to push him to learn things earlier. He found basic math and fractions much easier than his brother had, and I wrongly assumed that meant his entire math-learning track would be faster. It wasn't. It was simply different. He learned some things more easily than his brother, but other things—spatial concepts and the ability to do more extensive problem solving, for example—did not develop in him until he was closer to twelve or thirteen. I do regret having pushed him inadvertently, because I had damage control to do with him last year (which thankfully seems to have worked out by this year).

My two older children confirmed what made sense to me all along: being patient and expecting that a child will master math concepts on their own timetable does work. Not requiring them to learn "third grade fraction operations" in third grade does not mean they will be permanently behind, or harm them in the end. However, I still do sometimes have a bit of doubt that makes me wonder if I'm doing the right thing by my kids—until I see the results.

As they say, third time's a charm, right? With my third child, Hannah, now age eleven, I just tried to follow her lead and her signals with math all along. I have given her a lot of math enrichment experiences—she has grown up with math readers, as I started integrating those in our math library when she was about three years old. And lately I've been writing a lot about her, because she is now in the "golden age" of math learning that my boys experienced. The difference with her is that, so far, she has no negative baggage whatsoever—and I'm trying to keep it that way.

Doing Decimals

Hannah has been wanting to learn algebra, and seems to have a mind more wired for algebra than my other kids at this age, so she has been going through a book called *Access to Algebra and Geometry*. She hit a snag in that she never really learned decimals before this, so she and I have been going over her decimal understanding recently. Because she could relate it to money, her understanding and ability to perform operations on two decimal places was rock solid. But when she got to the third place and beyond, she struggled with the abstractness of it. She got some great ideas on how to approach decimals from reading *Math Doesn't Suck* by Danica McKellar, but needed to put them into practice.

A few weeks ago we decided to go back to basics and use money as manipulatives. I had a $10 bill, a $1 bill, ten dimes, and ten pennies, and we arranged things and discussed the progression: going right, you divide the unit by ten to get one-tenth, going left, you multiply by ten. Then she extended it on paper all the way to a billion on the left, and a millionth on the right.

When we were talking about it, I mentioned that it became abstract because we don't split pennies into fractions. Hannah instantly brightened up and said, "Yes, we do! The gas tax, remember?"* Well, I do remember that she asked me last year about the "$\frac{9}{10}$" next to the price of gas, and I had explained to her that this was a fraction of a penny. She related quite correctly that if we could have cut that penny up in ten pieces, one of those pieces would be a tenth of a penny, and, looking at the chart, a thousandth of a dollar. And that if she could then cut that tenth of a penny into another ten tiny pieces, those would be ten-thousandths of a dollar.

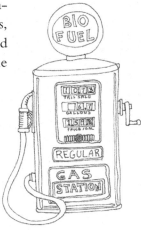

We also realized that, while she'd been "taught" this before, the whole "ten" vs. "tenth" thing had never really sunk in because she isn't a print-oriented kid. She is more auditory, and the words are so similar she just never picked up on the "th" being the key to understanding how this is expressed in writing. So we practiced enunciating that "th" at the end to emphasize being on the fraction side of the decimal, going back and forth from the whole units.

We usually think of money being limited to the penny unit, but apparently even some time ago she got the correct idea that we can split that unit up, even if we don't have a coin for it. And she also gets the fact that we pay a rounded-up price for gas because we can't split that penny.

What happened today was really fun, and a great illustration of how connections to things our kids understand can be so vital to enthusiasm and retention. We have been working on tying together all of Hannah's understanding of fractions with decimals and percents. I have a sample of a math test that she will be taking at the end of this month.† Each day before we sit down, I have been looking over a question I believe she does not know how to answer, thinking to myself, "What does she need to know to confidently answer this?" I start out our time together talking about, demonstrating, and diagramming the concepts needed to understand the problem.

The one we looked at today involved identifying, on a number line, a decimal number with several decimal places. While this seems simple to me, I know she has stumbled on similar problems in the past. So I started out with a very light-hearted talk about the number line: "This is where we've been, this is where you're headed". We started with counting numbers, then added the zero and talked about why it's

---

* While the exact origin of the $\frac{9}{10}$ths cent gas pricing practice isn't certain, it goes back to about the time the Federal government began to levy a fractional tax on gas in 1941. The $\frac{9}{10}$ths of a penny has stuck ever since, even though the federal tax fraction has varied over the decades, so this appears to be a marketing technique rather than a true passing on of the fractional gas tax.
† Our kids get to take choir, debate, drama, and other fun group classes with a homeschool co-op that requires each child to participate in annual standardized testing, so we were preparing for that.

important as a placeholder, a baseline, a starting point. We drew several number lines and reviewed real-life examples: the thermometer (she promptly got one out and compared it) and the time line. We talked about what these real-life examples use as their baseline, or zero. We brought up examples from many math readers we've read that exhibit these concepts.*

All of this is review, but I don't talk about it that way, nor do I imply she should already know it; you can "teach" a child something at eight, nine, and ten and they can still say they just "learned" it at eleven. But all that exposure makes the final learning with retention almost effortless—it's exciting, joyful, and lasting. Hannah is excited when she makes these recognitions, as she physically ties things together with notes we've made in the past that she flips to in her journal, or she'll run to the bookshelf to show me a *Foxtrot* comic or to the computer to show me a Webkinz† adventure.

Then I drew her the number line, setting her up to better understand the algebraic concept of real numbers, and we practiced writing some fractions on the line. She has a good grasp of this. We talked about abstract fractions we know exist, such as one millionth, which we can't draw on the line; then, the fact that these fractions can still be split further to get infinitesimally small fractions. She asked me to write the word "infinitesimally" on her notes, because she liked the word so much. (*The Cat in Numberland*, by Ivar Ekeland, does a good job setting up scenarios for this understanding.)

Next we reviewed decimal places, and I had her draw a number line, and place various decimal numbers on the line. She had no trouble with this either. We used notepaper turned sideways so that the lines could be divided evenly. When she plotted 1.7 and 1.8, I asked her, "Where would 1.75 be?" She knew it would be halfway between 1.7 and 1.8. So I knew her understanding was solid enough to pull out the test question and ask if she could answer it.

She got it right away, when I know she would have struggled had we not spent the half-hour ahead of time going over all her understanding, placing what she understood about fractions and decimals in the context of the number line. She only began to be motivated to learn how to do operations with fractions using more abstract numbers (beyond the intuitive ½, ⅓, and ¼) a couple months ago, so this is all

"It is like planting seeds when the ground is fully prepared and the season is right, as opposed to trying to plant seeds where these conditions are not met—for the same level of effort, you get so much more out of it."

---

* Our list includes *Less Than Zero* by Stuart Murphy, *Math Smart Junior* by Marsha Lerner, *The Number Devil* by Hans Enzensberger, and *Riddle-Iculous* by Joan Holu.

† *Webkinz.com* is an internet site where kids take their animated stuffed animals on adventures.

pretty new to her still. But she is grasping and retaining it very well. She also has a prodigious attention span for this, because she is making all these connections.

It is like planting seeds when the ground is fully prepared and the season is right, as opposed to trying to plant seeds where these conditions are not met—for the same level of effort, you get so much more out of it.

We moved on to connecting fractions to decimals, decimal notation, and then percents. Percents fascinate her, but she hasn't been able to fully understand them until now, other than the "common" percents of 10%, 25%, and so on. Today, I just wrote out a bunch of fractions and Hannah converted each of these to decimal notation and percents. Because I made them up, we encountered all kinds of interesting things, as opposed to predictable problems in a workbook. Then we talked about at least one real-life application of each answer. This seems to be vitally important to her.

We had a problem that ended up with 23%, and she shook her head at that one, saying nobody would advertise something as 23% off—it's an uncommon percent. I said she's right, people think in terms of 20% or 25%; odd percents are not convenient. But I told her that in real life, there are 23% off sales. Let's say there was an item regularly priced at $22. If you use a $5 off coupon, they are giving you about 23% off. We worked out the math, and she saw that this was a way retailers could make savings easy for consumers to understand. She was satisfied that we had a tangible example of this.

When I gave her 3/2 to convert, she hiccupped a bit on a real-life application of 150%, because she had always related the smaller percents more to a percent off, like a sale discount. She and her sister have been using the Webkinz coupons for the store, and estimating their savings very closely. So less than 100% was natural. But I said you can't have more than 100% off, because that would bring the cost to zero. Well, she pipes up and says, "Wouldn't 150% off mean they pay *you* to buy the item?" And I had to admit that made sense! Then she told me about a *Foxtrot* comic where this logic had applied, and how it made more sense to her now that she understood the math better. We also walked through examples of how we run across 150% in real life—for instance, if there were ten car thefts in our neighborhood last year, and there was a 150% increase in car thefts this year, how many more car thefts were there? She correctly figured out that this meant there were fifteen more this year than last year.

When she got 8% on another problem, she related this to getting a raise or a pay cut. I am amazed at her innate sense of what percentages

"We talked about at least one real-life application of each answer. This seems to be vitally important to her."

naturally apply to real-life scenarios. I asked her how she knew 8% was a reasonable pay raise, and she referred me to her *Math Doesn't Suck* book.

We also dealt with fractional percentages; again, she had to work through a real example in order for the concept to make sense. And then we worked through one other number-line problem on that sample test, discussing how she should be thinking about what two whole numbers the fractional number is between, and bar the area it should be in, before selecting her answer—estimating an answer before figuring it.

A Golden Age for Math

"Hannah is gaining a very strong number sense along with her procedures, and is taking charge of her own education to ensure that there are no 'black boxes.'"

We spent well over an hour today on this, and could have gone longer if she didn't have some place to go—she was not fatigued or wanting to stop. Hannah is gaining a very strong number sense along with her procedures, and is taking charge of her own education to ensure that there are no "black boxes."* She isn't satisfied until she can internalize her learning with at least one real-life example, sometimes many, and connect the dots with her math reading and previous notes she has kept. She is now joyfully and enthusiastically mastering concepts that a traditional curriculum would have expected her to master sooner—instead she spent the time learning algebra early last fall. I am thrilled to be her learning facilitator and mentor, rather than being a teacher with a passive student, wondering if anything is really sticking.

I think every child's golden age might be different for math, just as it is for reading and language development. With my three older kids for math, it has happened to be right around eleven and twelve. I tutored a girl a few years ago, however, who needed a lot more time before comprehension became easy for her.

Sarah's parents were more frustrated with her apparent lack of math ability than she was, as her slower development was in stark contrast to her younger brother's. He was math-gifted and learning trigonometry at eleven. But when she graduated early from homeschooling high school and took algebra at our local community college at sixteen, she really got math for the first time, and enjoyed it, having been lucky enough to get a great teacher.

I had tutored her the year before—we had worked through the chapters that were within her reach in Harold Jacobs' *Mathematics: A Human Endeavor*. I recall thinking during our tutoring sessions that my

---

* A calculator is an example of a black box. You put something in, and you get something out, but you don't know how it works, really. Many people treat math procedures this way, but if you don't understand how it works, it's not really math.

biggest contribution to Sarah and her family was giving them some out-side perspective that Sarah was not math-handicapped. Given time it could come—if she wasn't convinced by then she could never do it.

My daughter Hannah is formally mastering these concepts quickly now because she has been exposed to them for years and years through math readers, science and living math projects, natural conversations, and day-to-day activities. Sensing her cues along the way, I knew that expecting that she master and retain what she was exposed to was unrealistic. I might have managed to get her to master long division sooner if we had repeated the procedure over and over, but she would not have understood what she was doing.

Spending that time instead developing her sense of number, of proportion, of relationships—it was much better allocated. We have just recently gotten to formally converting decimals to percents, but she very naturally and comfortably estimates percents in increments of tens and fives in her everyday conversation. She has the innate sense of it, and now all we're doing is plugging that into the formal operations necessary to advance into formal algebra, where she wants to go next.

Why would it be so exciting for me to see Hannah exhibit a high level of true understanding of fractions, decimals, and percents at eleven? A few weeks ago I went to my son, Nick's, hybrid school (where he goes two days a week) to help tutor in the math lab. A girl a few years older than Hannah (I'll call her Tammy) was there working on her pre-algebra homework. The assignment she struggled with had to do with a table of blood types: O, A, B, or AB, and Rh + or −. There were a number of questions that asked her to interpret the data and express it in terms of percentages, forecast how many people in a given group would have a certain blood type, and so on.

Tammy's first question to me was how to enter $\frac{85}{100}$ into her calculator. As I helped her out quite a bit over the next forty-five minutes, I realized the following:

She didn't know that a fraction can be expressed as a division, i.e., that $\frac{85}{100}$ is the same as 85 divided by 100, or 85 out of 100. She didn't understand the basic idea of a ratio—a relationship between two numbers, a proportion.

She had been taught all the right procedures, but she did not know what they were used for, and consequently, she didn't know what procedure to use for what application.

When I tried to interpret the meaning of something—"$\frac{85}{100}$ means 85 out of every 100 people; this is what 85% means"—she just didn't want to process it. She asked me again how to put the numbers into her calculator. All she wanted was to write down an answer, so she could be done with her homework.

I could see by Tammy's work that she was conscientious and wanted a good grade. She had a good mind and desire to learn, but she'd been trained that math learning is memorizing and applying procedures, not thinking about the meaning of the numbers. Her initial answers to the questions were preposterous, and the only reason she knew they were wrong was by looking at the answer in the back of the book. She had no idea how to make a sensible connection between the information given and the processes she knew.

Nick has the same teacher for his algebra class, and believes she is very good. She attempts to teach through relevant examples, and she has the kids work on projects and activities designed to help them relate to and retain what they are learning. When a middle-school student like Tammy has had so many years of math instruction geared toward getting the right answer on the page, it can be hard to benefit from that style of teaching. It must be so hard for a student to do something different after years of this.

When I was hanging out on a math teacher list for a while, there was a physics teacher who kept preaching, over and over, the importance of kids developing proportional thinking, that without this, they would be nearly incapable of understanding the higher-level mathematics needed for physics and other applications. Some kids glean this understanding and skill simply from learning the operations of multiplication and division, but others need to experience this kinesthetically or visually to understand proportions and relationships between numbers. Too much attention on procedures and operations can actually cut off this development.

Today I think I felt more than ever before that Hannah was demonstrating her growth in her ability to think proportionally. Knowing how important this foundation is to all her future math, I was deeply gratified.

GAME
Place Value Risk

adapted by Sue VanHattum

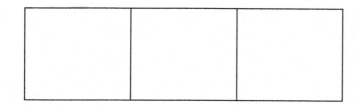

What You Need

Any number of players, one die (regular is fine, but ten-sided, with 0 to 9 would give a more interesting game), and the board you see above copied onto scrap paper.

How to Play

One person rolls the die (players take turns getting to roll the die), and all players place the digit in one of the spaces on their board. Repeat two more times.

Scoring

Your score for this round is the three-digit number you created. Play another round, and add your new number to your total. First to reach 5,000 wins.

Variations

- Change the board to use four-digit numbers, roll four times, and try to reach 50,000.
- Put one extra space off to the side on your playing board, for a free cell, and put any one digit there.

Naming

If you think your kids might like this game, add to the appeal by making up a fun name for it.

Advice from Living Math Forum

by Julie Brennan

Proportional Reasoning

Kate asked: *Could you explain to me exactly what proportional reasoning is?*

Proportional reasoning is the ability to see relationships between quantities (which could be objects, or distances, or time—anything that is being measured or counted) in proportion to each other, which is eventually translated to numerical notation. An extremely simple example of this is an everyday type situation—we might say that it takes a gallon of paint to cover two walls. How many gallons of paint does it take to cover eight walls?

If you understand that the proportion is 1 gallon for every 2 walls, then you know that you have to multiply the 2 walls times 4 to get the 8 walls. Therefore you need the 1 gallon times 4 to get 4 gallons of paint. This example is so simple, it really is intuitive for many kids—they get this kind of exposure from real life. For example, doubling or halving or otherwise adjusting cooking recipes involves proportions.

I see proportions begin to become more abstract when they involve fractions or less intuitive numbers, or when they work backwards. An example: A fifteen-foot tree casts a ten-foot shadow at a certain time of day. How long a shadow will a six-foot tree cast at the same time of day?

To answer this, you have to be able to understand that the basic proportion of tree to shadow is 3 to 2. If you understand this, you see that 6 is twice 3, therefore the shadow must be twice 2, or 4.

The most common error I notice is kids adding or subtracting, rather than multiplying or dividing, to move between proportions. For example, in the above situation, they can see there is a difference of 5, and therefore say the shadow of the 6-foot tree is 1 foot. But that shows a lack of proportion; if you draw a picture anywhere close to scale, you can see that 15 to 10 is nothing like 6 to 1. In fact, when we first start working on problems like this, we always draw them out to scale to see the proportions first.

A sense of number and quantity, and relationships between numbers, can begin very young. We've naturally played with numbers and quantities, both with words (we're a very verbal family) and with objects, reading aloud and reenacting the scenes in the books we read with real objects. Years of this gentle interaction and exploration begin to give a child a sense that an additive pattern such as even numbers (2, 4, 6, 8, 10, ...) grows differently from a multiplicative pattern such as the doubling pattern (2, 4, 8, 16, 32, ...). And books like *The King's Chessboard*, by David Birch, Demi's *One Grain of Rice*, and the *512 Ants on Sullivan Street*, by Carol Losi, can all give great visuals of the differences between these. So by the time they get to juggling these kinds of numbers in more abstract fractions and problems, they have pictures and experiences to attach them to.

I recall my daughter, Hannah, running across the old question, "How do you split two things evenly among three people?" She has two very memorable experiences to draw on. One is a PBS *Cyberchase* episode she watched when she was five or six, where the kids had to split two apples exactly evenly among the heads of the three-headed dog or they were in trouble. She never forgot that each apple was split into thirds, and each dog got two thirds. Second, when she was around seven or eight, we were reading a Laura Ingalls Wilder book aloud, and we ran into the story of Laura and Mary getting two cookies from someone. On the way home, they agonized over wanting to eat the cookies themselves, but knowing they needed to share with their sister Carrie, and not knowing how to evenly divide the cookies. In the end, they erred on the side of caution, split one cookie between themselves, and gave the other whole cookie to Carrie. My daughters found it so funny that they didn't think to divide the cookies up into thirds! Between these anchors, this idea of dividing and sharing proportionately is very real, and it gives a real sense of what ⅔ can be—two wholes divided three ways.

I like to focus on the most basic meaning of proportion and how it very often means a relationship between two quantities or numbers that extends to a general population. This also helps us interpret information in an information-overload world. If we see some data and calculate that 41.2% have some characteristic, being able to see that this means that roughly 4 out of 10 or 2 out of 5 have that characteristic makes it much more understandable. It is proportional reasoning that enables me to make sense out of this.

On Not Retaining Math Facts

Sandy asked: *My sixteen-year-old daughter used to be an eager math learner, but her math sessions with her tutor have become increasingly frustrating because she doesn't seem to retain math facts from one session to the next. What can I do to help?*

Some kids don't retain math facts, no matter how much they try, until they actually use them, and use them a lot. My oldest son never became proficient and quick with them until he took algebra and practiced factoring—a lot. We learned to just let him use a reference chart before that, and he learned to "leap" from facts he knew to facts he didn't, which took more time than instant recall, but he got by with that. He had the concepts down, and an algebra class clinched his speed of recall.

My guess is, the tutor has created the block by referring to the fact that your daughter is slow on memory recall. The tutor could have a very valid issue from her point of view, though; if she has, say, an hour to tutor, and your daughter is slow at working on problems because of recall, this could be limiting what she can do in the tutoring sessions.

Now and then my daughter, Hannah, will become very slow on recall of certain facts because she is working hard on learning something different. Lately she's been spending a lot of time on decimal operations and their interaction with fractions and percents, so her recall of her 6 and 9 facts seemed to evaporate. Then she did a review for her SAT testing next week and we realized she was very slow, not because she didn't know how to do the problem, but because, for instance, her brain wouldn't switch over very well to something like dividing 36 by 9 and knowing the other factor was 4. This made it very slow going for us indeed, and if I'd only had an hour with her, we wouldn't have covered much material. When kids are learning new concepts, it is very common for other concepts that were learned previously to temporarily be "lost" while the new concepts are being absorbed.

> *"When kids are learning new concepts, it is very common for other concepts that were learned previously to temporarily be 'lost' while the new concepts are being absorbed."*

The tutor's interaction seems to be doing more harm than good, so you might consider discontinuing that. Any chance your daughter could learn from video lessons, like the Teaching Company's *Basic Math* series?

I do think that focusing only on math facts at sixteen years old, when concepts are understood, can be very limiting. I guess I'd pose it this way. If you are learning how to use a hammer and you are clumsy with it, do you think you might learn better how to use it by simply hammering away at the same spot over and over, or by actually putting a project together? There is an introductory period of learning how to use a tool, but no one ever really knows how to use a tool until they use it for a purpose. Math facts are like that for many of us; it was like that for me.

The Math-Hater Years

Mary asked: *You wrote that nine and ten could become the "math-hater" years. I need more of your insight. I've got two boys who love math, but now, even though my eight-year-old loves math and can do so much more than what he is given, he's giving me attitude. He is going down the "math hater" path, so to speak. I can't let this happen! When he was five, his math skills blew me away. Now it is so hard just to get him to do a page of math. How can I turn things around?*

I have no scientific study to support my observation, just nine or so years on homeschool email lists hearing moms say their second, third, or fourth grader started to hate math after previously enjoying elementary math. I believe the reason Michael, my oldest, felt this was because his development was very asynchronous—he had learned to read easily and had a high reasoning and problem-solving ability, but computation and arithmetic just didn't seem to have any relevance to him, not without some context. All his motivation and enjoyment completely wilted at age eight.

But it can be like this for any kid. Just pick up any K–2 math book, and you'll most likely see pictures and mathematical representations with the numbers. By third or fourth grade, you'll start seeing a lot more numbers and little else. I recall how much my daughter, Emma, loved the green DK *Math Made Easy* book for ages six to seven. The next one was OK, but the blue one for ages nine to ten was a sea of arithmetic problems without all that cool stuff that gave her something to relate to. I noticed that Miquon does virtually the same thing. I suspect that this transition, from math that kids can relate to, to math that becomes more and more abstract, is one reason for this common timing in lost motivation and enjoyment in math learning.

I figured out that context and relevance were utterly essential for Michael to enjoy and really learn math. My youngest, Emma, who's nine, has learned on a very similar track, and it has been the same for her. Games, math literature, and puzzles provide a context for the math she does. She can spend hours a day with games and reading math books. If I use a text, I am using *Primary Grade Challenge Math*, which is mainly problem solving; yes, it's math, but all in fun contexts she can comprehend. Drill takes place in games or art projects. (She loves art, so drawing and decorating a multiplication chart on occasion is something she enjoys.) Michael loved math books so much he asked for them for his birthday and Christmas; that was how we collected the entire *Murderous Maths* series when the only place you could get them from was Amazon UK.

The key is, how can I blend math with things Emma enjoys doing? I have listed a lot of math readers on my website (*LivingMath.net*) and emphasized math readers on the Living Math Forum, because I found with my own kids that that was one way to learn math I didn't know existed until a few years ago. Michael and Emma are language-oriented, love to read, and hate the sight of a math workbook; for them, math literature and activities saved us. But that may or may not be what inspires your kids; you'll have to discover that.

My kids have picked up on my love of history and learning about people, so reading aloud and discussing books like *Mathematicians Are People, Too*, by Luetta and Wilbert Reimer, has also been a big part of our math education. There is very little math in these books themselves, but they inspire us. After finishing the series for the first time my oldest son, who had told me he hated math at the beginning of that year, told me he might want to become a mathematician! I did not care that the books had no sums or math exercises—they had helped accomplish the ultimate goal, instilling a desire to learn more through the inspiration of others' stories. My own enjoyment in these stories comes through in my readings, so it has been a favorite series for all my kids.

My middle children, Nick and Hannah, have had times where they went wild with math, and times when they slowed down; they didn't need context to enjoy math all the time. They weren't as big readers as my other two. I did a lot of reading aloud, they played a lot of games, but in contrast to my oldest and youngest, had I given them stacks of math readers to read, they would have learned to hate it that way too (with the exception of the earliest picture books and the *I Love Math* series, by Time-Life, which have been loved by all my children).

Michael seemed gifted and loved learning everything, including math. And then, at eight, it all started to dissolve with the formal math work. We started to try to avert this using Pam Sorooshian's ideas;* he loved to read, so he ate up the Marilyn Burns books as well as the *Murderous Maths* series, by Kjartan Poskitt, and Theoni Pappas' books. I was still learning how to relax myself, so I felt the need to keep some math going all the time—but how, when, and what he learned was what I learned to leave up to him. He was an excellent self-teacher!

After homeschooling for nine years, he decided to go to high school for various reasons, mostly social. He is a senior now, and what has surprised me is how much he does enjoy math. He signed up for AP statistics and another math-based science class this year, even though he didn't have to take any more math. (I recall being good in math myself,

---

* See the chapter by Pam Sorooshian later in this section.

but relieved when I finished the required courses; I didn't take another class until years later in college.) This from a kid who at eight absolutely hated arithmetic. (Problem solving and geometry, however, were loads of fun, so obviously it wasn't "math" he had a problem with!)

My kids do much better without a lot of direct teaching from me, so I provide a lot of resources, and I'm there to help them understand things they want to understand. Sometimes I do teach when I'm asked, or if I think they're ready and held back by a lack of understanding of a concept. But our own school experiences can make it hard for us to teach without being tempted to "help them master" a concept that they may or may not be ready to master. What we never learned in school was the concept of playing around with math, allowing ideas to "percolate," so to speak, before mastery occurs, and that process may take some time.

I believe that, as with reading or other subjects we learn, having frequent exposure to ideas above our mastery level in a non-threatening medium, or experience without requiring mastery, makes it easier to master those concepts later when the time is ripe. I've seen this happen over and over with my kids and math. We see this in other learning pursuits as well. Kids learning to play music learn better when exposed to listening long before they play. We've all seen kids who seem to understand science or history lessons later on because they've had lots of relaxed, discovery-related experiences in their younger years to build more formal knowledge on.

It's about finding out what they love, how they love to learn, and trying to find a connection between math and those things. Sometimes it just takes time, and that is *not* something our culture allows us much of. But homeschooling does allow us to slow the pace when motivation is low or they need some "percolation" time, and to speed way up when they are in a learning spurt and want more and more. This is the learning meadows concept Patricia Kenschaft describes in *Math Power*—allowing for kids' naturally uneven pacing lets them each catch their own wave—ready to shoot forward when the moment is right.

Deep Arithmetic—Classics from the Mathematicians

adapted by Sue VanHattum

Getting to One

Here's an open question in math (meaning no one knows the answer).

Play this game:

- Start with any whole number.
- If it's even, divide by 2.
- If it's odd, multiply by 3, and add 1.
- Repeat with this new number, creating a sequence of numbers.

Does this sequence *always* reach the number 1?

Here's an example: We randomly pick 6 to start with. It's even, so we cut it in half and get 3. That's odd, so we triple it and add 1, getting 10. Even, cut in half, get 5. Odd, triple and add 1, get 16. Even, half is 8. Even, half is 4. Now 2. Now 1. We got a sequence of nine numbers (6, 3, 10, 5, 16, 8, 4, 2, 1), ending with 1. If we had kept going, 1 is odd so we'd triple and add 1, getting 4, and we'd have a 4, 2, 1 loop that just repeats.

Which numbers give short sequences, and which give long sequences? What's the longest sequence you can find?

Of course mathematicians have checked this out on computers, and it does reach 1 for every number they've checked so far. But no one understands why, and no one is really sure it won't fail for a number so big it hasn't been checked yet. This problem is called the Collatz Conjecture, after Lothar Collatz, who first proposed it in 1937.

Lots of kids enjoy playing around with this. You could also change the rules. What if we said, for odd numbers, multiply by 3 and *subtract* 1?[*] Does this always reach 1, too? How else could we change the rules?

---

[*] This idea comes from Gord Hamilton, at: *MathPickle.com*

Number Squares[*]

Put a different number at each corner of the outer square. At each midpoint put the (positive) difference between the two end numbers. Repeat. What pattern do you see? Does it end before you get to the seventh square?

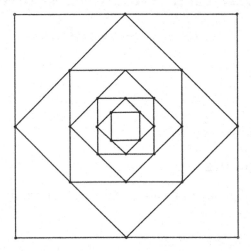

You don't have to put the numbers on a square. You can just write four numbers in a row, and the next row will have the differences (including the difference between the first and last numbers). Will you always get to a row or square of all zeros? How many levels can you go before it settles down?

Suppose I start with 1, 6, 10, and 15. 6 − 1 = 5; 10 − 6 = 4; 15 − 10 = 5; 15 − 1 = 14. So my next row will be 5, 4, 5, and 14. Here's what I'll get:

I got 7 rows. Can you find numbers that will take more than 7 rows to settle down to 0? Are there any sets of four numbers that will never settle down to 0?

1	6	10	15
5	4	5	14
1	1	9	13
0	8	4	12
8	4	8	12
4	4	4	4
0	0	0	0

---

[*] Josh Zucker introduced me to this one. Diffy Box is one of its many names. You can find a list of math papers on it at: *MathEd.uta.edu/~kribs/diffy.html*

Jimmie made something called a Squidoo lens about Living Math (at squidoo.com). I asked if we could modify it for the book, and she said yes. —SV

Transitioning to Living Math: How to Put Down the Textbook and Breathe Life into Your Lessons

by Jimmie Lanley

Yes, it's hard, very hard, to set aside the math workbook and the orderly progression through an outlined curriculum, and shift to what seems to be a messy, random bunch of games and hands-on activities.

You love the concept of living math. You know that it's fun. You even know that your children would learn through it. But there are still those nagging concerns: What about gaps in their math learning? What about drill? What about memorization? What about standardized tests? When will I find time to prepare all these games and clean up after all these messy activities?

Here's my own journey from textbook prison to living math paradise. Okay, it's not quite so glamorous as that! But this is how I shifted my thinking and am (still) transitioning to a living math approach.

I'm not a math expert or even a math person. I think in words not numbers. I have trouble remembering which number bus takes me downtown, but I can easily remember the names of all the stops on the way. This is just one homeschoool mother's attempt to try to make some sense of math instruction and make it enjoyable along the way. Come peek into my journey.

Step One: Thinking About It

It all started with a book, *Family Math*, by Jean Kerr Stenmark, recommended to me by a mom who spoke at a homeschool conference I attended. I found a used copy and read it over. Like many resource books, it found a comfy spot on my bookshelf and was promptly forgotten.

Over our years of homeschooling, I've slowly incorporated more and more of Charlotte Mason style learning.* I'd already added in artist study, composer study, nature study, even poetry and Shakespeare. We were using living books for history and science. Math was the last hold-out. I had read about a living math approach—using living books and real life tasks instead of textbooks and worksheets. I already understood what Charlotte Mason herself had written about math instruction. I liked the ideas in theory. But to actually use them? It seemed ridiculous.

These were my objections:

* If I don't follow the book, I'll leave out important math ideas.
* I'm not strong enough in math myself to guide our learning without a curriculum.
* I love living books, but how can they teach math? I mean, math is numbers.
* If my daughter Mel does a lot of math games but never does any drill or any worksheets, how will she be able to perform on standardized tests in the future?

But as I read more and more, and tears during math lessons became more and more frequent, I knew something had to change in our math instruction. I was reading blogs that described using living math, and I liked what I saw in their approaches.

Step Two: Games One Day a Week

"I could see that playing a game elicited excitement that a worksheet never could."

Finally, I committed to having one day a week with math games. That was my first step. Nothing changed except for that one weekly game day. I would try to pick a game that went along with the topic we were studying in our Singapore math book. Family Math's games are set up by topic, so it's easy to find a game that fits what you're studying. Those days were grand successes in terms of attitude, learning, and motivation. It kept me searching for more answers about living math.

We played fraction games; we made a huge number line from 1 to 20 with multiples of each number made from a gazillion tiny paper squares; we rolled dice and dealt cards. We both started to look forward to our weekly math game day.

---

* In the late 1800's Charlotte Mason, a teacher educator, advocated a natural form of education using what she called living books—books that would deeply engage the child, often classics.

I began to get serious about planning more extensive changes. I could see that playing a game elicited excitement that a worksheet never could. If the arithmetic skills were the same, then why not learn them in a fun way versus a dull one?

Step Three: Experimenting with Games, Activities, and Math History

We started playing with math games and activities every day, using the Singapore Math textbook as a supplement, pulling it out every now and then but not daily.

I pored over Julie Brennan's Living Math Through History lesson plan information,* hoping it would be the answer to my quest for a rich math curriculum filled with games and living learning. The lesson plans are more math theory and math history than arithmetic. You travel through history chronologically, seeing how math was used and what math discoveries were made.

Once I bought the lesson plans, I realized that this wasn't going to be a complete solution. It was a good addition, but it was not the whole picture. There are activity ideas for each lesson, but it's not a complete math curriculum. You still have to round it out with your own games, math activities, and arithmetic lessons.

The lesson plans have book suggestions, but there are too many, so you have to pare it down. I finally decided on a group of books and placed my order! I chose books from the living math curriculum list plus a few more general math books to pique Mel's interest.

To go with Lesson 1, titled Math is Everywhere, I used *The Great Number Rumble: A Story of Math in Surprising Places*, by Cora Lee. I was a super introduction to living math. It got us thinking and ma us go off on tangents—exploring tessellations, Fibonacci numbers, and prime numbers. Although the storyline is a bit contrived, this book is a very fun introduction to the idea that math is all around. The book also has one-page biographies of famous mathematicians, though we prefer *Mathematicians Are People, Too* for good biographies.

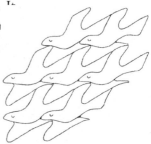

After that, we started using the Brown Paper School books (*I Hate Mathematics!* and *Math for Smarty Pants*, both by Marilyn Burns). They are written to kids with that "try to trick the grown-ups with this math problem" kind of humor.

---

* More information at: *LivingMath.net*

Through this investigation and experimentation process, I've come to grips with my former fears about the living math approach:

"If I don't follow the book, I'll leave out important math ideas."

This is a common fear with homeschooling. Gaps are inevitable, whether your child is educated at home or in a traditional setting. Get over it and move on with learning. Actually, there are many online guides that you can use to periodically check that you're covering it all. One example is the Math Curriculum Focal Points, published by the National Council of Teachers of Mathematics.*

"I'm not strong enough in math myself to guide our learning without a curriculum."

That's all the more reason to make math fun and engaging—both for me and for my daughter. My natural tendency is to avoid math. But by being more proactive in designing our curriculum, I'm becoming more interested in math. That excitement rubs off on my daughter! And again, I can still use my Singapore math texts as a guide for the skills to cover. The *how* to cover them is up to me.

"I love living books, but how can they teach math? I mean, math is numbers."

Wrong! Numbers are one aspect of math. But logical thinking, problem solving, and mathematical reasoning are all parts of math education.

"If Mel does a lot of math games but never does any drill or any worksheets, how will she be able to perform on standardized tests in the future?"

Taking a living math approach doesn't mean that she never does any drill and never fills in a workbook page. Those things simply become supplements to the real-life activities instead of being the core.

Step Four: Getting Clearer on My Goals and Approaches

As I revamped our math, I realized that I wanted to decide on some goals, and what we'd need to do to reach them.

The Goals:

- an appreciation for (even a love of!) math (definitely no fear of math)

---

* *nctm.org/standards/content.aspx?id=270*

- the ability to think mathematically and problem solve
- a basic understanding of math in history
- fluency in number operations

It would've been nice to start my journey with these goals, but to be honest, I had to plunge into this living math journey and flounder around a bit to discover what my goals were.

How to implement them? For us it seems to be a three-faceted approach:

- a chronological study of the developments in math history, including biographies of famous mathematicians
- math experiences—games, activities, puzzles
- arithmetic—drill, practice, skills

Step Five: Where We Are Now

I am working the plan! We aren't really spending much more time on math than we used to before the big shift, but the time is so much more productive. There is no "open and go" curriculum that covers all that I want our study of math to cover. So I'm picking and choosing, making it up as I go.

I'm using the outlines from the Living Math History Lesson Plans, for the history and for some of the activities. And I'll keep using Singapore math for the arithmetic. But for the rest of the experiences and games, I'll have to be the most creative—searching for goodies online, using my *Family Math* book, and trying to incorporate math into our daily lives as much as possible. It's not cut and dried.

To weave the arithmetic and games together, I pull out my Singapore math textbook and look at the overall units—measurement, time, or fractions, for example. Then instead of starting with the textbook explanations and workbook exercises, I search for games, puzzles, activities, or living books to introduce and practice the concepts and skills in a fun and living way. I'm also trying to incorporate more math notebooking into our studies. So I'm using graphic organizers and notebooking pages plus writing prompts about math.* After experiencing the math concepts in various ways, then we move to the workbook as a review or wrap up. By that time, Mel has confidence and proficiency in the skill and performs very fluently. The three areas overlap into each other quite a bit, and that's a wonderful, holistic perspective on math!

---

* Notebooking is done by the students. They put written ideas, drawn or printed images, and other relevant things into a notebook as a record of learning.

"It's fascinating how a worksheet brings tears of frustration, yet a silly game with identical problems is 'fun.'"

Mel has loved the shift to living math. She was pleased to stop using textbooks and workbooks, and do games instead. She adores the games, in fact. It's fascinating how a worksheet brings tears of frustration, yet a silly game with identical problems is "fun." It seems that with math instruction, the packaging is of utmost importance. She's using Life of Fred[*] now and really enjoys it. She even commented that a recent trip to a museum was not as fun as "normal" school with Life of Fred.

The shift was easy for her, but hard for me. It means a lot more planning and preparation on my part. And the lessons themselves are more time intensive for me. But for her it's delightful, and so it's worth it. Her newfound confidence with math and love of math are both huge payoffs of the living math approach.

---

[*] *StanleySchmidt.com / FredGauss / index2.html*

GAME
Math Card War

by Denise Gaskins

Have your children been struggling to learn the math facts? Math Card War is worth a thousand math drill worksheets, letting your children build calculating speed in a no-stress, no-test way.

You will need several decks of math cards. Don't rush to look for these at your school supply store. Math cards are normal, poker-style playing cards with the jacks, queens, kings, and jokers removed. Make one deck of math cards per player, each with a different back for easy post-game sorting. A math deck contains forty cards, so a single game of Addition War lets each child work twenty problems and hear their opponent work twenty more—and if your children are like mine, they will rarely want to stop at just once through the deck.

As my students learn their math facts, they need extra practice on the hard-to-remember ones like 6×8. With a normal deck of cards, however, I find they turn up far too many problems like 1×9 or 2×7. To give a greater challenge to older children, I make each player a double deck of math cards, but I remove the aces, twos, and tens. This gives them each a fifty-six-card deck of the toughest problems to calculate.

Basic War

War, a classic children's game, is the basis of all our math-practice variations. In case you haven't played it, here's a pretty standard set of rules for the game:

Each player puts one card face up on the table. The player with the greatest number wins the skirmish, and captures all cards on the table, creating a prisoner pile. Whenever there is a tie for greatest card, all the players battle: each player lays three cards face down, then a new card face up. The greatest of these new cards will capture everything on the table. Because all players join in, someone who had a low card in the initial skirmish may ultimately win the battle. If there is no greatest card this time, repeat the 3-down, 1-up battle pattern until someone breaks the tie. The player who wins the battle captures all the cards played in that turn. When the players have fought their way through the entire deck, count the prisoners. Whoever has captured the most cards wins the game.

I've often been amazed how such a simple thing can keep my kids occupied for hours. In our variations, because the math card decks are smaller than a regular card deck, we give each player their own pack of cards. We don't shuffle the decks together at the beginning.

Math Card War Variations

For most variations, the basic 3-down-1-up battle pattern becomes 2-down-2-up. For advanced games, however, the battle pattern is different: in case of a tie, the cards are placed in a center pile. The next hand is played normally, with no cards turned down, and the winner of that skirmish takes the center pile as well.

ADDITION WAR: Players turn up two cards for each skirmish. The highest sum wins.

ADVANCED ADDITION WAR: Turn up three (or four) cards for each skirmish and add them together.

SUBTRACTION WAR: Players turn up two cards and subtract the smaller number from the bigger. This time, the greatest difference wins the skirmish.

PRODUCT WAR: Turn up two cards and multiply.

ADVANCED PRODUCT WAR: Turn up three (or four) cards and multiply.

FRACTION WAR: Players turn up two cards and make a fraction, using the lesser card as the numerator. Greatest fraction wins the skirmish.

IMPROPER FRACTION WAR: Turn up two cards and make a fraction, using the bigger number as the numerator. Greatest fraction wins.

INTEGER ADDITION WAR: Black cards are positive numbers; red cards are negative. The greatest sum wins. Note that -2 is greater than -7 is.*

---

* Negative 2 is greater than negative 7 because it's to the right on a number line, or because being $2 in debt makes you richer than if you were $7 in debt.

INTEGER PRODUCT WAR: Black cards are positive numbers; red cards are negative. The greatest product wins. Note that two negative numbers make a positive product.*

WILD WAR: Players turn up three cards and may do whatever math manipulation they want with the numbers. The greatest answer wins the skirmish.

ADVANCED WILD WAR: Black cards are positive numbers; red cards are negative numbers. Players turn up four cards (or five) and may do whatever math manipulation they want with the numbers. The greatest answer wins the skirmish.

REVERSE WILD WAR: Players turn up three cards (or four or five) and may do whatever math manipulation they want with the numbers. The answer with the lowest absolute value (closest to zero) wins the skirmish.

---

* Negative times negative is a lot like the opposite of the opposite, putting you back where you started (positive).

I met Melanie and her family through my math salon. Then I began to tutor her son, who loves math more than anyone else I know. —SV

At the Eye of the Hurricane: Learning How to Support My Gifted Kids

by Melanie Hayes, Ed.D.

Ryan and Alannah

My son and daughter have exceptional minds. My husband and I are intelligent, well-educated people, but by some freak of nature our children are vastly smarter. It has taken us some time to realize just what that entails, how best to help them learn to live in the world, and how to support their quest for knowledge. Despite the fact that I am a professional educational consultant who specializes in meeting the needs of exceptional children, it took me several years to wrap my head around how exceptional my children are and what to do about it. To understand how they each respond to math, the bigger picture of their learning experiences in and out of school needs to be told.

According to IQ scales, my son, Ryan, is profoundly gifted. He demonstrates all the abilities and disabilities that are often assigned to that designation. He has a prodigious memory, sophisticated sense of humor, rapid processing abilities, advanced logic and reasoning, intense curiosity, unusual creativity, high energy, long attention span, extreme sensitivity, advanced reading skills, and extensive vocabulary.

He also has autistic-like behaviors, issues with sensory overload, a lack of social skills, obsessive-compulsive behaviors, perfectionism, anxiety, insomnia, and overexcitabilities. He was diagnosed as being developmentally delayed at six months of age, and by the time he was two, neurologists told us it was very likely he was on the autistic spectrum (a diagnosis that was later proved wrong). Often teachers don't like him; he can be disruptive, uncooperative, and combative in the classroom.

His disabilities are more visible than his abilities. When they first meet him, most people think of him as autistic rather than gifted. He is twice exceptional, or 2e, the gifted community's term for gifted children who also have disabilities.

His twin sister, Alannah, also demonstrates all of the above abilities, but regularly masks them in order to fit in with her friends. She does not share her brother's disabilities and is much more successful at coping with the stress of daily life. She is socially skilled and generally well-liked by her peers. She has developed the ability to hide her perfectionism, anxiety, and overexcitabilities and can usually pass for a "normal" kid. She has a wealth of knowledge and diverse interests, consistently scores very high on standardized tests, is respectful to her teachers, and friendly and cooperative with her classmates. Her focus is on creativity and imagination, topics that generally don't elicit amazed comments from strangers. Her teachers think she is a bright, creative, well-behaved girl. As often happens with gifted girls, she has not been challenged in the classroom; the extent of her abilities goes undetected, and teachers don't truly understand her or teach to her strengths.

Trying School

I have been a classroom teacher and educational consultant and I hold a doctorate in educational leadership specializing in the needs of gifted and twice exceptional children. I knew that most gifted children are not accommodated in our educational system and I didn't have high expectations of our local kindergarten, despite the fact that the school was recognized as one of the best in the Bay Area. I didn't expect that Alannah and Ryan would be intellectually challenged, but I figured it was kindergarten, how bad could it be? I liked their teacher. She was very open-minded and assured us she would try to make sure my kids had appropriate work. The principal said they were used to working with gifted children and did not see any problems with accommodating my kids. I thought it would give my children a great social opportunity. Alannah would get the daily playtime with friends that she craved, and Ryan might learn some social skills and maybe even make a friend.

Alannah went into the classroom enthusiastic and excited to make new friends and learn new things. After the first few weeks of school, she lost a bit of her initial enthusiasm, but seemed to be doing okay. She obeyed her teacher, followed the routines, and did her work (although because she worked slowly and meticulously, she ended up staying in to finish her work through many recess periods). Despite some initial social struggles, Alannah seemed to be making friends and generally trying to fit in.

But in May we found out that a little girl in her class had been making fun of her, had stealthily broken her crayons and torn up her work, and had managed to convince the other little girls not to play with Alannah. She eventually ended up pulling Alannah's glasses from her face and stomping on them during recess. We hadn't realized she had been subjected to months of bullying until the incident with the glasses. Alannah lost a great deal of confidence in herself that year but we only realized it after the school year was over.

Ryan did not do well in kindergarten from the start. He was very nervous about going to school and being separated from me. I stayed with him for the first few days and he finally felt okay with me going to my classroom just down the hall. However, after a few weeks of kindergarten level work, he became extremely frustrated. He refused to do any work, disrupted the classroom, was socially inappropriate, regularly hit and pushed his classmates, hit the teacher, and generally made his sister embarrassed to be his twin. I talked with his teacher and she agreed to let him do third-grade math workbooks and have more time to read books at his level. We agreed to let him come down to my classroom when he was having a meltdown, but nothing worked. His anxiety continued to rise; he began to eat his clothes, literally chewing off the cuffs of his sweaters, shirts, and jackets on a daily basis. He refused to use the bathroom and tried to hold it all day, resulting in publicly wetting his pants nearly every day. He began to obsessively hoard garbage. He had food rituals. Boredom and anxiety were shutting him down socially, emotionally, and intellectually.

One day he just stopped trying to learn. He stopped reading, exploring, asking questions, spouting facts. As things worsened, I made an agreement with his teacher to just let him come to my classroom every day after she had taken roll. Most days he sat quietly on his own in the corner of my reading lab while I worked with struggling readers. Sometimes he colored pictures or read a book, but mostly he just fiddled with paper clips, rubber bands, or other things on my desk. Ryan marked each day off on his calendar as he slowly plodded toward that light at the end of the tunnel called summer. When June rolled around, it was obvious that public school was out of the question for Ryan; we felt lucky to have made it through to the end of the year.

Up to this point, I had felt my own professional experience and knowledge would guide me in supporting Ryan, but now it became clear we needed a professional diagnosis to figure out what was happening.

We consulted with his pediatrician, who referred us to a psychologist and a neurologist. The psychologist tested him and told us he was "off the charts," but an IQ test was only one piece of the complete picture. So we made appointments and met with experts, who used multiple measures to identify his needs and abilities. The less-conventional indicators of intellectual talent like interviews, questionnaires, portfolios, and checklists helped us form a better picture of who Ryan is and how he learns, and helped us make more informed decisions about how to proceed.*

Meanwhile, because of all that was happening with Ryan, Alannah was quietly flying under the radar. Her shutdown was stealthy, unnoticed by any of us. She began to compare herself to others. She became extremely hard on herself—perfectionism gone wild. If she couldn't do it perfectly the first time, she wasn't going to do it at all. This perfectionism was exacerbated by her brother's early reading, writing, and math skills. To her, it seemed that Ryan could just magically, instantly, do all the difficult stuff. So rather than compete, she simply avoided reading and math. She stopped asking hard questions or challenging herself to try new things. She began to work very slowly and carefully and her unfinished work piled up on her desk. We took her unfinished work home and I spent extra time with her after school to get caught up. Despite her academic and social struggles, overall she seemed happy and we felt she was learning and growing in that setting.

Looking back now, I see how far off the mark we were. We should have advocated for our daughter to ensure she received an intellectually, socially, and emotionally appropriate education. But we were overwhelmed by the more-pressing problem of Ryan, so we missed her quiet desperation. I wish I had been more proactive and looked below the surface. I wish I had worked more closely with her teacher. I wish I had trusted my own instincts about my daughter's needs and abilities. Several studies have shown that parents are correct about eighty percent of the time in identifying their child as gifted (Silverman, 2009). I knew she was gifted; I just didn't realize how gifted and how much we had underidentified her abilities. We should have taken her for the same tests and assessments as Ryan. As her parents, we have intimate knowledge

---

* This reaffirmed my belief that gifted children should be identified using multiple measures. Standardized methods for identifying gifted children tend to underrepresent girls, children with behavioral problems, children with disabilities, children from low-income families, children from minority cultures, active boys, and children who have difficulty concentrating and performing when stressed or under time constraints. Jean Peterson, at Purdue University, wrote, "Test scores should never 'define' a person, no matter what they may reveal about his or her intellectual or achievement potential…All tests are imperfect measures."

of her strengths and weaknesses and could have been a great resource in designing a program that worked well for Alannah—but we didn't do it.

Realizing we had dropped the ball, we decided not to make the same mistake for first grade. We did our research, checked out schools, and made some decisions. I wanted to try a school for gifted children. I felt they would be experienced in dealing with kids like mine and I would not have to reinvent the wheel. Our biggest hurdle was the prohibitive cost of most private schools. We finally found a small, unconventional startup school for gifted kids that would trade my teaching skills and consulting advice for my kids' tuition. My kids were not excited about going to a new school. Ryan was not excited about going to school at all. Despite their initial misgivings, we started school that fall.

The school was held in an old mansion set on acres of beautiful, natural terrain. The structure of the school day was open and free-flowing, with lots of time for self-selected projects and play. My children began to enjoy going to school. They started to show interest in learning again. Alannah found friends who shared her interest in animals, fantasy, and drama. They got her jokes, they were interested in what she had to say, they loved her invented games. She really began to bond with this small group of peers. Ryan found a kindred math spirit in a fellow student, and they spent hours talking about and playing with math ideas. They ran back and forth across the room excitedly contemplating math, stopping only to write something down. They read books and played games.

The school provided a high degree of flexibility and freedom, tolerance for unconventional behavior, academically-advanced curriculum, mentoring, and social skills training. They empowered children to make educational decisions and worked at maintaining an emotionally-safe environment. Things were looking really promising for our children's education until the school lost its funding. Then it all began to unravel, and once again, we were looking for a solution.

My children loved that unstructured private school. They were devastated when it failed. Alannah sorely missed her friends and Ryan just seemed lost. We tried to regroup and find a temporary solution. I was worried about Alannah missing her new friends; I felt the solution would be to put her back in our local public school with her old friends. I knew that wouldn't work for Ryan, so I kept looking for him. I was optimistic; I have seen gifted children thrive in a wide variety of settings. There are public and private schools with programs designed to meet the individual needs of gifted students. The hallmark of those schools is a willingness and flexibility to accommodate each student and provide appropriate intellectual, emotional, and social support. Each child is unique and their needs should be evaluated on a case-by-case basis, because what works for one gifted child does not work for all gifted children.

In Ryan's case, we found it particularly difficult to find a solution. Most schools we looked at were unwilling or unable to provide adequate flexibility and understanding of his needs. After months of frustration and disappointment, we ultimately decided to try homeschooling. I quit working and began homeschooling Ryan his second-grade year. I use the term "schooling" loosely because he refused to do anything remotely academic with me. Considering the issues he was struggling with and all that he'd been through, I let it go. I became an unschooler by default. I stopped trying to make him learn and just let him sit in his room and play. I took him to the Exploratorium and let him play. I took him for nature hikes and let him play. In short, I dropped all my expectations and just let him play.

Alannah began to notice that Ryan was getting a lot of time to play. She resented that he was having so much fun with Mom every day. She started to throw fits about homework and began to say she was bored in class. She complained about her school uniforms and refused to get up in the morning. Her weekly reading scores began to slide. Her teacher commented that she was becoming "very chatty." By this time, I was so exhausted with trying to be two places at once that I decided to pull Alannah from school as well. I can't say that decision was made with her best interest in mind. I wasn't looking at her as a child who was desperate for a change. I didn't see the signs of underachievement. I didn't realize that she was quietly shutting down. I was simply trying to keep everything from falling apart.

Coming Home

Once she was home, I was more worried about her staying on track with her peers, so I designed an elaborate curriculum for her to do with me. We worked on reading, spelling, and math almost every day. We did science and social studies. I stuck to the state standards and benchmarks. We set aside the mornings to do "school." (Ryan avoided the morning school time by sequestering himself in his room.) At first, Alannah didn't seem to mind—she enjoyed the one-on-one time with Mom every day. She dutifully did her assignments and quizzes. I felt we finished out the school year successfully; we had the completed workbooks to prove it. As we wrapped up the year, I began to plan for third grade, imagining I would design such a compelling curriculum that both my children would join me for lessons at the kitchen table each morning.

When Alannah saw what I was up to, however, she put a stop to all my plans by announcing that she wanted to be an unschooler too. I said no. I reasoned that Alannah didn't have the same problems as Ryan, and I felt she should keep up with her peers. As I was arguing with her about it, I had an epiphany. All my professional knowledge about gifted girls as underachievers suddenly came slamming into perspective. It was one of those, "Hello, are you just seeing this now?!" moments. With perfect clarity I saw exactly what had been happening to my daughter over the last three years.

Her potential had been untapped, her abilities overlooked, and her love of learning snuffed out. I felt physically sick. Through my focus on her brother, I had let my daughter down. I, a feminist teacher who took such pride in my efforts for equality, had treated my daughter with gross inequality. I hugged her fiercely and told her I was sorry for not seeing that she was hurting too. I promised her I would give her the same opportunities as Ryan from now on.

So we threw out the traditional schoolwork and became radical unschoolers. We all played. We learned by doing things. We traveled, we read, we cooked, we crafted, we gardened, we raised animals, we shopped, we watched TV. That year of playing was a turning point for all of us. My children regained their love of learning and I regained my perspective. All of my previous efforts to teach my children paled in comparison to what they began to teach themselves, each other, and their parents. I began to learn how to be a mentor and facilitator to their explorations. I stepped back and gave them the space to grow. I reconnected with all the things I had loved about learning, the wonder and curiosity of life. I spent my time researching places, people, tools, and materials to facilitate their quests. It requires an enormous amount of time, energy, and resources to homeschool this way, but it has been well worth it.

We have been on this path for over a year now and my children's intellectual growth has far exceeded my wildest expectations. They are both showing incredible growth in many subjects. For example, Alannah has emerged as an inventive creator of math games like Rental, where she rents out her dollhouse rooms complete with family stories and calculations for income and expenses. Ryan has been working with a math professor[*] for the past three months and she recently informed me that although he did not yet understand algebra when they started, he is now

"All of my previous efforts to teach my children paled in comparison to what they began to teach themselves, each other, and their parents. I began to learn how to be a mentor and facilitator to their explorations."

---

[*] Sue VanHattum, the editor of this book.

working on and understanding a great deal of calculus. From all indications, what we are doing is successful. I regret that I didn't have the presence of mind to give my children those opportunities right from the start of their school years; but, like most healthy kids, they are resilient and seem to have bounced back.

Ryan is learning to manage life's stress and making great strides toward finding a balance in life. Alannah has found social circles through 4H and drama club and loves being the master of her fate. I am in the middle of a big, messy, and wonderful educational experiment. I am learning to encourage independence and confidence in my children's quest for knowledge. Through their own trial and error, they are learning to trust their intuition and follow their hearts. I'm finding that I don't have all the answers and that my approach is not always what works best for them.

My kids have gone places intellectually that I could never have taken them. I have come to realize that the best learning comes from offering my children opportunities for high-level abstract thinking and discussion, active inquiry and experimentation, and a creative approach to problem solving. I have seen that each child's learning is unique. While both of them are given the same unschooling opportunities, their individual approaches are completely different.

Ryan: Loving Math

Ryan's approach is purely mathematical. He is passionate about math, intellectually on fire, and entirely self-motivated to learn. He reads math textbooks for fun, memorizes theorems, invents math games, and researches math on the internet. He eats, sleeps, and breathes mathematics; in fact, his whole world is seen through a mathematical lens. Looking back at his early childhood, I can now see that he has always loved math.

When he was eighteen months old, we gave him a little board book, *Color Farm*, by Lois Ehlert, that showed farm animals made from cut paper shapes and he pestered us to tell him the names of all the shapes. "Mom, what's that shape that makes the thing on the chicken's head called?", "Um, a sort of elongated half circle thing?" I replied. He looked at me very seriously and asked, "But what's its real name?" To find the answer, I went to some geometry websites and looked up shapes, because even though it was a children's book, it had many shapes I didn't know.* When he (and I) had learned all

---

* The elongated half-circle thing doesn't actually have a name. I'd describe it as part of an oval. —SV

the shapes in *Color Farm,* he began looking for books with new and different shapes and wanting to know what they were called. We finally got him a geometry book that illustrated a wide variety of shapes.

Within a few weeks he could easily identify more complex shapes, some 3-dimensional, including the rhombus, tetrahedron, and dodecahedron. Despite poor fine motor skills, he struggled and persisted until he could write the names of all these shapes and draw them. Once when we were in a restaurant, in an attempt to keep him calm and busy, we gave him paper and crayons. He began to draw his favorite shapes, while chanting and writing their names. As you can imagine, he drew surprised responses from those around us.

By the time he was two, he would search through the board books in the library for anything connected to numbers. He quickly exhausted the library's collection of counting and sorting board books and began asking for more books about numbers. We scoured the library shelves for picture books on adding, subtracting, fractions, probability, exponents, and so on; any math topic we found in a picture book was checked out and devoured. By the time he was three, Ryan was reading fifth-grade level books and checking out more complex how-to math books. He read everything from *The Golden Ratio* by Mario Livio, to *Anno's Mysterious Multiplying Jar* by Mitsumasa Anno. I initially tried to select his books in an appropriate sequential order, starting with the basics, but Ryan began to self-select books and refused to let me dictate what he should check out. So I let him check out any math books that caught his eye.

When they were five, we gave our kids their own laptops and several educational games. We linked them to lots of fun educational websites. Ryan read the Magic School Bus book about how computers work and began to check out books on computers. By six he was an expert at navigating the computer and began to seek out websites on his own (with parental supervision, of course). He was continually seeking new information to fill in his big picture; he learned about fractals, phi, and pi before he learned how to subtract large numbers. Ryan was fascinated by ancient mathematicians and knew several archaic methods for computation. He loved large numbers—words like vigintillion and googolplex rolled off his tongue with ease. He read math books for hours each night. He could not get enough math.

We joined a math club. We fostered friendships with other children who were math nuts like Ryan. He was finally able to interact with kids who understood his way of thinking. When he is playing with someone who loves math as he does, he seems to be lit from within. We have come to see that it is essential for him to have the opportunity

to exchange ideas, solve problems, and work in a collaborative group with other children who are his true intellectual peers.

Math for Ryan is a big joyful game and he often takes on very scholarly topics in a playful way. Any down time, driving time, or waiting time is spent engaged in math and logic games with us. He is now much more advanced at math than I am, so our conversations often consist of him explaining something to me. He loves math jokes and tricks and often confounds us with stumper problems. He adores building 3-D geometric shapes from Magna-Tiles and playing with Cuisenaire rods, LEGO pieces, and math board games like Equate. We have learned a great deal about how fun math can be while playing with our son.

He invents many of his own math games and plays them with anyone who is willing. He uses materials like LEGO bricks in unconventional ways; for example, he builds mazes or models of Conway's Game of Life* with them. He loves all math tools—like his compass, slide rule, and calculator—and spends hours learning how to use them properly. We are fostering his learning by finding a rich variety of books, materials, and curricula for him to explore. I am no longer concerned with a comprehensive curriculum or the state standards and benchmarks because Ryan is already so far above them that they are a moot point. Ryan is now free to pursue his passion for math in an organic, hands-on, experiential manner, which in turn is preserving his love of learning.

We usually think of mathematics as a series of steps, starting with the foundational building blocks and eventually building a stairway to higher mathematics. We don't move students up the stairway until they have mastered each previous step. We feel compelled to make sure they thoroughly understand algebra before we allow them to try trigonometry or calculus. For mathematically-gifted children, this lock-step method can kill their creativity and their desire to fit the pieces of the overall mathematical puzzle together.

The learning style of some mathematically-gifted children† is more akin to a hurricane; they stand at the eye and watch all the information

"To the casual observer or bewildered teacher it often seems disjointed and messy, but wonderful things are happening within the eye of the hurricane."

---

* In 1970 John Conway invented the Game of Life, which is most easily played on computer. The player sets up an initial configuration of "living cells" on an infinite grid. The following rules then determine what happens generation after generation: A cell becomes alive if it has exactly three living neighbors. A live cell can only stay alive if it has two or three living neighbors. Some initial configurations create traveling patterns. Others create blinking patterns. Most small configurations die out. This game is a fertile field for mathematical research, and is the best-known example of cellular automata.

† Editor's note: … along with many children not identified as gifted.

swirling around them. Their curiosity urges them to reach into the hurricane and pull out bits and pieces of mathematical data. They ponder and experiment until they fit those bits and pieces into their prior knowledge and come up with the whole picture. To the casual observer or bewildered teacher it often seems disjointed and messy, but wonderful things are happening within the eye of the hurricane. These children are making deep connections, internalizing knowledge, and building concepts that will allow them to experiment and try out their own theories. Teaching mathematically-gifted children requires an open mind and a willingness to throw out most accepted notions of how to teach math.

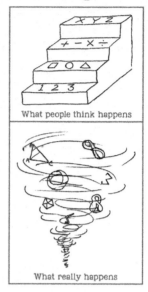

Learning Math

What people think happens

What really happens

Ryan has a nearly-photographic memory and reads prodigiously on the subject of math. Consequently, he has incredible background knowledge of formulas, mathematical theorems, and mathematicians and their contributions throughout history. We try not to be intimidated by his knowledge; we realize it is how he is wired. We know that his math abilities have surpassed us, so while he is technically a third-grader, it was apparent that he needed to work with someone who really understood math. A few months ago we found Sue, who's the perfect teacher for Ryan. She is a math professor who thinks outside the box, delights in learning differences, and plays with math. She loves math as much as Ryan. We knew she was the right person to help him fill the gaps in his knowledge and introduce him to new math topics, while allowing him to continue to think and explore freely.

Ryan is now exploring mathematics with Sue in weekly private tutoring sessions. They are studying algebra, trigonometry, calculus, and number theory. Sue is sometimes surprised to find Ryan understands difficult concepts, yet at the same time doesn't know how to do something as simple as long division. This asynchronicity doesn't concern her, however, because she knows the missing pieces will be naturally filled in as they work—she understands the hurricane. Ryan learns material at such an accelerated pace that Sue usually only has to show him something once and he can master it. She is good at explaining not only the computations, but also how and why they fit into the big picture.

Sue also understands that Ryan learns unconventionally; for example, he learned much of his algebra through playing with a graphing calculator. She is comfortable with an alternative approach to teaching. She sees herself as a learner as well as a teacher, and the dialogue between

Sue and Ryan is open and free-flowing.* She has been teaching him the importance of proof in higher mathematics and his understanding of why and how to do this has grown tremendously. She recently showed him the Wolfram internet site† and encouraged him to test his hypotheses there when he wasn't working directly with her.

Sue acts as a guide and mentor for Ryan; she presents him with increasingly sophisticated ideas as well as helping him with the practical application of his knowledge. She is not afraid to radically accelerate Ryan in math. She is skilled at knowing when to step in and challenge him, and when to step back and let him explore. We are lucky that he gets to work with such a gifted mathematician who can follow his thought processes and help him weave his scattered learning into a coherent framework.

We have learned how important it is to match the teacher to the student. In Judy Galbraith's book, *The Gifted Kids Survival Guide*, she asked gifted children what they value and desire in a teacher or mentor. Some of the traits they listed were: understands them; has a sense of humor; supports and respects them; is flexible; intelligent; open to exploring new ideas; and resourceful. Sue offers all of that. Ryan is thriving and learning at a pace that suits his hunger, although he wishes he could work with her every day.

Alannah: Dealing with Math

Alannah has an entirely different approach to life. While Ryan is an introvert, she is an extrovert. She is a natural leader. She often comes up with engaging ideas that make her the center of games and play with other children. She has always been the more assertive twin; she alternates between directing Ryan's activities and worrying for his well-being. She is the driving force behind all of their shared activities. She designs games and activities that often keep them occupied for hours. It is very interesting to watch them play; Alannah has a way of engaging Ryan thoroughly by including math in their games. For example, she may want to play with little animal figures, but to ensure Ryan's cooperation, she will ask him to design and build her a geometrical zoo out of Magna-Tiles. If he is already building or playing and she wants to join in, Alannah will create a scenario to include both their interests.

---

* Editor's note: When Ryan offers an insight I hadn't thought of, I will often say, "Thank you, Professor Hayes." I love seeing his eyes light up at that.

† *WolframAlpha.com*, a 'computational knowledge engine'.

Recently Ryan was building a marble run and Alannah joined in and suggested they use the pieces to build an egg factory. The next few hours were spent designing and building an elaborate chicken farm, egg factory, and processing plant out of the marble run pieces. The marbles were the eggs, of course, but they also made the chickens out of marble run pieces and designed them to hold the eggs until they laid them at the top chute. They outlined a business plan, invented customers, and worried about their sustainability and carbon footprint. It is rewarding for us to see our children pull in so many concepts to create their complex games. While Alannah's focus was on chickens and Ryan's was on physics, they were both playing with multi-level math concepts.

Alannah has heard a great number of obscure math facts living with Ryan. However, she refuses to let him teach her anything directly, much to Ryan's sorrow. He would love to be her teacher, but she is keenly aware of his advanced abilities, and her perfectionism rears its head. When he starts talking about math that she doesn't immediately understand, she will shut him off. We are aware that Alannah is a perfectionist and tends to be very self-critical. We try to help her by listening to her concerns and empathizing with her feelings. We are working with her to help her see that mistakes are an organic part of the learning process and often lead to discovering more sophisticated methods or solutions. It is helping Alannah to accept her abilities and not be so hard on herself when she makes a mistake or doesn't come in first. We have told her that her brain works differently than her brother's and both approaches are valid and important. We hope that Alannah's self-criticism will not shut down her creativity and self-confidence. I agree with Arthur Koestler's thought, "The principle mark of genius is not perfection but originality, the opening of new frontiers."

Alannah is not as focused on math. She enjoys math, is good at it, and readily uses it in her daily life, but it is not her grand passion. Yet she can hold her own in logic games, creative problem solving, and discussing grand concepts. When I teach Alannah any math concept using a hands-on approach, she grasps it easily. She also has an incredible memory for math facts, but it is tied to stories, scenarios, music, and play. She doesn't remember formulas and facts out of context. She can complete workbooks and quizzes successfully, but she is bored with that type of exercise. Alannah doesn't like workbooks, even electronic ones with awards and games. What Alannah craves is creating, playing, and socializing. When she is playing a math game with other people, especially one that she has invented, her math skills really shine.

Like many gifted children, Alannah is a visual-spatial learner. They are often overlooked and underidentified as gifted because most teachers don't teach the way these thinkers learn. Consequently, the typical approach to math instruction is doomed to fail. Alannah is a non-sequential thinker; in other words, she does not learn in a sequential, linear mode. She interprets numbers as an image in her right brain first, then that image has to be translated into a computation in her left brain. She will not be strong in memorizing math facts or performing timed math tests. It will take her a longer period of time to produce an answer to a problem. She will experience stress when she has to work under time pressure and her ability to recall information rapidly will be diminished. Is it any wonder that she was failing the timed math fact quizzes in school? Timed math tests will not give an accurate reflection of her math knowledge or abilities.

Filling in worksheets or memorizing multiplication facts will not enable her to internalize math knowledge. Visual-spatial learners thrive in an environment that allows them to utilize their creativity. Alannah works best when she can visualize concepts, create pictures or stories, manipulate materials, physically move her body, make jokes, tell how it makes her feel, and discuss her thinking.

"If she is presented with an overall concept, and then allowed to play with how the facts fit into that overall concept, she understands."

According to Dr. Linda Silverman, a leading expert on visual-spatial learners, these children are "sequentially-impaired." I agree with her; Alannah shuts down when she is asked to perform memorization drills in math. "Sequentially-impaired students cannot learn through rote memorization, particularly series of numbers, such as math facts. Since the right hemisphere cannot process series of non-meaningful symbols, it appears that these spatially-oriented students must picture things in their minds before they can reproduce them." Alannah sees things in whole pictures; if she is presented with an overall concept, and then allowed to play with how the facts fit into that overall concept, she understands. She can memorize facts if she makes up stories, draws pictures, or invents games around those facts. If she can engage her emotions, her creativity, or her body, she will remember everything. For Alannah, a picture really is worth a thousand words. Dr. Silverman's research has proved to be immensely valuable to me as a parent and home educator of my gifted, visual-spatial girl.*

---

* I highly recommend Dr. Silverman's website: *VisualSpatial.org*

Intense and Joyful

We have two very different learners in our home. We have come to realize that if we are to educate our children successfully, we must be willing to find unique solutions, not be bound by conformity, and not put limits on their learning. If we can achieve this, our children will not experience the frustration and boredom that often plague gifted children in the typical classroom. They will not be given more of the same type of problems to keep them occupied because they finished early. They will not be constrained by the lack of time, interest, or ability of their teachers. They will not be tempted to dumb themselves down to fit in nor to hold themselves back because it is not acceptable to surge ahead. They will not be bullied or belittled by classmates and teachers. They will not be misidentified because they don't think or behave like other children. We have learned that we must support them as individual people, celebrating their strengths while helping them mitigate their weaknesses.

Both of our children are unique individuals with their own approach to life. My husband and I have worked hard to create a home environment that celebrates individual differences, acceptance, and respect. We have tried to foster independent inquisitive thinking in our children. We try every day to generate positive peer and family interactions and to be emotionally supportive. Research shows that gifted children are highly sensitive to our emotions, words, and judgments; so despite the day-to-day exhaustion of parenting and homeschooling our kids, we try to model positive dialogue, respect, and kindness in our interactions. We hope to teach them how to use their intellectual strengths to develop coping strategies and successfully deal with stress and insecurities.

We also want them to learn how to point out mistakes, look at differences, and disagree with others in a positive, supportive manner. This is a long slow process. Ryan is truthful to a fault and will bluntly state his case without realizing he may hurt others' feelings. Alannah doesn't have that same problem with tact, but she does get impatient with friends who don't understand her, and can be stubborn in wanting things done her way.

Teaching and parenting our gifted children is an extremely demanding job. They have much more physical and intellectual energy and stamina than we can muster. But, like most parents, it is our first priority to give it our best shot. If we can help them reach their full potential, we are giving them a precious gift.

We love and appreciate our children for who they are as human beings, not just for their gifts and abilities. However, I feel strongly that gifted children should be valued for the thinkers they are and the doers they can become. They have the right to an appropriate education and the future opportunities that holds. They have the potential to solve world problems, make our lives better, and open the future to untold possibilities. We, as teachers and parents, have the privilege and responsibility to nurture their learning and help them find their way to success.

Self-Referential
Number Square

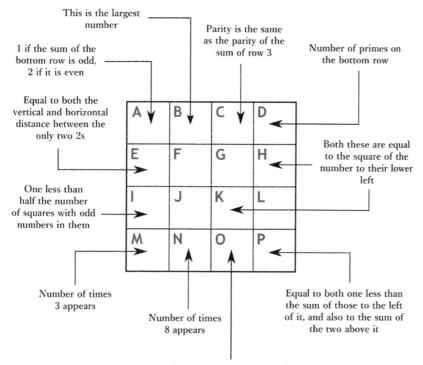

This is the largest number

1 if the sum of the bottom row is odd, 2 if it is even

Parity is the same as the parity of the sum of row 3

Number of primes on the bottom row

Equal to both the vertical and horizontal distance between the only two 2s

Both these are equal to the square of the number to their lower left

One less than half the number of squares with odd numbers in them

Number of times 3 appears

Number of times 8 appears

Equal to both one less than the sum of those to the left of it, and also to the sum of the two above it

The column that the unique 7 is in.
The number of different digits in the down diagonal.
The number of different digits in the up diagonal.

Fill in each square with a digit between 1 and 9
No digit may be repeated on a row or column

At the end of March in 2009, I posted a call for submissions for this project on my blog. The only chapter in the book that came from that call is Holly's. I'm so glad she found me. —SV

One and a Quarter Pizzas: An Unschooling Adventure

by Holly Graff

My daughter, Luna, like most babies, began to grasp the concept of quantity the moment she discovered the delight of placing her foot in her mouth. If she tired of the one, there was always the other. But somehow there was never a third. Our bodies, in all their beautiful symmetry, are mathematical! And as Luna discovered her own body, she couldn't help but discover math. Like all of us, she was immersed in mathematical concepts from the moment of her birth. So I never thought it unusual that Luna should love math.

Now she's eight and tends to eat erratically, generally having little interest in food, but then becoming absolutely ravenous every second or third day. This was a ravenous day, and Luna was busy wolfing down slice after slice of spinach pizza with her friend, Maya. Meanwhile, Maya and I were remarking on Luna's enormous appetite and amusing ourselves by tallying her slices as she ate them. The conversation went something like this:

> ME: You've eaten more than one whole pizza!
>
> LUNA: How many slices are in one pizza?
>
> ME: Eight.
>
> LUNA: And how many more than eight have I eaten?
>
> ME: Two more.
>
> LUNA: So eight and two...
>
> MAYA: That's ten slices!

LUNA (AFTER SOME THOUGHT): That's one and a quarter pizzas!

ME: How did you figure that out?

LUNA: Well, if there are eight slices in a whole pizza, then there are four slices in a half, and two slices is a quarter because a quarter is half of a half.

Learning Has No Schedule

Luna's understanding of fractions is derived from everyday activities such as cooking, measuring, and handling money. She has never had a formal math lesson, nor has she ever completed a worksheet of repetitive practice problems. Luna is an unschooler, and as such she has the freedom to learn within the context of her own activities and interests. Rather than conforming to a prescribed curriculum, she continually constructs her own learning by culling meaning from raw experience. As a facilitator in this process, I have tried to show Luna that math is in no way a series of dry facts to be memorized. I have tried to emphasize that math is a powerful tool and a way to describe and enhance our experience in the world.

Luna's learning is not tied to any externally imposed schedule. She is free to mull things over, to process ideas for as long as she desires. There are no deadlines to be met and no evidence required of her learning. I simply trust her to be curious and motivated, and to learn at her own pace. After all, millions of years of evolution have honed the human brain into a fine, responsive instrument for the purpose of seeking out knowledge. And just as Luna learned to walk and talk organically, without force or coercion, I believe that she will learn everything else she needs to know—including math—as a result of her natural interaction with the world. This postulate of unschooling, that children can and should be trusted with their own education, can be difficult to explain to others. But I think breastfeeding provides a great analogy.

Like unschooling, breastfeeding involves a lot of trust. It's so common to see new mothers examining baby bottles after a feeding, noting the volume of milk consumed and expressing some degree of either surprise or dismay at their observations. They tend to feed their children according to a prescribed schedule, usually suggested by a pediatrician. In contrast, a breastfeeding mom has no quantifiable evidence of her child's nourishment. She trusts her child to communicate when she is hungry and to drink until she is full.

As an unschooling mom, I am similarly lacking in any quantifiable evidence of Luna's academic progress. I have no test scores and no report cards, no ounces of milk to cite as proof of her intellectual nourishment. Much of what she's taking in, like breast milk, is invisible to my eyes. But I trust her to drink of the knowledge for which she thirsts, and I trust her to do so until, for the time being, she's had her fill.

Indeed, unschoolers believe that the most profound learning often takes place silently and invisibly, in between activities and away from prying eyes. It is here that all those pieces of information, having been shaved from active experience, are pulled inward to jostle against one another in various combinations and arrangements until gradually, or sometimes suddenly, a new understanding emerges. This takes time, and time is one of the greatest gifts of the unschooling life.

"Time is one of the greatest gifts of the unschooling life."

Luna often experiences such moments of revelation, discovering key math concepts over time through her own thought and exploration. While reading a recipe, for example, she recently came upon the measurement, 1.5 cups. She'd seen the decimal point used in this way before and through experience understood that this was just another way of writing 1½. But on this particular occasion, a new connection was made.

Luna said, "Oh, so is that because the five could go up to ten, and then ten would mean another whole cup?" When I told her yes, that she was absolutely right and that's why we call it the base-ten system, she said, "I knew that because five is one half of ten, and if 0.5 means one half, then if the five went all the way up to ten then that must mean one whole."

The joy that I felt upon hearing my daughter construct her own understanding of the decimal system was akin to the joy one feels upon watching her toddler take her very first step. For some time Luna had been collecting her experiences with numbers, quantity, fractions, and probably a dozen other ideas, turning them over in her mind, processing them. And on that day, within that context, she fit them all together to make a new and more sophisticated connection. This idea would not have had nearly the same significance if I had simply told Luna that it was so.

Visual Models

A few days later Luna told me that she'd thought of a good way to explain how zero is used as a placeholder in the base-ten system. "You can think of it like a vending machine that sells drinks or something," she said. "Even if one of the spots runs out of bottles, there's still a place there. Zero is holding the place until it gets more." When Luna has been mulling over a concept in her head, she often comes up with interesting visual models to aid her understanding.

This is another hallmark of unschooling. Children are not restricted to the models and formulas taught by others. They are free to create their own. This allows for more flexibility and creativity when approaching a problem and also allows children to draw on their own strengths and preferred learning modalities. Luna is a strongly visual learner in general, so it comes as no surprise that she would often describe her understanding of math in terms of a visual model like the vending machine.

As a visual thinker, Luna loves to create art and has always been very interested in symmetry. She often incorporates symmetry into her artwork and invents symmetrical patterns. When she first began adding two numbers together, the problems that she was able to figure out immediately, without pausing to count in her head, were the following: 2 + 2, 3 + 3, 4 + 4, and 5 + 5. Other problems, those involving two different numbers such as 3 + 4 or 6 + 3, required more time and thought, and she didn't always solve them correctly. I believe that her strong ability to double numbers is an extension of her symmetrical visualization skill. I find that fascinating, and it is a gift that will serve her well in the development of her mathematical ability. If Luna were in school, her teacher would probably focus on the problems that had given her trouble rather than on this very obvious and exciting pattern in her work. One of the benefits of unschooling is that Luna will always be regarded as an individual. I will always have the time and ability to try to understand her. I may not always succeed. But because I know my child so well, I have the ability to recognize her strengths and help her build on them.

Alternative Algorithms

Given so much freedom, Luna often devises original strategies when performing calculations in her head. How's this for an alternative algorithm? During an extended stay in Paris last year, Luna asked how many days we had left before going home, and I said six. Then she asked, "How many hours is that?" So I said, "Well, there are 24 hours in a day, and…" Before I could do the mental math and provide her an answer she began it on her own. I happened to be writing at the time, so I jotted down exactly what she said, "Well, 24 is almost 25, and a quarter is 25 cents, and there are four quarters in a dollar, so four 25's is 100. So if I had four 24's then it would be taking away 4 from 100. So… 100, 99, 98, 97, 96. 96 is four 24's. Four, five, six… So we need two more. So we need half a dollar now. So half a dollar's 50. Take away 2 from 50. So that's 48. So add 48 to 96."

Here things got a little tricky because 48 and 96 weren't so easy to add in her head. But after trying it a couple of different ways, she decided to make the 96 into 100, add the 48 and get 148, and then subtract the extra 4, giving her a final answer of 144 hours left in Paris.

At the time, Luna would have been in second grade. By this point in traditional schooling, there is much emphasis placed on memorizing "basic facts." A second grader is expected to know basic addition and subtraction facts and to have begun memorization of the multiplication tables, often rattling them off by rote. "Two times two is four, three times two is six, four times two is eight…"

Luna hasn't memorized her "basic facts." She doesn't know the multiplication tables by heart. She still even counts on her fingers a lot of the time when solving some basic addition problems. But when in her daily life Luna encounters a math problem that she's interested in solving for one reason or another, she always finds a way to do it. Always.

More importantly, it never seems to occur to her that for any reason she *couldn't* do it. While a problem like 24 hours times 6 days might be completely uncharted territory for her, she approaches it with confidence. She makes use of what she knows to extrapolate into what she doesn't. Her problem solving process is always creative and fascinating. She doesn't always solve problems correctly, and sometimes her process is so meandering that she forgets what she was trying to solve in the first place! But I'm not concerned about these things. I see her playing with math, manipulating it, using it, and owning it.

Luna is much more interested in working problems in her head than working them out on paper. She prefers to talk the problems through, describing the steps as she performs them in her head. I think that's great. I was always good at math, but because I was taught one "correct" way to work out problems in school, I've always felt very dependent on pencil and paper. If there's none available, I'll even use a finger to "write" invisible numbers on my palm so I can keep track of their positions as I borrow and carry. It was only in grad school, when I had to do more advanced math, that I finally started to break away from these school-imposed restrictions and started to feel comfortable manipulating numbers in a way that suited me.

Because Luna was never told that there's a "right way" and a "wrong way" to work a problem, she's already comfortable juggling numbers around in her head, pretending they're 25's instead of 24's because that's what works for her, and then later taking away the extra ones she gave them earlier. *She* is in command of those numbers. She calls the shots. As I said earlier, math is a tool. Like a hammer. You can wag it menacingly over a child's head. Or you can put it in her hand and watch her swing it.

Every good math teacher I mention it to already knows and loves this game, though they may give it different names. My version goes like this...

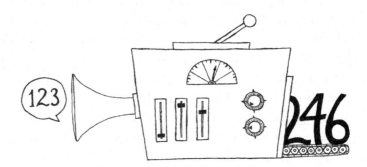

A student comes to the board to be the scribe, and makes a chart with two columns, labeled "class" and "Sue," or sometimes "in" and "out" or x and y. You could even use "raw materials" and "finished product," or other fanciful names. A beautiful machine may be drawn above the chart. Though I've seldom done this with my adult students, the playfulness of it can help students take risks—a necessity for true learning. With younger students, a volume button is fun too.

I call on students at random to give me a number, "any number." As the scribe fills it in, I give the output for this number, which the scribe also fills in. Perhaps the rule in my head is double and add 1. Jana says 3, and I say 7. I call on Yung, who says 5, and I say 11. If I haven't done so already, I now remind the students that they mustn't say the "rule" when they think they've discovered it. They can just call out my number—the output. The next person I call on says 9, and before I say anything someone else calls out 19. I know that person has figured out my rule, but they haven't wrecked the game for anyone else.

We usually keep playing until most of the students have seen (in their mind's eye) the rule that turns each input into its corresponding output. If the rule is too complicated, I might have to give suggestions for strategies. Organizing the input in increasing order can be very helpful if the group is stuck. If you're new to leading the game, you may tend to use rules that are too complicated. Start with one operation before moving to two, and be aware that subtraction and division are harder to recognize than addition and multiplication. I've found that something as simple from my side as ten minus their number is a very hard rule for students to get.

Drawing the input–output pairs as x,y-coordinates on a graph is a wonderful extension for a lesson that includes graphing.

I use this game in many contexts: to introduce problem solving or functions, to help students understand domain and range, to go with graphing, to help students see the difference between the graphs of different sorts of functions, and sometimes, just to lighten the mood.

The Math Haters Come Around

by Tiffani Bearup

My daughter Caitlin's thinking is very non-linear, especially in regards to math. This has made finding a math program impossible, since they are all based on a number line. I see her style of thinking as more like this ouroboros symbol.

As nervous as it made me to drop all math curriculum, I'd read enough John Holt[*] to know that I needed to trust her, rather than force her into doing a curriculum that was unsuited for her style. Working with numbers naturally—doing things like cooking, sewing, shopping—gave her a great number sense and literacy, which I hadn't seen earlier, and life was good.

Vedic Math

Then I happened upon a Vedic Math book.[†] I'd abandoned my search for a math curriculum from anywhere here in the West, and had gone Eastward. Vedic math comes from India and is quite trippy compared to how we learn it over here. It is mostly done mentally (great for kids who don't like to write), working from left to right (great for speed and harder to get confused), and based on breaking numbers down into smaller units (nice and simple). When I leafed through the book, instead of a number line I saw a number circle, like this one.

It's a Vedic ten-point circle. Just like the Ouroboros symbol, only for math! I checked out the book, and brought it home to study and share with the kids. Caitlin immediately responded to it. For instance, in the ten-point circle, you see that directly across from each number is

---

[*] *How Children Fail* and many others.
[†] *Vedic Mathematics Teacher's Manual, Voume. 1*, by Kenneth Williams

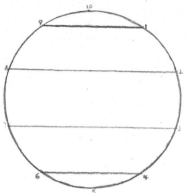

orresponding number, and they coincidentally add up to 10 in every case. ::pause for effect::

This was quite dramatic for both Caitlin and me because, up until we saw that circle, we each would add numbers by adding on by ones. 7 + 3 was us going, "seven, eight, nine, ten." 7 + 4 was us going, "seven, eight, nine, ten, eleven." It's very laborious to do it this way, but that's the only way we knew to do it. Finger counting at its finest.

All of a sudden, we realized that if we could remember which numbers added to 10, it was a jumping off point. 7 + 4 was just 7 + 3 (that's 10!) + 1. 7 + 5 was just 2 more than 7 + 3, and adding 2 on to 10 is much more automatic than counting up by fingers. By pegging numbers that add up to 10, we saved our mental energy and could work with numbers more quickly. I suspect that most of you reading this already do that; my son, Stuart, and my husband (who are great at math) had already figured it out. I had never realized they were using a basic concept to do math so speedily—I always wondered how they could count up so fast.

Once Caitlin and I grasped the concept of making 10, we quickly learned how to apply this to doing *multiplication*! ::pause for effect:: Did you hear that? I said MULTIPLICATION! The two of us! At the table! Doing multiplication! Without crying! Here's a quick tutorial (from *VedicMaths.org*) to explain how we did it.

Suppose you need 8 × 7. 8 is 2 below 10, so 2 is the 'deficiency' for 8, and 7 is 3 below 10, so 3 is the deficiency for 7. Write your multiplication column style (with the 7 below the 8), and next to each number write its deficiency. Think of it like this:

$$
\begin{array}{r r}
7 & 3 \\
\times\, 8 & 2 \\
\hline
5 & 6
\end{array}
$$

You subtract crosswise 8 − 3, or 7 − 2, to get 5, the first digit of the answer. And you multiply vertically, 2 × 3, to get 6, the last digit of the answer. That's all you do. See how far the numbers are below 10, subtract one number's deficiency from the other number, and multiply the deficiencies together.*

In fact, because multiplication had tortured us for so long (don't even get me started on how I didn't get an ice cream party with the other fourth graders who had memorized their facts up to 12, while I was still stuck at my 3 tables) we did it while giggling, like, "Look at me! I can do it!"

And this is how our math program started. Encouraged by our newfound success with addition and basic multiplication, Caitlin and I

---

* Editor's note: And if you'd like to think about this like a mathematician, now see if you can figure out why it works.

decided this Vedic math stuff was worth learning more about. Stuart is always up for doing math, and he was all in. So every morning after we eat breakfast, we clear the table, make some hot chocolate, and do math for (I'm not kidding about this...) *an hour*! Sometimes more. It's not uncommon for Caitlin to spend longer than Stuart doing math, because the patterns and number relationships are simply delightful, especially for someone who was so tortured by it before.

The highest recommendation for any education book is one from an unschooler, simply because if my kids didn't like it, we wouldn't be doing it. For an hour! Every day! If you have a math phobia, have dyscalculia, greatly dislike math, or have a child who fits any of those, definitely check Vedic Math out.

Quick math trick to divide any number by 5:

* 23 divided by 5
* Take the number. (23)
* Double it. (46)
* Place a decimal point one place to the left. (4.6)
* There's your answer!★
* 83 divided by 5
* 83 + 83 = 166
* 16.6
* !!!
* 77 divided by 5
* 77 + 77 = 154
* 15.4
* !!!

You can do the same for multiplying by 50, 500, 5000, etc. Just keep moving the decimal number over to the left, as many times as the digits in your number.

Viva la Math!

The Nine-Point Circle

In Vedic Math, there isn't just a ten-point circle, there's also a nine-point circle as well. And we love circles around here—circular logic, circular thinking, circular donut, whatever—if it's a circle, it's good.

"There isn't anything very fun about a bunch of numbers in a long line, but wait 'til I tell you what happens when you wind those boring numbers up into a circle."

★ Editor's note: Can you treat this technique as a mathematician would, and figure out why it works? This one is pretty straightforward. A good way to start is to try very easy numbers. For example, 15 divided by 5 is 3. Try the Vedic procedure. Double 15 to get 30, move the decimal to the left, and you get 3. Now can you figure out why it works for five times any number?

The nine-point circle is tons of fun, especially to someone who has learned to hate math and numbers. There isn't anything very fun about a bunch of numbers in a long line, but wait 'til I tell you what happens when you wind those boring numbers up into a circle.

Play along, if you'd like. First, take a circle and put nine lines like spokes on it. 9 is up top, then going from 1, label the lines until you get back to 9 again. Then, keep going with the 10 placed alongside the 1, 11 alongside the 2, 12 alongside the 3, etc. Do this for as long as you have room, or until you want to stop. This is when it starts getting fun.

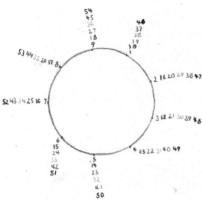

Pick a spoke, any spoke. Let's say, spoke 4. Now look at all the numbers coming off from that spoke: 4, 13, 22, 31, 40, 49, … There's something interesting about them. They go up by 9, yes. But they do something else, too. Stuart, who is our math whiz, couldn't see anything else. Caitlin, who is our mathphobe, got it in an instant. It's all about the patterns! "The numbers all add up to 4! 13…1 + 3 is 4! They all do that!" And they do.

She was excited at this point, and wanted to see if the pattern held true for every spoke … which it does. In fact, you can place any number on the correct spoke by figuring out the digit sum (numbers added together until there's only one digit) and putting it on that spoke.

Well, I'm happy to say that the mathphobe, who is good at avoiding adding numbers at all costs, wanted to take big long numbers and keep adding the digit sum until she could put it on a spoke. We started with birthdays. Hers is 8/17/1996. So, her digit sum would go like this:

$8 + 1 + 7 + 1 + 9 + 9 + 6$ turns into $8 + 8 + 10 + 15$, which turns into $16 + 25$, which turns into $1 + 6 + 2 + 5$, then $7 + 7$, then 14 which turns into $1 + 4$, and then 5.

You might notice we took some extra steps, dividing up the larger numbers—it's because neither of us likes to add big numbers like that, so we just broke them up first, and continued on.

Eventually we discovered things, like … a 0 doesn't move you around the circle, so you can ignore those, and … a 9 moves you around the circle, but keeps you on the same spoke, so you can ignore those.

Stuart had the best birthday to show that: 8/19/1999. The long way to get the digit sum is like this: $8 + 1 + 9 + 1 + 9 + 9 + 9$ turns into $9 + 10 + 18 + 9$, and that turns into $19 + 27$, which turns into 46, and then $4 + 6$ turns into 10, which gets us $1 + 0$, and that becomes 1! (Note: Stuart adds big numbers better than we do, so it's a bit quicker for him.)

But we can "cast out the nines", meaning, ignore them since they keep us on the same spoke anyway, so his number becomes: 1

Just like that! He didn't have to add anything! (Well, except that 8 and 1 turned into a 9 and got thrown out.)

We spent an afternoon adding digit sums—it became obsessive, especially when we realized we could get rid of the 9's to shorten our number. My birthday was kinda fun, but not like Stuart's. 11/12/1972 (Now you know how old I am … all in the name of math…)

I cast out the 9, as well as the 7 and 2 because those make 9, so my number became 11/12/1… 1 + 1 + 1 + 2 + 1, or 3 + 3, or 6.

We looked to see if anyone shared a spoke with anyone else. I'll tell you what—for two girls who hate to add, Caitlin and I couldn't stop doing this. It makes for a fun little game.

Go ahead…try it!

Pretty Patterns

Alright, party people. The last few pages of introduction to the Vedic nine-point circle have been fun, but I've been dying to get to the point where I can show you what you can really start to do with it…and now is the time!

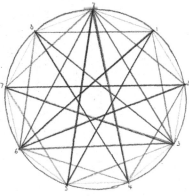

I thought the nine-point circle had a limited amount of fun until I started studying a Vedic illustration like this one, which looked more artsy and less mathy. And, well, that's the point. Art, math, philosophy … it's all the same. In fact, the basis for this type of math is centered on sixteen Vedas, or sutras. I haven't delved deeply into the sutras at this point, either for Math Mondays or in my own studies, because honestly we are having so much stinkin' fun with the nine-point circle still. We haven't moved on yet!

So, gather around you everyone who claims to hate math (yourself included!), and arm yourself with a nine-point circle.

The first thing you need is someone who loves math. I know, they can be obnoxious and spoil the "I hate math" fun, but you need someone to do the multiplication tables for you. Luckily, Caitlin and I have Stuart nearby. If you don't have someone like this available, use a calculator. The point of this exercise isn't to see how good you are at memorizing multiplication tables (I still haven't done it!) but to find these super cool patterns in the circle. So, don't get bogged down in the numbers. Free your mind to do other things like draw lines in pretty colors!

The second thing you need is to start writing down the multiplication tables. The designated math lover will love this. Then, the designated math hater can start taking those numbers and 'graphing' them on the circle. For instance, start with 1. Multiplying in order, the multiples will be 1, 2, 3, 4, 5, 6, 7, 8, 9, 10, 11, etc. When you graph them on the circle, it looks like this:

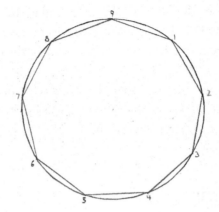

You may have realized that 10, 11, etc., are all two digits and ungraphable on the chart. Good for you! This is why I talked about digit sums first. If a number is more than one digit, add the digits together until it becomes a number between 1 and 9. Then graph it. You may have realized that the multiples of one have a cool pattern on the circle…they are an endless loop. 1 to 9, 1 to 9, 1 to 9, repeating forever, no matter how big the numbers get…the digit sums repeat the pattern.

Now look what 2 does:

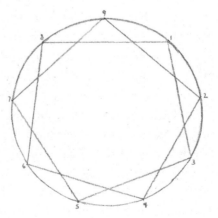

!!! It is also on a repeating loop. Can you work it out? Have the designated math lover show you the multiples of two, and then when you and the other math haters graph it, you can appreciate its pattern.

But just wait until 3. You won't believe it. You will be amazed and overjoyed. Because math haters may not like numbers, but we all love a good picture…a nice shape. And when we realize that numbers can make lovely shapes, all of a sudden the numbers that we hate so much begin to hold a certain appeal. So … I bring you … 3 …

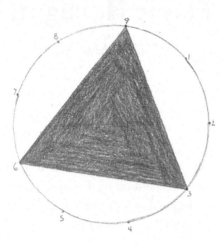

Can you *stand* it?! Didn't your mind look at that and think, "I've got to multiply 3 over and over to find out how this triangle is possible!" Ours did. In fact, Stuart wasn't done with some other computations, so Caitlin and I were doing the 3's ourselves and almost fainted when we saw the pattern on paper, with the numbers … and we hadn't even graphed it yet.

We stopped here for the day. For the first time in my life, I spent that night thinking of numbers. What patterns would the multiples of 4 make? What about 5? … and 6?

We've made number patterns like this for the past couple weeks, each day uncovering a couple new shapes, and each night leaving me to ponder the shapes that numbers make. I even started figuring out multiples of 15, people! Me! The biggest math hater around. But we discovered the triangle shape in number 3, then 6, then 12, and I had to know if it continued the pattern for 15. (A pattern in a pattern!)

And if the pattern holds for multiples of 3, why wasn't 9 a triangle? And, what pattern was 9 if it wasn't a triangle?

And next thing you know, we're wondering if multiples of 3 seem to be triangles, are multiples of 9 just a dot? So Caitlin and I started figuring out multiples of 18, 27, 36, etc. Sometimes mentally if the calculator was busy. And, well, I'll just let you do the graphing for those—I've spoiled the surprise on too many numbers already.

There is an entire wall of our breakfast nook devoted to our colorful little drawings. I must admit, this is the first time I've looked forward to doing math. Caitlin, too! And maybe … you, too!

Magic Hexagon

by Michael Hartley

Fill in numbers so the grid has each number from 1 to 19 just once, with each row and diagonal adding to the same number. (Each cell is in one row and on two diagonals.) If you like this puzzle, you can find lots more at Dr. Mike's Math Games for Kids.*

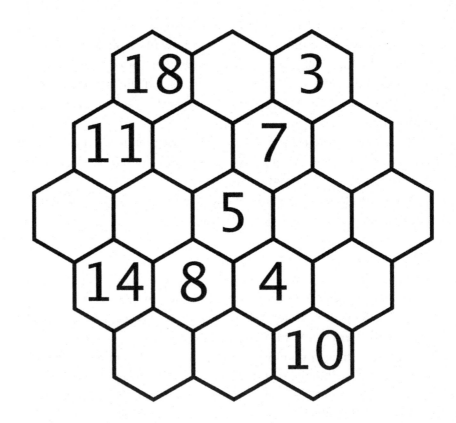

---

* Dr-Mikes-math-games-for-kids.com/magic-hexagon-worksheets.html

Malke blogs at The Map is Not the Territory (located at MathInYourFeet. blogspot.com), about the journey toward math she is taking with her daughter and about her math and dance program described in the Passionate Teachers section. —SV

Mapping the Familiar

by Malke Rosenfeld

There was a bright blue sky up above, and at ground level there was frozen fog. The result was a morning delicately dressed in sparkles. Perfect for a walk.

Down the driveway. Pick a piece of lavender, covered with millions of tiny ice crystals. Which way do you want to turn, left or right? Next intersection, right or left?

We walked through the fog, already burning off. We could feel the sparkles entering our lungs with each breath.

Busy road and cars zooming. Three choices, right, left, or straight ahead. "Mama, I used to be afraid of those trees, but I'm not any more." We pick tiny pine cones off the tips of the branches.

Next crossroads, "Mama, that's University Street down there, let's go there." Thinly frozen puddles alongside thinly disguised reading practice: "What does that P stand for, do you think?—That one with the red circle and the cross over it. What does the rest of the sign say?" I ask.

Right turn down University and an old dog barking at us across the lawn. "Mama, I used to be afraid of dogs, but now I just don't like their licking."

Find two sticks, clap them together, and then we're marching. Left turn. Right turn. Rose Street! Find the stone pig, march on home. "I wanna make a map!" the girl says.

She wanted red and blue like the roads in the atlas. We recalled which way we turned and what we saw. We remembered the crossroads, one block at a time. All of a sudden, she notices corners and the geometry of the street layout. "I always thought the blocks went in a circle. I didn't know they were squares." The things she loves go on the map (friends' house,

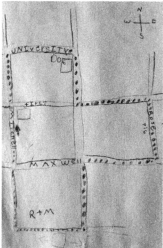

"All of a sudden, she notices corners and the geometry of the street layout. 'I always thought the blocks went in a circle. I didn't know they were squares.'"

stone pig) as well as the things that "used to" frighten her. Her long battle with anxiety has its landmarks as well.

It may not be to scale, but when we go out again this afternoon to follow our map, the issue of scale might come up. I'm also pretty sure we didn't get all the streets on there, especially at the end of our route, but next time we'll bring paper and make some notes as we walk.

Mapping the familiar twists and turns and landmarks of our neighborhood—bodies first, memories second, paper and pencils third. I marvel at the human brain inside my six-year-old daughter's head that is so driven toward representation of her experiences and activities; driven toward it even though she is still just learning to decode print and to write using "the rules."

She makes maps of other kinds, too. Sewing "patterns," also not to scale, but clearly a sequence of steps mapped out.

I recently read a fascinating article in the New York Times[*] about teachers taking their young students on walking field trips as a way to develop literacy. This kind of activity is literally a step in the right direction. Without concrete, kinesthetic, physical experiences like these, no child can fathom the meaning behind the marks on the page or develop full mastery of the human brain's greatest gifts. The order needs to be sensory experience, then memory, then symbols, not the other way around.

---

[*]*NYTimes.com/2012/02/13/nyregion/for-poorer-students-an-attempt-to-let-new-experiences-guide-learning.html*

Racetrack

adapted by Sue VanHattum

This game has charmed generations of young racing enthusiasts, along with math and physics students. I've gotten most of my information on it from Wikipedia,* but I remember playing this game myself as a kid.

This game may help players gain intuition about velocity versus acceleration, about vectors (which show distance and direction), and about some basic physics.

What You Need

A copy of the grid below (or your own track), two or more racers

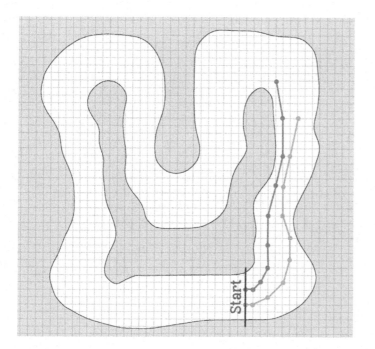

---

* *en.wikipedia.org/wiki/Racetrack_game*

How to Play

- Each racer uses a different color to mark their path, and chooses a starting position at an intersection point on the Starting Line.
- On your first turn, you go one unit in any direction. You'll travel from your starting position to one of the 8 neighboring intersection points (left, right, above, below, and diagonally).
- On each turn after that, you must first go the same direction and distance (your speed) as your previous turn, but then you can move to any of the 8 neighboring intersection points. Draw your path as a straight line from your previous position to your final position for this turn. This is your new direction and speed.
- If you go too fast (too far in one turn), you'll have trouble getting around curves. (If you hit a wall, start over at the beginning. Or you can agree that the penalty is to lose one turn.)

Variations

Check the Wikipedia entry for variations, or make your own rules.

This is edited from transcriptions of a few of Pam Sorooshian's talks at the annual California Homeschooler conference. Her marvelous prompt cards make good reminders for us all. —SV

Radically Sensible Ideas: Math Advice for Unschoolers

by Pam Sorooshian

Schooling

I remember being so compliant in high school. I did the math, but it didn't mean much to me. What changed me was my first female math teacher. She was a radical feminist in 1967, and she wanted girls in math. I got A's but I didn't know anything. She got me to join the math club, chess club, and computer club, and I got an identity as a feminist. My role in the women's movement was to do well in math. Then I majored in economics, so I had to do the math.

When I majored in econ, I finally really learned math, after all those years in high school as a math fake. Why do I think I was a math fake? Because in eleventh grade, the year before my teacher asked me to join the math club, I had an "Ah-ha!" moment where I suddenly got it that multiplication was just repeated addition. The adults think kids are understanding more than they are. (You're probably doing that with your own kids—they say the right things, you think they get it.) Here's what's even worse: several years later in college I had taken advanced math classes, and I finally realized, "Oh yeah! And division, that's repeated subtraction!!"

The existing methods of teaching math don't work, period. They turn people away from math in droves; they are counter-productive. I think you're better off to not *let* your kid learn any math—because they can learn it later if they're not math phobic. I've seen serious estimates

"I think you're better off to not let your kid learn any math— because they can learn it later if they're not math phobic."

that around 85% of kids are math phobic. Is it different in other cultures? It's still pretty bad, but they're a lot more like I was—compliant. They expect to be confused, and they're more tolerant of being confused and bored.

It's not the difficulty of math that's the problem. It's not because it's hard. It's because of the way it's taught. You shouldn't feel bad about yourself if you have math anxiety; you should feel angry. That's the appropriate response. You've been mistreated; you've been abused. It's still going on—it's happening to all these kids. They're being damaged.

When I had kids and we decided to keep them out of school, I thought about math. The one thing I don't want to do is damage my kids; I don't want them to come out of the experience hating it. I just want to do no harm. What's the worst-case scenario? That they turn 18 and they can't add or divide? That won't happen. Those things come up in real life. There's a reason why basic math was invented. It wasn't invented by mathematicians, it was invented by farmers. It's practical.

A Long Division Story

There are these points where people lose it in math: division, fractions, and algebra. They say, "I was fine up until…" I had a little worry in the back of my mind. I was wondering, "Where will long division come up in real life?" But I just decided I wasn't going to worry about it. I figured that they couldn't come out worse than the high school seniors I've been teaching. They come out of twelve years of schooling and they know nothing.

Here's what should be a natural development…

A couple of years ago my daughter was thirteen; she wanted to go see *Cats* on Broadway. She was a *Cats* fanatic—she had seen it over a dozen times. We drove two hundred miles to go see it once, in costume. She has recordings of it in every foreign language it's ever been recorded in. So this is extreme.

She wanted to go see it before it closed on Broadway. They had threatened to close several times, and then they would move back the date. She found out it really was closing in three weeks.

When she learned how high airfares were, she asked, "Can we drive, mom?"

I was doing laundry, walking back and forth, and just said, "Maybe…"

"How long will it take?"

"You figure it out."

She asks me, "How far is it to drive to New York?"

"I don't know, over 3,000 miles, say 3,300 miles."

Then she asks, "How many miles can you drive in a day?" This was a teachable moment. I could have made it easy, but I let her do the figuring. My wheels were turning; I didn't want to make it too easy. I said, "I don't know. Let's see … probably like 350 miles in a day."

I didn't make it nice easy numbers. I admit that I was aware of that when I did it. If it turned out to make her uncomfortable, and if she had a problem, I was right there, ready to say, "Why don't you just try 3000 and see what it would be if we could go 300 miles in a day?" Because that would be an easy way to do it. And I thought that was a good thing to know—that's how real people do math in their heads. Like all those people you're impressed with, who sit around and do the math in their head. That's because they're really good at simplifying the problem to make it doable. Nobody's doing 3300 divided by 350 in their heads just like that. Neither could she, but she didn't seem concerned about it. And I was busy so I didn't pay attention.

At one point, I looked over and she'd gotten a piece of paper and had written 3300 at the top, and subtracted 350 and gotten the answer, and then subtracted 350 again and gotten that. She already had a tower of numbers. And just as I was looking over, she went, "Oh no! I'm gonna have to do it all over again!"

I said, "What's the matter?"

"Ohh! I made a mistake at the top!" She was miserable.

She'd misread her own handwriting. She'd read one of her zeros as a six. It was the second or third subtraction and she'd done a whole bunch of them. She said, "Oh, I don't want to have to do it all over again!"

I said, "Well, I can show you a shortcut way to do that."

Just that, not letting her know how eager I was to show it to her. She said ok. I said, "Only here's the thing. You have to really want to know it, because I have to show you some other things first. I can't just show you that one right away. I've got to show you a simpler one, and then another simple one, and then a little harder one, and then you can do this one."

She's never seen the notation for doing long division. I had to show her that. I showed her 3 into 6, "This is how you write down 6 divided by 3, and you put the answer right above it." That's the level we were starting at. She knew what 6 divided by 3 was. I said, "Now, if it's 60…"

She said, "Then it's 20."

I said, "So you can do it this way. 3 goes into 6 two times, and you can put the 2 right there. And 3 goes into 0 zero times, and you can put the 0 right there."

Then I showed her another one. I just made it one tiny step harder. We did about four of them. She got the pattern. I said, "Now you're ready to do yours—it's has a lot harder numbers." And I asked, "Do you want to try it now, or do you want me to do a harder one first?"

She said, "Oh no, I'm ready." She sat down. It was kind of hard, but she got it. I kept myself busy. I didn't want to hover and make her nervous. I was folding towels, and she got it.

She went from misery to thrilled. "I can't believe you never showed this to me before. It's so cool! I can't believe how many times I made those subtraction towers, and I could have done this!"

I said, "I know," and paused. Then, "By the way, that's called long division."

And she went, "No! I don't get it. Everybody says they hate long division. And this is so cool."

You can't imagine how my heart was just singing—I did it right! Remember she was way past the age where they teach long division. Schools spend weeks on teaching the long division method—not the meaning of division, just the method for long division. This was 30 minutes. And she's fine now—totally caught up, and in college. She recently said she's thinking of being a math teacher. I said, "Yeah?"

"They're so bad! They don't understand students' questions."

We didn't end up going to New York then, but we saw *Cats* three more times. And we just took a trip to New York City and saw six shows.

Do You Need a Curriculum?

I've talked with unschoolers who use commercial math programs to support their children's interest in math. I love math and have at least one child with a lot of aptitude for it, who has enjoyed it since she was little. I teach college-level economics, which includes a fair amount of math, as well as statistics, and I've been tutoring high-school-age kids in math. I am very aware of what these older teens can do and what they understand in math—after many years of taking math classes. They can "do" math if it is presented to them in a textbook format. They have very minimal understanding of what they are doing, why it works, why they'd want to do it. They can't generalize the techniques to utilize them when an appropriate situation presents itself, and they can't combine techniques to solve more complex problems.

As an unschooler, I would seriously warn people away from supporting their young child's interest by providing math programs or textbooks. I very honestly feel it is not a good idea for kids to use any kind of program to memorize multiplication facts, for example, and I mean that especially for those kids who have a natural interest in mathematics!

Yes, support their interest, but do it through conversation, games, experiences, responding to their questions as they arise.

Relax and let them develop conceptual understanding slowly, over time. Don't encourage them to memorize anything—the problem is that once people memorize a technique or a "fact" they have the feeling that they "know it" and they stop questioning it or wondering about it. Learning is stunted. I've talked to a lot of people who say they didn't understand until they were adults that multiplication was just a short-cut way to do addition or division was a short-cut way to do subtraction. They thought of multiplication and division as "facts," just something to memorize and use.

The biggest danger is that thinking of math like that, as a series of things to memorize and use, means that kids don't expect it to all make sense. They don't expect to understand why and how things work. It soon begins to seem normal to them that they don't fully grasp math; they feel it is beyond them to truly understand it. "Doing math" without understanding what they are doing is very discouraging, and people frequently report that they spent years feeling like they were going to be "found out" or it would "catch up to them" eventually. Even students who got good grades will later admit that they felt like fakes and it was very unpleasant. This is one of the most common sources of the epidemic of math anxiety we have in this country.

Some of you are still feeling a need to get some sort of program. Be aware that there's not one right way to do things. Stop your search for the perfect program! Asking "What's the best one?" is a nonsense question. There are bad programs, but there's really no such thing as a "good" program. Ask whether it works for you. It changes constantly as your kids change.

One guiding principle: The child is the learner; don't get a program that meets *your* needs. Some people want to give their child the education they wish they'd had. Don't do it.

"Once people memorize a technique or a "fact" they have the feeling that they "know it" and they stop questioning it or wondering about it."

Games and Math

Arithmetic is not mathematics. I want to talk about the underlying idea of what mathematics is. What do mathematicians do? They play games. Think about what a game is—what makes something a game? Pleasure, fun, challenge, strategy—it's all of those, and it's something to solve. There are rules to games. The rule says you can only put one piece on a square, you roll the die, and you can only move how far the die says. It's not a game if it doesn't have some setup like that. Mathematicians invent games. If this happens and this happens, then this will happen. It's a bunch of rules and an outcome. What they really do is they tweak the rules to see what will happen. Like in Monopoly, they'd make a new rule like, "You can trade properties only if they're the same colors." Even with a simpler game like Candyland, what if you could choose to go forward or backward? That's what mathematicians are doing. They'll tell you that. If you think about mathematics that way, as game playing, then maybe it won't be so threatening.

Kids start out enjoying making up games. Sometimes they get told they can't change the rules of games, and they get real rigid about how they play. Try to help them get over that because breaking the rules, redefining the rules, figuring out why the rules work the way they do, or what would happen if you changed one of the rules—that's a really critical part of math; that is what mathematicians do. They make up games, they change the rules of existing games. Once in a while they make up a really new, cool game. Mathematicians don't add and subtract; they don't even add fractions or do algebra. Mathematicians figure out the rules of what we would call games, and they call it games themselves. It's not trivial; that is real math.

Parents have come up to me after I've given a talk about unschooling and math and they've said, "I really don't like playing games." My response is that they probably had bad game-playing experiences themselves as kids—probably someone was really competitive and made them feel stupid. That has ruined game playing for so many adults. Another possibility is that they tried playing some games with their kids when they were little, and the games were boring, but the kids wanted to play over and over. My answer is sort of blunt: "For your kids' sakes, get over it."

Playing games is a really fun and easy way for kids to develop mathematical thinking along with a lot of basic number skills. There are lots of different kinds of games, so try out new ones until you find some you do like. And heal your own hurts over being bullied or shamed while playing games by being extra sweet to your own kids while playing lots of games with them. Encourage them to fool around with the rules— change the rules and see how it changes the way the game plays out. That is real mathematical thinking in action. Also, word games, story games, pretend games, and picture games all involve a lot of mathematical thinking—it doesn't have to be number games.

Today I overheard someone saying, "These people all just play games—like they're gonna learn math from that." Little did she know...

> *"Breaking the rules, redefining the rules, figuring out why the rules work the way they do, or what would happen if you changed one of the rules—that's a really critical part of math; that is what mathematicians do."*

Unschoolers and Math

Sometimes people bring up the possibility of unschooled kids getting older and developing the attitude of "I can't do math." In an ideal unschooling-friendly world, our kids wouldn't develop this attitude because they'd know that they can learn what they want to learn when they want to learn it. And I've worked pretty hard to make sure my kids have developed that attitude. But we live in a society that is overflowing with math anxiety; as our kids get older they are, unfortunately, more and more exposed to a lot of negativity about math. It is a free-floating societal math anxiety—just out there. Everywhere. We see it in jokes, in books, in movies, in conversations that they might just fleetingly over-hear. There is so much of it that it's like the air—we don't even notice it's there unless we pay close attention.

And as our kids get older, they are hanging out more and more with people who don't share our unschooling attitude that it is "never too late." They might even get teased, or they might just get some blank looks or confused comments, or just absorb the idea that math is hard, and all of that can have an influence on how they feel about their own abilities. This is why I think unschooling parents ought to really talk about their educational philosophy with their kids, help them under-stand that it is a conscious thought-out choice being made for specific reasons. Our kids aren't immune to catching some of the anti-math atti-tude that is out there. Their friends who go to school will be absolutely certain that formal math is essential and that it has to be started early and continued, year after year. And they will talk about it like it is hard and miserable. Our unschooled kids can start to feel like they won't be able to do it when they decide to—that it'll be too hard for them.

I've talked a lot to my kids about school math and why all their schooled friends talk about math with so much negativity. Even so, my kids each had a lot of trepidation when they started taking community college math courses. It was a huge relief to them to find out that they could easily be at the top of their math classes, in spite of not having done any formal math throughout their childhoods. They didn't start with algebra, they started with lower-level math, but it was all very easy for them. Then they moved on to algebra and that was easy, and pretty enjoyable sometimes.

Surely a math education should do more than produce a poor imita-tion of a cheap calculator, but that's what I get in my students. They can do the rote work, sort of. They can't think; they don't understand the concepts. All the schools are really trying to do, in thirteen years, is get them to be able to do the mechanics. We don't need to do that.

What *do* we want?

If you want to help a child with what it takes to be good in math, help them with:

- Persistence, patience, and a willingness to start over
- Concentration
- Hope (This is number one for mathematicians. When they start, it's on a slim chance. They'll do six years of work, hoping. They're not solving pages of problems.)
- Ability to recognize similarities among differences
- Ability to recognize patterns
- Finding joy in math (This is the main thing they need to be good in math, or at least they have to like it enough to not be routinely negative.)

My goals for students would include understanding what math is, where and how it's used and what mathematicians do; appreciating the pervasive role of math in our culture; and having the ability to use math in real ways. To achieve these goals, there are just two things we need to do: *Don't* create math fear/avoidance/phobia, and *do* support an interest and talent for advanced math when it occurs.

GAME
Dotsy

by Leonard Pitt, Cinda Heeren, and Tom Magliery

What you need

Five dice and a copy of the scorecard below for each player.[*]

Goal

Satisfy as many expressions on the scorecard as possible.

How to play

Roll the five dice. Decide if you want to keep any of them, set these aside, and roll the remaining dice again. Keep some more if you want, and roll the rest one more time. At the end of these three rolls, you must choose one expression on the scorecard that is satisfied by the five dice, and take the score for that expression. If no expression can be satisfied, then you must score 0 points for one of the expressions. The game is over after each player takes ten turns.

---

[*] Make your own to create variations, or get more copies of this one at: *MathManiacs.org/lessons /04-boolean/dotsycard.html*

Dotsy Expressions	Score	Game		
		1	2	3
(at least one odd) OR (at least one even)	Largest die			
(at least one odd) AND (at least one even)	Largest die			
(at least three odd) OR (two pairs)	5 pts			
(at least three 1s) OR (NOT any 2s)	5 pts			
(at least four odd) OR (at least four even)	10 pts			
(at least two 2s OR at least two 4s) AND (at least 2 odd)	10 pts			
(NOT any 3s) AND (NOT any 4s)	15 pts			
NOT (any 5s OR any 6s)	15 pts			
NOT (any pairs)	20 pts			
(three of a kind) AND (at least 19 points)	Sum of all dice			
GAME TOTALS				

I met Lavinia at the community college where I teach, and I loved her story. —SV

A Young Voice: An Unschooler Goes to College

An Interview with Lavinia Karl

Q: *Tell me about your math courses.*

I graduated in 2009 from Knox College, a small liberal arts school in Galesburg, Illinois, with a BA in mathematics, minoring in biology. Until I started taking classes at Contra Costa College (the local community college) when I was 14, I had never taken a formal math class. So I started with the basic arithmetic class.

My parents weren't really into math, but they weren't uncomfortable with it either. My mom's a nurse, and my dad's a carpenter. He knows that sort of math really well, but not things like calculus. When I got to that, I was on my own.

Q: *Did your parents encourage you in math?*

No, they just threw books at me. I read a lot of books, and listened to books on tape. I read more books than most people do. I did a lot of art, and I did science at Lawrence Hall of Science. It wasn't until I got to Contra Costa College that I started to focus more on math and science.

I'd say, "I think I should do some math," and my mom would get me a workbook. I'd do it until I was bored with that. I played with blocks and LEGO pieces a lot. There was a very math-oriented home-schooling family we knew, and the mom did a math class with a lot of creative word problems and puzzles. I took that class.

I did math stuff that I wasn't aware at the time had any connection to math. I took chess for a while; I played a lot with puzzles and logic games; I played a game that's very similar to Set; I was really into brainteasers.

I also got *Top Secret Adventures.** It's a bunch of puzzle games. You get one a month. It's a mystery with thieves stealing priceless artifacts. You figure out which one stole what, and you learn about the country it was set in. You had to solve math puzzles to get information. I loved that game.

Q: *Did you know before college that you were interested in math?*
I didn't, actually. I liked everything. It was just another interesting thing. I knew that I liked doing strings of addition problems and puzzles. But I was more into reading books. I loved that I could spend the whole day reading.

When I started at Contra Costa College, I was taking math every semester and loving it. I started with the arithmetic, and went through all the algebra and calculus classes, and kept on going. I didn't want to stop taking math, and I figured the best way to get to keep taking math was to major in it. Then I'd have to do it. I had a lot of good teachers there. They didn't make it inaccessible or esoteric. They were available, and willing to talk to me about it for as long as I had time.

A big part of the reason I liked it so much was that I hadn't expected to be good at it, and when I found out I was, that felt good. I figured: I can do this, I think I'll keep doing it.

"I had never learned the standard ways to do things. I could do things with pictures, but I didn't know the algorithms."

Q: *Did you learn anything in that first arithmetic course?*
Oh yeah. I was fourteen when I took that course. I had never learned the standard ways to do things. I could do things with pictures, but I didn't know the algorithms.

Q: *Was it harder at the four-year school?*
Yes. It was much harder. Their math department likes to pretend that you're Ph.D. students. It was a huge jump. Most of the math classes are taught at Ph.D. level. It was really hard. But I made a lot of friends who were still at the point where it was easy for them, and we worked together.

For a brief period I thought I didn't like math any more. Then I did an independent study on cryptography. And I loved cryptography—still do. I realized it wasn't that I didn't like math. I really loved number theory and set theory; I just didn't like topology and statistics, the classes I had taken because they fit in my schedule.

---

* *store.highlights.com/puzzle-book-clubs/top-secret-adventures*

Q: *Was learning how to do proofs hard?*

Yes. I had never written a proof in my life that was at the level they were expecting. I was the only person in my first class who hadn't already done those proofs. I took a symbolic logic class, and that was really helpful. I liked that class.

Cryptography got me interested in computer science. I haven't taken any classes in that yet, but it's the next thing I want to do.

Q: *What are you doing now?*

Right now, I'm living in an intentional Quaker community, working with high school students interested in peace, justice, and sustainability. I'm working in the garden, cooking, and helping them write essays. I'll be tutoring one girl in math next week. This is a semester-long program for the students. I went when I was seventeen, and it changed my life. Now I'm interning for one whole year. It's a small program; there are only eleven students this semester, and when I came there were only six.

I'm moving to Chicago next year. I want to take advantage of the fact that I'm still young and don't have a lot of obligations. I plan to live with a bunch of friends from college, and I'm applying to the Science and Industry Museum. I want to be the person who walks around and answers questions about exhibits; I'd like to work in the genetics area.

Q: *Do you wish your childhood background in math were different in any way?*

No. I think unschooling was the best decision my parents ever made for me.

Passionate Teachers:
Transforming
Classroom Math

Banded Torus, by Thomas Banchoff and Davide Cervone

Thomas Banchoff at Brown University and Davide Cervone at Union College created this image, Banded Torus, as part of a series exploring the torus in four-dimensional space. This series is featured in the Scientific American Library volume "Beyond the Third Dimension" (1996). To see more of this exploration, watch the animation: *math. brown.edu/~banchoff/art/PAC-9603/tour/torus/torus.html*

Introduction

Grades and Testing

Standards and schedules and grades, oh my! That doesn't sound like playing. And it's hard to imagine school without all that. How can you know your child is getting what they need without the school having standards and schedules and grades? It can be done, but it's not what we're used to. Sudbury Schools (described in the first chapter in this section) do away with all that. Other progressive schools modify the standards to reflect broader goals, make the schedule more flexible, and use portfolios of student work in place of grades. In *The Power of Their Ideas*, Deborah Meier describes Central Park East Elementary School, a very successful public school in Harlem that was able to do away with grades by replacing them with portfolios.

Young students start out with intense internal motivation to learn. But when they begin to pay attention to grades, that external motivation interferes with their own internal motivation. Students become less interested in learning, more likely to skim and pick the easy way through their tasks.*

The models provided by Meier's school and other schools in the Coalition of Essential Schools show us how to escape from grading, but it takes a community of parents who are willing to try something new and who know they can trust their children's teachers. It also takes somehow being outside the federal government's decade-plus mandate for standardized testing, which may be even more harmful than grades.

In her book *Different: Escaping the Competitive Herd*, Youngme Moon, a business professor at Harvard, describes the power of measurement:

> *Measurement can cut both ways. In track and field, we happen to measure speed, and so we cultivate a nation of speedsters. If we happened to measure running style, we would cultivate a nation of gazelles. The*

> *"Central Park East Elementary School, a very successful public school in Harlem, was able to do away with grades by replacing them with portfolios."*

---

* "The Case Against Grades" (*AlfieKohn.org/teaching/tcag.htm*) is a quick summary of the harms of grading. Kohn's book, *Punished by Rewards*, goes into more depth.

minute we choose to measure something, we are essentially choosing to aspire to it. A metric, in other words, creates a pointer in a particular direction. And once the pointer is created, it is only a matter of time before competitors herd in the direction of that pointer.

In the 1980s and 1990s, a number of prominent hospitals agreed to make public their mortality rates. The agreement was considered a breakthrough in hospital openness, promising to give patients the kind of insider view into hospital quality that they'd never been privy to before. If a hospital's mission is to heal, then what better way to audit the performance of a hospital than to track the ultimate measure of that healing ability?

What soon became evident, however, was that a hospital's mortality rate is a function of an elaborate host of factors—including the type of patients it admits, the amount of experimental research its doctors conduct, and the degree of care it provides—each of which can heavily conflate the intended meaning of the metric.

To put it more bluntly, it soon became evident that the easiest way for a hospital to improve its mortality rate would be to stop admitting the sickest patients.

"Our measurements pull us in the direction of what we measure."

Along the same lines, Campbell's Law stipulates that, "the more any quantitative social indicator is used for social decision-making, the more subject it will be to corruption pressures and the more apt it will be to distort and corrupt the social processes it is intended to monitor."* Both Moon and Campbell show us how our measurements pull us in the direction of what we measure. Standardized testing can only measure the ability to choose among stated options. Creative abilities—quite necessary for real mathematics—are not measured by standardized testing and are therefore hard to nurture in schools controlled by that testing. Awareness is growing regarding these limitations, but until other ways to assess the quality of education are a part of public discourse, we'll have a long way to go to dispel this harmful practice.

Schooling

Schools have great potential, both for good and for harm. Generations of Americans have counted on schools to help their children get ahead. For some groups of immigrants—those who blend in racially as "white"

---

* Quote from: *en.wikipedia.org/wiki/Campbell's_law*

or who come from cultures that mesh well with schooling*—school has been the path to realizing the "American Dream." For them, school is where children can learn more than their parents ever knew.

Unfortunately, schools are also where our children learn to stand in line, to try to fit in, to do the work whether it makes sense or not, and to jump up when the bell rings. For African-Americans, U.S. schools have always been problematic. Segregated schools have always meant fewer resources for their children. And the schools are about as segregated now as they were before the Supreme Court decided the Brown v Board of Education case in 1954 (in some places more so, in some places less).†

Classroom culture is hard to change. According to James Stigler, author of *The Teaching Gap*, much of it is deeply imprinted in us, as what school *is*. "The scripts for teaching in each country appear to rest on a relatively small and tacit set of core beliefs about the nature of the subject, about how students learn, and about the role that a teacher should play in the classroom."‡ Many teachers who've tried teaching with more of a problem-solving focus can attest to how much resistance students put up: "That's not how math class is supposed to work! Just tell us how to do it!"

It's a conundrum, trying to figure out how to teach math in school without destroying the innocent love of it young kids have. Some people's solution is not to teach, but instead to let kids discover math through their own interests, when they choose. That's a more sensible idea than it may seem at first. But there are other solutions. Educational theorists talk about the "zone of proximal development." What that means is providing challenging tasks that the children would get stuck on alone, but can manage either in a group or led by a teacher. Stretching yourself that way can feel like a risk, though. If there is a right answer, then there are wrong answers too, and it takes some courage to be willing to expose yourself by sharing your ideas. So making classrooms into safe learning communities, where students support each other's thinking, is vital.

"Making classrooms into safe learning communities, where students support each other's thinking, is vital."

Our Chapters

Although Montessori schools call it work, their math program looks like one kind of play to me; in her chapter, Pilar Bewley describes a Montessori lesson on place value. Malke Rosenfeld ties math and dance

---

* Education has been a top priority in many Asian countries for over 1,000 years due to the influence of Confucianism and Civil Service Examinations.

† *Tolerance.org/magazine/number-37-spring-2010/feature/unmaking-brown*

‡ page 87

together, and Michelle Martin brings fantasy play into an upper elementary math lesson. As we move to high school, perhaps it's more accurate to talk about engagement than play in some of the best teachers' lessons. Each teacher featured in this section definitely brings passion into their classrooms, especially in their search for ways to help students engage with mathematics. I discovered these passionate teachers by reading hundreds of math teachers' blogs, and through the Math Teachers at Play blog carnival, which brings together exciting posts from dozens of blogs in each monthly issue.* (The math education books in the Book Picks chapter describe a number of wonderful books that add depth and complexity to the picture shown in this section.)

Good teachers have always worked valiantly to provide a rich learning environment for the children in their care, and to overcome the limitations imposed by the structure of schooling. In this section, you'll get a peek at a few teachers who discuss their work and their struggles online. One of the themes is how textbooks get in the way. We've ceded much of our power to textbook publishers, and finding ways to move beyond the textbook can be very powerful.

Lots of dedicated high school and college teachers have started blogging about what works for them (and what doesn't). Teaching is a complex art, and each of us does it differently. We all keep talking and learning, and the blogging is making a huge difference in our teaching. I'm looking forward to the time when more elementary teachers join the conversation. It's hard to change education, but this is from the ground up, and has a chance of really making a difference.

---

* *LetsPlayMath.net/mtap*

Teach Less, Learn More: Two Case Studies

by Sue VanHattum

Here are two radical departures from the norms of schooling: Benezet's in the 1920's and 1930's in the public schools, and Greenberg's in the 1980's in an independent school.

Benezet's Experiment

In 1929, Louis P. Benezet, superintendent of schools in Manchester, New Hampshire, was dissatisfied with the results of arithmetic instruction, and decided to conduct an experiment. It might seem contradictory to expect students to improve with less teaching, but his experiment meshes with child development. Children are more ready for the ins and outs of arithmetic procedures by fifth and sixth grade than they were in the earlier grades. They've figured much of it out for themselves, and are ready to get solid on the conventional procedures. Here's Benezet (from his series of three articles, published in the *Journal of the National Education Association* in 1935):

In the fall of 1929 I made up my mind to try the experiment of abandoning all formal instruction in arithmetic below the seventh grade and concentrating on teaching the children to read, to reason, and to recite—my new Three R's. And by reciting I did not mean giving back, verbatim, the words of the teacher or of the textbook. I meant speaking the English language.

The children in these rooms were encouraged to do a great deal of oral composition. They reported on books that they had read, on incidents which they had seen, on visits that they had made. They told the stories of movies that they had attended and they made up romances on the spur of the moment. It was refreshing to go into one of these rooms. A happy and joyous spirit pervaded them. The children were no longer under the restraint of learning multiplication tables or struggling with long division. They were thoroughly enjoying their hours in school.

For some years I had noted that the effect of the early introduction of arithmetic had been to dull and almost chloroform the child's reasoning faculties. There was a certain problem which I tried out, not once but a hundred times, in grades six, seven, and eight. Here is the problem: "If I can walk a hundred yards in a minute [and I can], how many miles can I walk in an hour, keeping up the same rate of speed?" In nineteen cases out of twenty the answer given me would be six thousand, and if I beamed approval and smiled, the class settled back, well satisfied. But if I should happen to say, "I see. That means that I could walk from here to San Francisco and back in an hour," there would invariably be a laugh and the children would look foolish.

I, therefore, told the teachers of these experimental rooms that I would expect them to give the children much practise in estimating heights, lengths, areas, distances, and the like.

"The effect of the early introduction of arithmetic had been to dull and almost chloroform the child's reasoning faculties."

Benezet chose the schools with immigrant families for his experiment, knowing that those parents were unlikely to complain about the departure from tradition. After a year he visited a number of classrooms, both experimental and traditional. The children in the experimental classrooms had been given more time to reason things out, to estimate, and to really think about what would make sense. The children in the experimental classrooms answered questions that required applications of math much more effectively than the children in the traditional classrooms did. For example*, on a visit to a fourth and fifth grade experimental classroom, he described how Niagara Falls had moved, due to the rock crumbling, some 2500 feet from 1680 to 1930. The students told him it had moved about ten feet a year, something the traditionally-taught students were entirely incapable of.

Perhaps this seems astounding. Not teaching the children math gives them a better foundation than teaching it?! It's certainly counter-intuitive. But standard instruction involves telling kids things to memorize without understanding, which works against the deep thinking and sense-making that is real mathematics. The measurement activities that Benezet had the students do instead gave them a forum for numeric exploration that kept them thinking about mathematical questions, without depending on a teacher to provide the "right answers."

You may also wonder why his experiment wasn't expanded across the nation, if it was a success. The problem is that schooling is mired in tradition, and no matter how useful a change is, it's not likely to be widely implemented without pressure from above. But that pressure is

---

* *inference.phy.cam.ac.uk/sanjoy/benezet/*

not likely to come with any deep understanding of children's needs and cannot be sensitive to local conditions.

Sudbury Schools

Let's look at an even more radical experiment. Sudbury schools started out following the model of Summerhill, a school in England where the students decide how the school will operate. Summerhill is a boarding school, and the Sudbury schools in the U.S. are not. The Sudbury schools are dedicated to teaching children democracy by living it in their daily lives at school. Also known as democratic schools, Sudbury schools are not what the word "school" brings to mind. The students do not have daily lessons, they are not required to go to class, and the children make all the decisions and all the rules, not the adults. Sudbury schools work quite well—the students work out their disputes in meetings that they run themselves, develop their individual interests, and move on to successful lives, following passions they might not have discovered in a more conventional setting.

Daniel Greenberg, a founder of the Sudbury Valley School, wrote *Free At Last*, a fascinating introduction to the approach of Sudbury schools. In the chapter titled "And 'Rithmetic," he describes a time when some of the students came to him and asked him to teach them math. At first he tells them, "You don't really want to do this. ... Your neighborhood friends, your parents, your relatives probably want you to, but you yourselves would much rather be playing or doing something else." But they convince him, and so they begin.

> *Sitting before me were a dozen boys and girls, aged nine to twelve....*
> *They wanted to learn to add, subtract, multiply, and all the rest....*
> *Basic addition took two classes. They learned to add everything—long thin columns, short fat columns, long fat columns. They did dozens of exercises. Subtraction took another two classes. It might have taken one, but "borrowing" needed some extra explanation. On to multiplication, and the tables. Everyone had to memorize the tables. Each person was quizzed again and again in class. Then the rules. Then the practice.*

> *They were high, all of them. Sailing along, mastering all the techniques and algorithms, they could feel the material entering their bones. Hundreds and hundreds of exercises, class quizzes, oral tests, pounded the material into their heads. Still they continued to come, all of them. They helped each other when they had to, to keep the class*

moving. The twelve-year-olds and the nine-year-olds, the lions and the lambs, sat peacefully together in harmonious cooperation—no teasing, no shame. Division, long division. Fractions. Decimals. Percentages. Square roots....

In twenty weeks, after twenty contact hours, they had covered it all. Six years' worth. Every one of them knew the material cold.

Greenberg was surprised at the speed—these students were not specially picked. They weren't "gifted." When he shared his surprise with Alan White, an elementary math specialist, Alan said, "Everyone knows that the subject matter itself isn't that hard. What's hard, virtually impossible, is beating it into the heads of youngsters who hate every step. The only way we have a ghost of a chance is to hammer away at the stuff bit by bit every day for years. Even then it does not work. Most of the sixth graders are mathematical illiterates. Give me a kid who wants to learn the stuff—well, twenty hours or so makes sense."

"In twenty weeks, after twenty contact hours, they had covered it all. Six years' worth. Every one of them knew the material cold."

Those mathematically-illiterate sixth graders came up in Benezet's account too. They give a hint at how pervasive and long-standing the problems with math instruction are. Traditional instruction focuses too much on memorization and explaining how to do something, when what is needed is a math-rich environment where kids can work on questions they pose themselves. Benezet and Greenberg provide very different solutions. Benezet's was to offer measurement activities, which provoked problem-solving. Greenberg's was to wait until the students came to him. The instruction sounds conventional, but when offered to kids later than usual, at their request, it likely helped them make many connections between things they had already figured out on their own.

The Sudbury approach may not work for everyone, but Benezet's solution shows us one way to respect the needs and interests of children within a conventional school format. There are others. The Montessori approach described in the following chapter is one, and the other chapters in this section give us a few more hints at what we might be able to do.

Preview

This game uses modular arithmetic, sometimes called clock arithmetic, to create an unusual variation on the classic card game of war. One of the greatest mathematicians of all time, Carl Friedrich Gauss, formalized the idea of modular arithmetic and then used it to solve many previously-unsolved problems and find entirely new results. With its use of small numbers, modular arithmetic makes calculations much easier, while preserving important properties of the original numbers.

We use modular arithmetic all the time. In fact, telling time is modular arithmetic. For example, 3 hours after 11 o'clock is 2 o'clock. We are all used to doing $11 + 3 = 2$ with time, which is an example of using "modulo 12"; mathematicians would write $11 + 3 \equiv 2 \bmod 12$, with that odd-looking three-bar equals sign (read "is equivalent to"). Gauss realized modular arithmetic could be used with "clocks" having any number of hours on them; for example, the clock below is modulo 7. If we are using n as our modulus, the numbers we use go from 0 to $n - 1$. (Notice that modulo 12 goes from 0 to 11. So clocks have a minor difference from the conventions of modular arithmetic. But since $12 \equiv 0 \bmod 12$, we won't quibble.)

Any number less than 0 or greater than $n \equiv 1$ can be seen as equivalent to a number between 0 and $n \equiv 1$. To use our original example, $11 + 3 = 14$. But 14 is equivalent to 2 modulo 12, because $14 - 12 = 2$, so we write it as $11 + 3 \equiv 2$ modulo 12. You can also think of it as finding the remainder when dividing, since $14 \div 12$ is 1 remainder 2, or $14 = 1 \times 12 + 2$.

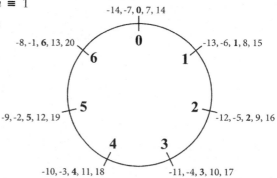

To find the value of a number modulo n, subtract n from your number as many times as necessary to make your result less than n but still not negative. If you start out negative, you'll be adding n until you get a number between 0 and $n - 1$. For example, modulo 12, -20 is equivalent to 4 since $-20 + 12 = -8$ and $-8 + 12 = 4$. The division idea is a little harder to see with negative numbers, but $-20 = -2 \times 12 + 4$, so it still fits. In fact, this division idea is a key connection in modular arithmetic.

The Game

What you need

one deck of cards, two to four players

How to play

Each player is dealt a hand of three cards. Pick the two cards that will give you the highest score, and lay them down. The player with the highest sum takes all the cards on the table. Everyone now draws two more cards. The round ends when the deck is used up.

For scoring purposes, black cards are positive, red cards are negative. The Jack counts as 11, the Queen as 12, the King as 13, and the Ace as 1. So the Queen of Hearts, for example, is a negative 12. A complete game is three rounds, each using a different modulus: first 11, then 7, then 5. The highest number modulo 11 is 10, since $11 \equiv 0 \bmod 11$; in modulo 7 the high number is 6, and in modulo 5 it's 4.

This is a game where 5 can beat 15. If you're playing mod 11, $15 \equiv 4 \bmod 11$, so the 15 becomes 4, and $5 \equiv 5 \bmod 11$, so the 5 stays at 5. And 5 beats 4. It turns out that 5 beats 15 in mod 7, too, since $15 \equiv 1 \bmod 7$, while 5 would stay 5. In mod 5, they tie, since both are equivalent to 0.

If two or more players are tied for the highest total, there is a one-hand playoff (just like in the conventional game of War) among the players who are tied.

At the end of a round, count the number of cards you won for your score and then shuffle up the cards for the next round.

Examples from a game

A hand from round one, modulus = 11

Player 1: black 3, black 2, $3 + 2 = 5$

Player 2: black J, red 5, $11 - 5 = 6$.

Player 2 wins. Since 5 and 6 are both within the range of 0 to 10, we don't need to do anything special in this hand.

A hand from round two, modulus = 7

Player 1: black 3, black 8, $3 + 8 = 11$; this is equivalent to 4 modulo 7.

Player 2: red 6, black 5, $-6 + 5 = -1$; this is equivalent to 6 modulo 7.

Player 2 wins again. Give us a break, will ya?

A hand from round three, modulus = 5

Player 1: black 4, red A, $4 - 1 = 3$; $3 \equiv 3$ modulus 5, of course!

Player 2: black J, black 2, $11 + 2 = 13$; that is $2 \times 5 + 3$, so it's also 3 mod 5.

War! Both players discard their extra card and draw three new.

Player 1: black K, red 4. $13 - 4 = 9 \equiv 4$ mod 5.

Player 2: black K, black 10. $13 + 10 = 23 \equiv 3$ mod 5.

Player 1 wins all the cards! Finally.

Variations

- For younger kids, start with all cards being positive, and just use modulo 12 until everyone's ready to try another modulus. It may also be helpful to have a number line handy for counting down.
- Use the cards you won in one round to play the next round.
- Try using a different modulus.
- Include multiplying. To add cards, place them side by side; to multiply, place one card sideways so the two are perpendicular.

I found Pilar's blog when she submitted an earlier version of this to the Math Teachers at Play blog carnival. I'm delighted to be able to include it here. —SV

Trust, Montessori Style

by Pilar Bewley

*Every unnecessary help is really
a hindrance to development.*
—Maria Montessori

Answer Versus Process

Five-and-a-half-year-old Roland asked me if he could multiply 8,696 times 10 using the stamp game. I was thrilled to see his interest in math taking off again after an unfortunate temper tantrum with the addition blank chart. I suggested he borrow a stamp game box from another classroom to supplement the one we have in ours, and he got started.

It took him a while to figure out where he would do the work, and then he painstakingly began to make 8,696 with the stamps... Six units, nine tens, six hundreds, and eight thousands... Leave a space and repeat... Six units, nine tens, six hundreds, and eight thousands...

He made the amount five times before it was time to go home, and he left his work out so he could return to it the next day. (Can you imagine what that looks like, once you've made 8,696 with little colored tiles ten times? How cool!)

"I'm going to get right back to work as soon as I change my shoes," he declared before leaving that afternoon. "I won't even talk to anybody!"

I waited eagerly for him to arrive the next morning, looking forward to the moment when he would put AAAAAALLLLLL those tiles together in neat rows by category, and he would have to exchange several times (not to mention his surprise at seeing all the units disappear when multiplying by ten).

Instead Roland came in, shook my hand, and said: "My dad told me that all I have to do is add a zero to 8,696 and I'll have my answer, because when you multiply by ten you just add a zero."

Photo by Jessica Welsh.

"My dad told me that all I have to do is add a zero to 8,696 and I'll have my answer, because when you multiply by ten you just add a zero.'"

My heart sank. Oh no, Dad! You robbed your son of such a cool experience! He was getting ready to see what ten times 8,696 looks like, and would have discovered the process that takes place during multiplication. He won't be doing multiplication tables for at least two more years in public school—the answer doesn't matter yet, but the process could have really taught him something valuable.

Needless to say, Roland lost steam immediately and I had to use the "You took out the work, now you have to finish it" argument to get him to complete the task. It was clear that the thrill of discovery and the pride of achievement and hard work were gone, zapped, extinguished. He made a million excuses to delay completion of the task, and worked carelessly and without focus.

Trust Your Child

I wrote the story above on my blog, and a reader asked:

So if I were a parent, how would I know I'm not supposed to help? I've always heard parents should be involved in their kids' education—hearing this story makes me think that even if I have the best intentions, I might not always know when I'm doing more harm than good. What's the right approach here?

Before I answer, I want to make clear that even Montessori guides are guilty of "teaching" at some point in their classroom journey. (I know I am!) By "teaching," I mean wanting the child to know the answer so badly (because you feel it would help them make a leap in understanding), that you point it out to them, instead of guiding them through the sometimes arduous and frustrating process of discovery. With that said, here are some of the lessons I've learned and some suggestions that might help parents better understand and value the Montessori approach to child-led discovery.

Trust is the key concept that must not be forgotten. Parents and teachers must trust the effectiveness of this method in order to benefit from it. And the method works by trusting children's innate drive and fundamental right to explore the world around them, make their own discoveries, follow a process of trial and error, and come to their own conclusions. Unfortunately, trust is a difficult quality to embrace. How can we move toward it?

Let's take the first point: Parents and teachers must trust the effectiveness of the method in order to benefit from it. You cannot trust something you are not familiar with, so it is essential to familiarize yourself with the method. You ask: How would I know I'm not supposed to help? I answer: By learning about Montessori!

If you visit a foreign country, you will probably experience culture shock; the more different the country is from yours, the bigger the shock. The same can be said for Montessori. The Montessori method is completely different from the type of educational system most of us grew up with. There are no bells, no homework, no awards, no punishments, no grades, no praise, no points, no tests, no assigned seating, no worksheets, no honor roll, no detention. You simply cannot expect to spontaneously understand something so different and unfamiliar. Only those who get past the culture shock of a foreign country can truly enjoy their experience in it, and only those who get past the culture shock of Montessori will truly see the benefits it provides.

The best way to educate yourself about the method is to visit your child's Montessori school and observe a classroom in progress. Watch how the children interact with the materials, the environment, and each other. (Note: Your child will probably act differently because you are there, so look at the other children to see how your child would normally be behaving.) Observe the level of trust and respect the teacher has for the children, and how it is reciprocated. Listen for the lack of verbal praise and the abundance of aha! moments. Make notes during the observation, without passing judgment on what you see. Then call your child's teacher or the head of school and invite them to clear up your questions.

"There's a fine line between guiding your child's development and pushing it in the direction you think it ought to go."

Many schools also provide free parent education courses and informal chat sessions with the head of school, so take advantage of them! Ask whether your child's school would consider hosting a "Silent Journey," which is a three-hour evening session where parents get to explore the materials their children work with during the day. Don't forget to attend Parent's Night, where the children give their parents lessons on materials they've been working with. And educate yourself by reading quality Montessori books. I recommend starting with *Montessori Madness: A Parent to Parent Argument for Montessori Education*, by Trevor Eissler.*

These experiences will hopefully change your approach when you feel the need to become involved in your child's education. Wanting to be involved is fabulous, but there's a fine line between guiding your child's development and pushing it in the direction you think it ought to go. Which leads us to the second point: We must trust children's innate drive and fundamental right to explore the world around them, make their own discoveries, follow a process of trial and error, and come to their own conclusions.

---

* I've made further recommendations on my new blog, at: *TheFullMontessori.wordpress.com/ recommended-reading*

Is this hard to do? Oh, you bet it is! Leaving questions of ego aside, we all want to share our knowledge with our children with the goal of helping them expand their horizons and be successful in life. But giving our children the answers is tantamount to giving them a fish, while guiding them in the process of discovery equates to teaching them to fish. One will feed them for a day, the other a lifetime.

So let's say Roland came home and told his dad, "Hey Dad, I'm multiplying 8,696 by 10 at school!" We all know by now that saying, "Well, you just tack a zero onto the end of the number" is the wrong response. What's the right one? Perhaps, "Oh wow, tell me more!" If the boy explains how he's in the middle of an exercise with the Stamp Game, and tells you how it works, you will have seen his mind in action—much more fun than telling him about that zero at the end. If he says he's frustrated because he wants to keep working on it, then you'll want to empathize with his frustration, or tell a story about a time you persevered.

A dad who has done his research knows (from observations, parent education sessions, and from working with the Stamp Game himself in Silent Journey) how the exploration of math evolves in the classroom, trusts the teacher's ability to put the child in touch with the right material and guide his progress, and trusts his child's ability to overcome obstacles and complete his work of discovery.

If the child is not working on the problem at school but is curious about the concept of multiplication, then the dad could explain that multiplication is when you put the same number together a certain number of times. Grab some beans or pebbles, and invite the child to make eight, ten times. Let her make ten piles of eight beans, and then count them with the child. Voila, your child has discovered multiplication and you guided her in the process! She obviously won't figure out the rule of multiplying by ten from doing one multiplication exercise, but you will have planted the seed. If she wants to do more exercises with you or by herself, that's great! You should definitely suggest that she ask her teacher what material she can use to practice multiplication in the classroom, and give the teacher a quick call to let her know about her budding interest. You are now much more involved with your child's education than if you had given her the answer!

The concepts they're learning at school and the things they're curious about are all around us, so use their curiosity to open up doors. If Roland likes to help in the kitchen, Mom can ask: "Roland, I want to serve four dumplings on each plate. I have six plates. Please help me figure out how many dumplings I need to steam." Let him take out the dumplings, put them on the plates, and count them. Voila, multiplication in everyday life! And by the way, when he's done helping, instead of saying "good job," say "thank you." He didn't do it to receive an evaluation, he did it because he loves to help. As I see it, this drive to help and be involved is Mother Nature's way of putting children in touch with experiences that will help them develop profound knowledge, the depth of which will never be found in workbooks or educational videos.

Especially for the Primary child who is discovering math and writing, what's important is not the answer, but the process. Mistakes are bound to happen during the discovery process, and here's where most parents (and Montessori teachers early on in their classroom journey) panic. We've been educated in a system where the only thing that matters is the right answer, no matter how we get it. Getting the wrong answer is equated with failure, so as adults we quickly jump in to correct. However, we learn more from making mistakes than from getting the right answer.

I constantly work with children who don't seem to be understanding a concept one day, and then a few days later suddenly "get it" (sometimes without revisiting the material). Research shows that the brain sometimes needs time to make sense of the input it has received; I've learned to trust this process after seeing this phenomenon manifested over and over.

Consider what Thomas Edison said when criticized for repeatedly failing to design a working light bulb: "I have not failed. I've just found 10,000 ways that won't work." Ponder how much knowledge he was able to glean from each so-called "failed" attempt. Wonder at the resiliency that kept him focused on the goal. Trust that your child was born with the same drive.

As a guide, many-a-time the children are my best teachers. When one of my older students wants to help a younger one, I always tell the older one to ask if the younger one would like help before jumping in. This teaches respect for the discovery process and lets the younger child know that I trust in her ability to figure out the answer on her own. Interestingly, if asked for help, the older children will only provide the necessary support for the younger ones to get past the immediate obstacle. They seem to be keenly aware of the little one's innate abilities, in a way that we lost touch with long ago. We should model our behaviors after theirs, being available when needed but never offering unnecessary help.

Children trust us. Shouldn't we reciprocate?

Start with a standard 8½ by 11 inch sheet of paper.

Can you fold it to show an exact length of six inches—without using any measuring devices?

After you've found one way, can you find another way?

How many ways can you find?

Try again. This time, start with paper that's 8½ by 14 inches, and find a way to fold it to show six inches.

What if you had a 10 by 14 inch sheet of paper? Could you find a way to fold that to show six inches?

Can you figure out a system to check whether your folding method will work for any dimensions, without actually doing the folding?

This is a good one to try in groups.

Can you make up your own puzzles like this one?

Malke helped me to understand how dance and math could be connected. She blogs at MathInYourFeet.blogspot.com and has a website at MalkeRosenfeld.com. —SV

Math in Your Feet: Integrating Math and Dance

by Malke Rosenfeld

Decades of research shows that movement is a necessary element in learning and brain development—for children it is essential. My program for elementary students, Math in Your Feet, combines traditional percussive dance and elementary-level mathematics, making the abstract world of mathematics concrete and personally relevant. The journey of bringing math and dance together includes a little wooden platform, a trail of blue tape, and the precise communication of both dance and math ideas through a tool I developed called Jump Patterns.

The Power of Limits

I am a traditional percussive dancer of Appalachian style flatfooting and clogging, and Canadian step dancing. I have spent most of my dance life performing and teaching on a three-foot by three-foot square dance platform. Most cloggers, step dancers, and tap dancers do not regularly work in such a small space. For me, working within the confines of my dance board was born out of necessity and eventually influenced the course of my creative life as both an artist and a teacher.

Stephen Nachmanovitch, in his book *Free Play: The Power of Improvisation in Life and the Arts*, includes a chapter titled "The Power of Limits." His chapter inspired me to think about how limits not only enhance creative problem solving but are actually a requirement of such a process. Creativity—and all the intensity and surprise that it implies—requires of us resourcefulness, flexibility, ingenuity, and the necessity to think outside the box. Which, in my case, meant staying in the box!

When I was touring and performing with my band, Cucanandy, many of the venues we played were not dance-friendly. We performed on tiny stages, often carpeted or tile-over-cement. As a dancer whose feet were the percussion section, my dancing contributed to the overall musical experience of our show and the sound of my feet needed to be consistent every time I performed. It's practically impossible to sound good on cement, plus it's really bad for the body. So, I bartered dance lessons with a specialty carpenter who created a beautiful wooden dance platform with the capability of producing high end, mid-range, and bass tones. The design of the platform was in itself limited to whether or not it would fit into the back of a Toyota Corolla hatchback, a compact three feet by three feet.

I didn't start dancing until my mid-twenties, which is another limit I have had to work with in the course of my career. The reason I mention this is that, compared to a child's learning process, which is quite holistic, an adult learner often approaches new learning self-consciously—self-conscious in ways that both help and hinder. Having learned percussive dance at a somewhat late age, I remember very clearly not knowing how to dance.

For this reason, I remember perfectly the day when I realized the creative potential of working within the limits of my dance platform. I was still quite new to percussive dance. As I listened to a song the band was working on, I realized I had no steps in my current repertoire that would work. I remember looking down at the platform and noticing the outer edges of my space, which I normally avoided because I didn't want to fall off. I remember thinking, "Look at all the different directions I can go in!" This insight inspired and generated a whole new set of dance steps and, eventually, the final choreography for the piece.

That moment eventually led me to creating Math in Your Feet, where students, with a basic vocabulary of percussive dance movements, do creative work within the limits of their own square dance spaces while making meaningful connections to mathematical topics.

Teaching Below the Surface with Math in Your Feet

During the Math in Your Feet residency, in which I work with elementary students, each class has a group dancing time to warm up and learn clogging, a little each day until they have some mastery of basic steps by the end of the week. The bulk of our class time, however, is spent with partners engaged in creative work. This effort is done in what I call a personal dance space: a scaled-down version of the portable square dance platform on which I teach and perform. Mine is brown wood, theirs are blue tape. Mine is three-dimensional, theirs are two-dimensional. Mine is three foot by three foot and theirs are two foot by two foot.

On the first day we work exclusively as a large group and the tape on the floor in our dance space is a simple three-sided rectangle. The kids line up with their toes on the tape and face toward the center of the space. This way everyone can see me and what my feet are doing. By the second day of our work together I've managed to tape out about fifteen pairs of blue dance spaces. Inevitably, on that day the kids walk into the room and, knowing nothing about what is going to happen in our class later, go directly to a box and sit down. There's something about having a space of one's own, and these boxes just pull them in.

We never talk about the setup of the room, but since we focus quite a bit on transformation and symmetry in this program I try my best to make sure that, if asked, I can draw an accurate line of symmetry down the middle of our dance space. This drawing, done by a fourth grader, was drawn from memory, back in her regular classroom. Notice the basic symmetry of the space. This isn't exactly what the room looks like (not enough squares), but you can draw a perfect line of symmetry from top to bottom of this picture.

Learning from a Square

By now, you're probably wondering what the kids *do* in all those squares taped on the floor. Well, there's quite a bit of learning going on as they experiment and create foot-based dance patterns using a tool that I developed called Jump Patterns. This tool breaks down the elements of percussive dance into three categories: foot position, type of movement, and direction.* The great thing is that while students are engaged in the challenge of creating their own dance patterns, they are also learning from the square itself.

---

* You can read more about the development of Jump Patterns and how they integrate with math content and practices on the publications page of my website: *MathInYourFeet.com*

What can you learn from a square? Well, before you can learn from a square you first have to understand it. And, to do that, it's best for you to have a chance to experience *squareness* using use all your *senses*. As Albert Einstein once said, "Learning is experience. Everything else is just information."

To start, you need to see it. You've probably been looking at squares all your life. You can correctly identify a square and find examples of it in your environment. But do you really understand it?

Possibly. You might be able to give some facts about a square (number of sides, number of vertices, measurement of angles, etc.). You may even be able to draw one or all four of the lines of symmetry through a square. But if you're a fourth grader being asked to make your body execute a move on the diagonal, it's actually pretty hard for you to do that without a visual reference. That's where tape comes in.

So, *look* at your taped two-foot by two-foot square on the floor and sit inside it. Use your fingers to *touch* and *trace* the taped parallel sides, the vertices, and the equilateral sides. *Touch* the directions forward, back, left, right, and both the diagonals; while you do this, *say* the words that identify the locations on the square as you touch them.

By now, it's probably safe to say that you are oriented to your two-dimensional dance space. It's also likely that you have become inordinately fond of this little piece of property you call home and are unwilling to let anyone usurp your territory. (Ahh, to be nine again…)

It's also time to count up how many *senses* you've used so far to further your understanding of *squareness*. Let's see—seeing, hearing/saying, and touching. There's actually one more sense you need to use and it's not smelling or tasting. It's your *vestibular system* (which provides your sense of balance and spatial orientation).[*]

Okay, so now it's time to *stand up* and utilize your body for some high-powered learning. Put your *feet together* and *stand* in the center of your space. *Jump* forward, *jump* center, *jump* back, *jump* center. *Split* your feet to the sides of the square. *Split* your feet to a diagonal. *Turn* your body right, towards the first side. *Turn* toward the next side. *Turn* toward the third side. *Turn* toward the fourth side. How many times did you have to *turn* to get all the way around? How far, in fractions, did you *jump* on each turn? How far was each turn in degrees?

If you *jump* and *turn* half way around your square, how far have you gone? How many jumps will you need to get all the way around? If you

> *"There's something about having a space of one's own, and these boxes just pull them in."*

---

[*] Carla Hannaford's book, *Smart Moves: Why Learning is Not All in Your Head,* shares extensive research showing the importance of the vestibular system to learning.

start your movements facing forward, *jump* and *turn* 90 degrees to the right and then *jump* and *turn* 180 degrees to the left, where will you end up?

Are you learning anything new from a square yet?

Teaching Below the Surface:
A Preschool Digression

I love tape. You can learn so much from tape on the floor, whether it's in the shape of a square or just a simple line dividing space in half. Simple floor tape allows me to manipulate an environment and encourage physical exploration of that environment. It's a powerful tool for teaching below the surface, something that makes a bigger impact when you don't talk about it because it's just there.

A few years ago I went to Indianapolis to view "The Hundred Languages of Children," a traveling exhibit about the Reggio Emilia approach to early childhood education. Reggio Emilia treats the environment of the classroom and other spaces as a "third teacher." I was drawn to the part of the exhibit that focused on movement and dance as one of the "hundred languages" with which children express themselves. I watched a video at the exhibit that showed the children's first experiences with an old factory space—a huge room, empty except for two rows of large, white columns. The children were running around and between the columns, peeking around them, and interacting with their friends, all movements and ideas that eventually turned into a formal piece of choreography.

I wondered how I could encourage that kind of exploration without having an empty factory on hand. And then it hit me—I could create an environment out of tape. I could define three-dimensional space using two-dimensional lines and colors. Sometimes I use the painters' tape—blue, low tack, comes up easily off both hard surfaces and carpet—that's easily available at hardware stores. There is also the floor tape that P.E. teachers use, which comes in lots of fabulous colors.

Why am I so passionate about floor tape? Let's see...

• Straight Lines, Take 1: A simple straight line taped down a hallway becomes a pathway. It also divides the space in two, and provides a chance to walk on it or jump over it. Best of all, one can march (or walk, or skip, or slide, etc.) rhythmically down it singing "As I was marching down the street, down the street, down the street..."

• Straight Lines, Take 2: When my daughter was three her teachers put down a straight line of tape to help the class line

Movement Variables

FEET	Together	Right
	Crossed	Left
	Split	

MOVEMENT	Jump	Hop
	Slide	Turn
	Step	Touch

DIRECTION	Forward	Back
	Diagonal	Right
	Center	Left

up before leaving the classroom—a simple, visual learning strategy. Later in the year I saw pictures of what else the kids had done with the line. They had used their large blocks to build a wall the length of the tape and then lined up their animals and cars alongside it. A wonderful example of how a simple alteration of a child's environment can deepen their experience and exploration of the space around them.

* Floor tape can define and redefine the space it's in. Large open spaces encourage a lot of endless running. The minute you create a large rectangular box on the floor, with corners, you now have enough of a visual to focus a preschooler's attention to *in* (the box), *out* (of the box), *around* (the sides of the box), *corners*, and *across*, all age-appropriate math terminology.
* A simple taped perimeter can highlight empty space, as in "Find an empty spot inside the tape and make a shape with your body."
* Tape two or more parallel lines down a space and see what happens when you sing "Down by the banks of the hanky panky, when the bullfrogs jump from bank to banky..."

Ultimately, I would love it if every preschool teacher would just put down taped lines in their classroom and then stand back to observe how the children interact with the lines. Start with one straight line and go from there.

And Back to Class

As my elementary students create their original Jump Patterns, they are thinking mathematically. The Jump Patterns tool breaks percussive dance into three main categories of movement variables, which include foot position, type of movement, and direction. These movement variables are analogous to pattern attributes, a tool used to analyze differences, similarities, and sameness in various situations. This is a key thinking skill needed to do math. In Math in Your Feet we use these attributes to first build and then analyze our creative work.

Elementary teachers often use attribute blocks in class. The classic set has five shapes, three colors, two thicknesses, and two sizes. In Math in

Your Feet, kids choose from five foot positions, six types of movement, and six directions to create *each* of the four beats in their Pattern A, and then they make choices again when they choreograph Pattern B. There are two other categories to work with as well, tempo and starting position.

Here's why it's a big deal. The math topics in Math in Your Feet have always been clear to me: concrete, kinesthetic experience with spatial reasoning, combinations, congruence, transformation, reflection, and rotation. These are the things kids and their teachers *know* are being taught. They've always been the selling points of the program because they are easily recognized and understood as math.

But, after years of working out connections between these topics and percussive dance, I knew there was more going on than simply learning *about* math. My hunch was that there was some real mathematical thinking going on; I just needed to figure out where it was occurring and how to explain it.

I've been working hard to figure out what it means to do math and now I know that when children are able to identify the elements (attributes) that they have used in their creative dance work, they are thinking mathematically. When they use this understanding to analyze and critique others' creative work, they are thinking mathematically.

The level of mathematical reasoning and thinking is really the most important aspect of this program, perhaps even more so than the concrete topics we cover. Also important is the way movement affects students' learning, especially in math. Engaging the vestibular system through intentional cross-lateral, rhythmic, and patterned movements improves learning. Math concepts are experienced first through the body. Firm grounding in spatial relationships (best learned through the body) is vital to a strong understanding of math concepts.

Words are connected to the movements and then used in reflective journal entries and in the process of recording patterns on the page. This everyday language is then converted to a more abstract symbolic language in the mapping activities. Higher-order thinking and problem-solving skills are strengthened during the process of creating, manipulating, combining, observing, transforming, and analyzing foot-based dance patterns. At the center of the students' experience is their role as creator, using just the elements of percussive dance and a few guidelines. There is nothing quite so empowering as being able to create something by yourself out of (almost) nothing.

GAME
Fizz Buzz

adapted by Michael Hartley

I loved this game in primary school. It's a great kids' math game, especially for those needing times tables help. The rules are simple, but force players to quickly analyze a number in several different ways. It helps push certain multiplication facts into long-term memory, by associating them with strong emotions—the excitement of the game, or the frustration of making a mistake. And by the way, it makes a decent ice-breaker game for adults too—except that adults seem to have more difficulty than kids!

To play Fizz Buzz, you need several people. They should stand or sit in a circle. One person is chosen to start the game, and players take turns around the circle. The first person says the number one. The next person must then say the next number, and so on. Each person takes their turn by saying the next number in sequence, but...

This is where the game gets interesting.

- If the number is divisible by three, the person doesn't say the number, instead they say "Fizz!".
- Similarly, if the number is divisible by five, they must say "Buzz!".
- These fizzes and buzzes combine together—for example, instead of fifteen, say "Fizz Buzz!" because the number is divisible by both five and three.
- When a Fizz or a Buzz is said, the direction of play is reversed (from counter-clockwise to clockwise, or vice-versa).
- Play until everyone is laughing so hard you have to stop.

Variations

When the first person starts off the game, they start by saying a number from one to ninety-nine. The second person says the following number (or the appropriate Fizz or Buzz).

The player must also Fizz or Buzz when the number contains three or five as a digit, so thirteen gets a Fizz, and fifteen becomes "Fizz Buzz Buzz!"

Add in multiples of seven, using "Woof!" If you're using the previous variation, numbers containing the digit seven would also get a Woof.

Make your own variation!

On my website, at *dr-mikes-math-games-for-kids.com/fizz-buzz.html*, I have directions for my favorite version of the game, along with an app that will "fizz-buzzify" any positive number you type in.

Michelle Martin teaches in the fourth/fifth grade classroom at Prairie Creek Community School, a progressive public charter school in Minnesota. I found her through her blog, The Rookery (PrairieCreek.typepad.com/herons). —SV

Dinosaur Math

by Michelle Martin

Teaching math can feel like a balancing act. On the one hand, computational skills are vital to math literacy. They must be taught and practiced. On the other hand, the beauty of the mathematics and its connection to the natural world are also crucial. Without exploring the wonder of math, it is dull and lifeless. Without knowing some foundational pieces, one is blind to the wonder.

These lessons from two days in October illustrate how we try to nurture both elements in our students. The first day, we did a pretty straightforward lesson on place value. We looked at how our place value system works and why it is an efficient system that had advantages over abandoned systems like Roman numerals and Egyptian glyphs. We briefly hypothesized why base ten might be so popular with humans. (Ten fingers, maybe?) We practiced reading big numbers. We learned how to place commas in numbers. We used place value to easily add large numbers together.

The next day the dino-math *hatched** out of a silly conversation we were having at our morning meeting. Kids noticed that we have ten fingers and we use base ten, and then we riffed on how a T. Rex would tell his mom he ate four velociraptors. I do a mean T. Rex impression and the class was convulsed in giggles—the perfect way to enter a "hard" math lesson. I chucked the planned lesson for the day, and we went with the dinosaurs, and eventually various other creatures with different numbers of digits.

I asked the class how the T. Rex would count. After all, it has only three fingers. I'll admit to a lot of roaring and stomping as I, the T. Rex, became more and more frustrated trying to write a note to my mother

---

* If you spend your days with nine to eleven-year-olds, you have to love puns!

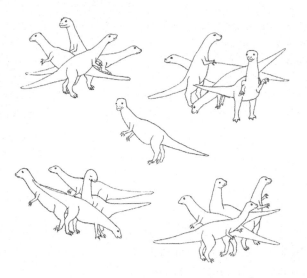

in which I wanted to tell her that I had eaten those four velociraptors.

The only digits I had were 1, 2, 3, and 0.* How could I write the quantity four? Suggestions abounded and eventually we hit upon a place value system, but instead of a group of ten being the next place value, four would be. At this point, about 10% of the class was really understanding what was going on. I added thirteen more velociraptors to the original four. Now how could I tell my mom? A new place value was needed, four groups of four. We practiced with a few more values and more heads started to nod. The dinosaur was feeling pretty good about things.

Another student then pondered, "What if you had a different number of fingers?" Instantly, I announced that we had landed in Hexadeciland—home of a species with sixteen fingers. They, of course, had a system with sixteen digits—0, 1, 2, 3, 4, 5, 6, 7, 8, 9, A, B, C, D, E, F. Kids giggled as they announced, "I'm going to be A this year!" "My brother just turned F!" Someone asked, "How old would my dad be in Hexadeciland? He's 54." We figured it out and then figured out his age in Dinosaur Base4. Students were howling to discover that I would be 203 in Dinosaur. More hands shot up, and we figured out ages for siblings, grandparents, great grandparents. At one point, a student was jumping up and down saying, "I get it! I get it!"

I love other bases and the way playing with them for a while can really shift kids' understanding of what they're doing in base ten, but it's a stretch for many of our kids. At different points, I re-assured students that they should feel very confused. Everything they had learned since pre-school was based on their ten fingers, after all. I also assured them that we were just playing and that they weren't responsible for being able to do this by themselves. But they left the room laughing and imagining different people they'd want to figure out in dinosaur. It was all just a little bit crazy—and wonderful. Our goal for the day was accomplished.

"They left the room laughing and imagining different people they'd want to figure out in dinosaur."

---

* As the lesson *evolved*, we realized the gap in our logic. With its three fingers per hand, the T. Rex should have counted in base three or base six. But base four had easier numbers to work with, which must be why we grabbed it in the heat of the moment.

PUZZLE
Alien Math

by Amanda Serenevy

Some scientists just found this alien artifact. What is it?!

Better Teaching Through Blogging

by Kate Nowak

I'm not out buying popsicle sticks right now.

If I weren't writing this I would be. Because my friend, whom I have never met, took the time to write about a class project. He turns the popsicle sticks (along with clothespins and wood glue) into catapults, which his students use to launch candy.* That sounds fun enough, I know, but then they use measurements from trial launches to predict the candy's trajectory, and are evaluated on how well they can hit a target.

Has blogging changed the way I teach? Before I started teaching, I was taught to design problem-based lessons. But when I started teaching, I quickly learned that procedure-based lessons yielded more reliable short-term results, though miserable long-term ones. I'm clawing my way back to problem-based design. I have blogging to thank.

Before I started teaching, I was told that daily written reflection was key to improvement. When I started teaching, written reflection got done last. And then not at all. Now I write reflections of my lessons several times a week. I have blogging to thank.

Before I started blogging, I could rely on about six people to hear my ideas and share their ideas with me on a daily basis. Now I have about four hundred people to share with, an at-times overwhelming wealth of resources. I have blogging to thank.

"Blogging" refers to three distinct but overlapping practices: reading blog posts written by others; writing posts on my own blog; and participating in discussions through the comments on my blog and those of others.

---

* See the Candy Launcher activity after this chapter.

I started teaching in 2005. My first year was predictably chaotic and inconsistent. I was too often flying by the seat of my pants, trying whatever seemed like it might work, practicing classroom management by coercion. I was grasping for anything to help, but more often than not coming up short. My colleagues were as helpful as they could be, but only had so many minutes a day to talk to me. I would turn to the Internet for lesson ideas, and when I was lucky, would end up at a blog post written by a thoughtful teacher who for some reason was moved to share a successful lesson.

I started reading a few blogs more regularly by remembering to visit them every few days. Every author came from a different location, type of school, and passion, all of which determined their viewpoint and emphasis. Here were teachers like me, not just slogging through their day-to-day, but having fun doing it. I wanted to have fun at work. I became a teacher because I love math and I love working with kids. These reflective teachers were reminding me that I was lucky to be in a challenging and important profession, and were miraculously taking the time to throw me a life preserver when I really needed it. Such succor inspires loyalty. It wasn't long before I figured out what the Google Reader hype was about, and checking my reader became as regular a routine as checking my email.*

Inevitably I experienced a desire to respond to these people. Ask a question, say thanks, leave a compliment or a criticism. Eventually I found the courage to actually leave those comments. You read and admire someone's words for a while, finally leave a comment, and then they respond to your comments and a dialogue starts—you feel like you are contributing to a community. That's very reinforcing. I spent several months discussing, arguing, and commiserating through the comment sections of other teachers' blogs.

> "More and more during mental downtime, like driving home from school, brushing my teeth, or supposedly doing yoga, I would find myself composing sentences and rough arguments for posts I thought I'd like to write myself."

More and more during mental downtime, like driving home from school, brushing my teeth, or supposedly doing yoga, I would find myself composing sentences and rough arguments for posts I thought I'd like to write myself. I had ideas. I was writing some comments that could easily stand as posts on their own. I had tried some creative things in my classroom that were successful, that I knew would be useful to people.

Early in the school year of 2008, I opened the shutters of my own professional blog, which I named f(t).† I found myself with no shortage of ideas for posts. I started with, and maintained, a rate of about two

---

* Editor's note: Google Reader is gone. I now use: *feedly.com*
† At: *function-of-time.blogspot.com*

posts per week. I found that I immediately enjoyed a small but engaged following of readers and commenters because of the relationships I had formed. I learned a few tricks, like leaving my full name and web address when I leave a comment on another blog, so people can click through and find my writing. I began submitting my better posts to blog carnivals, which are enjoyed by a large audience. A few of my blogging friends gave me a boost by featuring one of my posts.

I write about five types of posts. Here's a start for a field guide to posts in the math teacher blogosphere:

Cool Lessons

These are by far my most frequent and popular posts. The ones that get shared, forwarded, linked to on other blogs, included in carnivals, and generally swooned over. A great one or two will quickly make you a rock star in the math teacher blogosphere for about a week.

My most downloaded document ever is "Logarithm War Cards"—a deck of cards you can print out so the students can play War by evaluating logarithms. But those would never have come to be without blogging. I read a post on Let's Play Math titled "This Game is Worth 1000 Worksheets."* The author, Denise, uses variations of War with kids to practice basic math facts. For example, each player can flip over two cards, and the player with the highest product wins. And I thought, hmm, I would like my high school sophomores and juniors to gain some of that automatic math-fact facility with evaluating logarithms.

So I made up a special deck of cards, tried it with a class, and it was a big hit. The basic idea can be used for anything, true, but Denise and I have different audiences. I turned around and wrote up a quick post—explaining the idea, describing how it went, crediting Denise, and sharing the document with the logarithm cards. It's been read now by thousands of teachers.

Complaining

These aren't my favorite posts, but the comments help me remember I'm not alone. My favorite complaint target is the overloaded, impossible-to-teach-well, mile-wide-inch-deep New York state math standards. (The Common Core standards, which value focus and coherence and include fewer topics, *might* help with this problem.) For now, I can't

---

* Let's Play Math is at: *LetsPlayMath.net* Math Card War is included in this book on page 135.

both teach for understanding and teach such that the New York exams show progress. My post "I Can't Do Both"* will give you the details.

Other teachers are also sharing these concerns online, but I have to say that for now, it feels like no one is listening. We need more federal and state education officials, test publishers, and administrators engaging with practicing teachers and responding to their concerns. When the current anti-teacher climate changes, the conversations and documentation we've provided on our blogs will still be there.

Advice

Once in a while I offer advice to new teachers, parents of math students, new bloggers, or random people who email me. I don't write a ton of these, because I still feel kind of "Who do I think I am?" about it. However, these have tended to be popular as well. To new bloggers I offered "Love, Your Fairy Blogmother,"† detailing what it takes to start a successful blog; I wrote "Math Around the House"‡ for parents, to give them ideas for bringing math into their kids' lives painlessly; and for new teachers, "Are You Sure You Want to Do This?,"§ because the first years of teaching are daunting.

Let's Talk Math

These come in two flavors: "Help Me with Some Math" and "Something Interesting I Noticed about Math." Normally when I get stumped, I can un-stump myself with a book or an Internet search, or by asking a colleague. There have been times, though, that I've had to turn to the blogosphere for answers. For example, it is demonstrably true that if there is a 75% chance it will rain on any given day in the next seven days, the chance it will rain on exactly five of those days is *exactly the same* as the chance it will rain on exactly six of those days. This is surprising, and I had a hard time understanding why it was true, so I posted about it.¶ I am lucky that I've attracted a number of actual mathematician readers who are wonderful commenters.

---

function-of-time.blogspot.com/2011/06/i-cant-do-both.html

†*function-of-time.blogspot.com/2010/05/love-your-fairy-blogmother.html*

‡*function-of-time.blogspot.com/2009/07/math-around-house.html*

§*function-of-time.blogspot.com/2012/06/are-you-sure-you-want-to-do-this.html*

¶*function-of-time.blogspot.com/2009/05/wait-what.html*

One day Nick Hamblet suggested on Twitter that we all blog about our favorite math theorems. My contribution to that blog party was "My Favorite Theorem,"[*] which starts out with:

I immediately chose Cantor's proof of the nondenumerability of the reals, for its counterintuitiveness and yet easiness to understand if you can hang with a pretty simple argument. It's the best way to show the uninitiated that math is beautiful that I've ever found. And not because you drew a pretty picture of a golden rectangle, but because the *abstract argument* all by itself is *beautiful* and, once you get it, makes you go ooh and aah. I've explained this to middle school kids, roommates, people in elevators, my mom, and one time (disastrously) a boy I had a crush on.

Help Me Improve My Lesson

These harness the collective power of the blogging community to help improve instruction. I am often stunned by the helpful comments I get. Readers suggest entire documents, links to videos, related "real life" applications, and whole other blogs I didn't know existed. A good example of how this works is my lesson introducing right triangles,[†] which I was not happy with. My readers got to work on it, and with their help I created a streamlined version with less scaffolding that worked much better.[‡]

Sometimes Twitter is the key to getting lots of help. When I wanted to better motivate the concept of proof in geometry class, I tweeted these 132 characters: "I need some false Geometry statements where drawing a counterexample is easy. Help. For example: All right triangles are isosceles." I got well over a dozen responses and crafted the lesson I describe in "Counterexamples in Geometry."[§]

And On and On

After years of blogging, I've found that my passion for participating in this community has been sustained by the ongoing interaction, opportunity for reflection, and high-quality resources I find to improve my practice. Some of my conversations have migrated to Twitter, where I find the feedback is more immediate, but less nuanced.

---

[*] *function-of-time.blogspot.com/2009/12/my-favorite-theorem.html*

[†] *function-of-time.blogspot.com/2009/04/introducing-right-triangle-trig.html*

[‡] *function-of-time.blogspot.com/2009/04/fixed-introducing-right-triangle-trig.html*

[§] *function-of-time.blogspot.com/2010/10/counterexamples-in-geometry.html*

I've also had the joyful opportunity to encourage and support teachers starting new blogs. Additional voices contribute to a richer, more valuable dialogue. Some months, when I am extra busy, my posting slows down, but I think I will always consider it an essential part of my teaching practice. As of January 2013, I'm working as a curriculum developer instead of a classroom teacher. Teacher support is a big part of my role in my new position,* and I rely on the relationships I've built through blogging. I'll likely find myself back in a classroom someday, and I can't imagine a time when blogging won't be integral to my work.

And those catapults? My students loved them. In our end-of-year survey, many cited that activity as their favorite and most memorable. It wasn't just fun. By applying their understanding of parabolas and quadratic functions to their catapults, their learning endured.

---

* At: *mathalicious.com*

ACTIVITY
Candy Launcher*

by Sean Sweeney

Each group of two or three students makes a small catapult, and shoots candies from it while it is on the ground. They measure how far each shot goes and how long it is in the air, and use that to figure out how far the catapult will fire when they place it up on a desk.

They then place a target where they think their projectile will land, and get points based on how accurate they are. I check in with each group regularly so they aren't getting too far off course.

This is probably my favorite project all year because it takes a large number of the things we've done on parabolas and puts it all together, in a "real life" situation. (While firing candies doesn't have much of a purpose, it's pretty easy to get them to understand the connection to ballistics, basketball, and anything involving throwing.)

I bought popsicle sticks (craft sticks, really), a few small pieces of wood, wood glue, and some small clothespins at the local crafts store and used some scissors and tape to make this:

The plans are pretty self-explanatory from the picture above. The clothespin sits on a base made from an inch or so of a popsicle stick cut with scissors, which leans on a platform made of four popsicle sticks.

---

* Editor's note: Try this after studying quadratics. Those equations will suddenly become real.

The basket to hold the candy is made out of paper taped into a circle. The guide rails on the sides help with accuracy. I added the firing mechanism to improve accuracy.

I think one of the reasons I like this project so much is that it actually works. When the kids are consistent and do their calculations correctly, they will hit the center of the target with ease. It's one of my students' all-too-rare opportunities to see that the math they did directly affects something real.

Making the Candy Launcher Catapult

Materials

- Two mini-clothespins (mine are 1¾ inches long; make sure the metal lies embedded in the wood so they are flat on top, because some aren't)
- Four popsicle/craft sticks (mine are 1⁹⁄₁₆ inches wide)
- Wood for base
- Wood glue
- Paper and tape
- Strong scissors (to cut craft sticks)

Construction

1. When planning to do this, leave plenty of time (maybe a day) for the glue to dry. [Note: Because the popsicle sticks are not originally designed to be assembled into Candy Launchers, you may need to press pieces together and hold them for several minutes in order to avoid gaps between the pieces due to warped wood, so you can create a strong bond with the glue.]

2. Cut three popsicle sticks in half. Four of these pieces will be used for the platform, with the curved ends pointing towards the back.

3. Put a light line of glue on each side of the four half-sticks, and stack these on the base. Make sure to leave enough room behind the curved end to mount the firing mechanism (clothespin). I left 1½ inches.

4. Add the guide rails, using the last two half-sticks.

5. Build the firing arm by gluing the clothespin to the curved end of a popsicle stick with the other end cut off, and gluing a one-inch piece to the other side of the clothespin, as in photo. (The flat end is held better by the firing mechanism, which helps it to fire more consistently.)

6. Wait for glue to dry some, and then glue firing arm onto end of platform.

7. Wait for glue to dry completely.

8. Position and glue down firing mechanism. This involves lowering the firing arm, whose glue must hold at this point. The back clothespin is positioned so that it just barely overlaps the back of the firing arm when it is all the way down. It needs to be far enough back that opening it allows release of the firing arm.

9. Allow glue to dry completely before using. (After building your first catapult, you can speed this process up by marking exact positions on your base, and only waiting for glue to dry at the end. This will allow your students to build a catapult in one session and use it in the next.)

10. Make a paper basket out of a thin strip of paper. Complete the circle with a small piece of tape, and use a bit of glue to hold the basket on. Having a basket that is just barely bigger than a candy lying flat helps accuracy.

Candy Launcher Competition

Overview

You will use your catapult (first on the ground, then on a desk) to launch candies into the air. Using a stopwatch and tape measure, you will measure how long each candy is in the air and how far it went.

Your goal is to use your floor launches to predict where the candy will land when you later do your desk launches. See the section below on using math to describe gravity to understand the math behind this.

When you move your catapult onto a desk, you'll use the equation you created to predict where the candy will land. Points are based on where your candies land on the target you have placed on the ground. You will only have four attempts once the catapult is placed on the desk.

Directions

1. Gather together: your catapult, candies, target, tape, stopwatch, and tape measure.

2. Place the catapult on the ground. Make sure it doesn't change position during tests. Fire a few practice rounds. Practice firing until your shots hit close to the same spot each time. If they're not consistent, your equation won't predict distance well.

3. One person is the "timer"; another is the "spotter." The timer will launch, starting the stopwatch while releasing the catapult and listening for the moment the candy hits ground. The spotter will mark exactly where each candy lands and measure the distance. Make sure to load the candy lying flat each time for consistency.

4. Once you get consistent times and distances for your launches, record the official time and distance for three launches. Now find your average time and distance. (For steps 5 and 7, you can either use time and distance from one flight or use your average time and distance.)

5. Your candy was rising for half of its flight, then fell for the other half. To find the time it was at its highest point, divide your time by two.

6. The time you found in step 5 is the value for t that you plug into $\frac{1}{2}gt^2$ to find the highest point your candy reached. You also need to plug in g, the acceleration due to gravity, which is 9.8 meters/sec^2, 980 centimeters/sec^2, 32 feet/sec^2, or 384 inches/ sec^2. You have now found *the y-coordinate of the vertex.*

7. To find *the x-coordinate of the vertex*, divide horizontal distance (from step 4) by two.

8. To model the path of the candy you now want to consider height versus horizontal distance. You have the vertex, so you can enter the h (x-coordinate of vertex) and k (y-coordinate of vertex) into $y = a(x − h)^2 + k$. Using $(0,0)$ as the coordinates of your starting point allows you to solve for a.

9. You now have the a, h, and k, making your equation complete— you now have y as a function of x. Simplify this to put it in

standard form ($y = ax^2 + bx + c$). You may also want to graph the flight of your candy based on your equation.

10. Measure from the floor to the top of the desk you'll use for your Desk Flight.

11. Adjust your equation for the height of the desk. (Remember that the y-intercept, c in your second equation, represents the starting point. It should be changed from 0 to the new starting height.)

12. Solve your new equation to find where the candy should land. (Use the quadratic formula to find the x-value for $y = 0$.)

13. You may want to graph your anticipated candy flight from the top of the desk. Make sure the units are consistent, and graph the x-intercept as accurately as you can.

14. Place the target where you expect your candy to land. You get four attempts. Count your top three scores and ignore the worst result. There are no practice runs here. The team with the highest total score wins.

Tips

- This firing mechanism allows you to just press a lever to fire. There is still room for some error here, so make sure to press the lever slowly each time. Make sure you are shooting consistently before you do official trials; start over if your official trials aren't close together.
- Practice until you can press the firing lever and the stopwatch button at the same exact time.
- This project takes me about two forty-minute classes, depending on class size and skill level. I'm sure it could be done faster with more space and more student independence.
- Having a variety of backup candies might be a good idea in case of allergies or dislikes. (I mean, what fun would it be if they couldn't eat some leftovers?)
- As with any lesson or project, I encourage you to change this to meet your own needs. Let me know what you come up with or if anything is unclear. (Email: seanwsweeney@gmail.com)

Recording Sheet

Print one for each group.

Flights from Ground	Time	Distance
#1		
#2		
#3		
Average		

Flights from Desk	Points
#1	
#2	
#3	
#4	
Total (of best three)	

Target

Enlarge as much as possible on an 8½ by 11 sheet. Print one for each group.

7

8

9

10

9

8

7

Using Math to Describe Gravity*

by Sue VanHattum

In the picture above, we see water shooting upward. Whenever you squirt water from a hose pointed up at an angle, it follows a similar path. Have you ever wondered why?

Math is helpful whenever we want to think about how something is changing. For example, the idea of velocity tells us how position is changing with respect to time.† If you are driving at 70 miles per hour, in one hour you will have driven 70 miles. In two hours, 140 miles. Mathematicians generalize this idea by writing distance = rate × time.

The path of the water in the fountain makes the shape of a parabola. The physics of gravity explains why the water follows that path. As the force of gravity pulls us toward the center of the Earth, it creates an acceleration—a change in velocity. When we are near the surface of the Earth, that acceleration is always 32 feet per second squared (downward). That's a weird unit, isn't it? It means that if you are headed straight down, your velocity will increase by 32 feet per second each

---

* The catapult activity was designed for students who've recently learned the math, so it doesn't explain the math completely. I've written this piece as background for teachers and parents.

† Unlike speed, which is just a positive number, velocity has direction, and can be negative to indicate a downward direction.

second. So when you drop something, one second later it has already gone from a speed of 0 feet per second to a speed of 32 feet per second. Over 20 miles per hour! In metric units, that would be 9.8 meters per second squared. (We'll mostly stick with metric from here on out.)

This acceleration affects the relationship between distance and time because the speed, or rate, is changing. In the driving example, if your speed goes from 55 miles per hour to 60 miles per hour to 70 miles per hour, it makes it harder to calculate how far you have driven.

When considering the physics of situations like the fountain, we can analyze the vertical and horizontal motion separately. Gravity isn't affecting the horizontal motion, so that stays constant.* When you throw something upward at an angle, gravity pulls straight down, changing the vertical component of the velocity. Since the horizontal part of the motion is constant, this gradually changes the direction the object is headed, making the parabolic path you see above.

But how do we know that it's in exactly the shape of a parabola? To see why it is, we'll start with a simpler experiment, throwing a ball directly up. Now the *path* is no longer a parabola, because the horizontal position is not changing. But, amazingly, if we were to draw a graph of height versus time, that *graph* would still be a parabola. To describe parabolas algebraically, we use equations like $y = at^2 + bt + c$. In our case, y is the height and t is the time.

We can figure out a lot about a, b, and c by using what we know about the physical situation. When $t = 0$, $y = a \times 0^2 + b \times 0 + c = c$, so c can be filled in by knowing your initial height. If we had no gravity (and no air resistance), what we threw upward would keep going up with a constant speed. So its height would be given by rate (velocity) times time plus initial height. Do you see why b is the initial velocity the ball has as it leaves your hand?

That leaves a. The value of a will always be half the value of the gravitational constant—hmm, why half? In one second, the acceleration of gravity would increase velocity from 0 to 9.8 meters per second. So the average velocity during that second is 4.9 meters per second. In t seconds, we would increase from 0 to $9.8t$ meters per second, with an average of $4.9t$ meters per second times t seconds, for a height change of $4.9t^2$ meters.

Now we can see the effects of initial height, initial velocity, and gravity combining to make an equation of the form $y = at^2 + bt + c$ for

> *So many ways to say the same thing...*
>
> rate × time = distance
>
> R × T = D
>
> velocity × time = height
>
> h = v × t

---

* If you were moving very fast, air resistance would slow you down. But at these speeds, we can ignore the effect of air resistance.

height versus time. Gravity will actually affect an object in this way no matter which direction it's pointed. And since the horizontal motion is constant, this same sort of relationship holds when we look at height versus horizontal position, although the values for a, b, and c will change.

When an object is launched at an angle, the value for a is determined by both gravity and the launch angle, b is determined by both the initial speed of launch and the launch angle, and c is still the initial height. To find the values for a and b, we can use the symmetry of parabolas across their vertex. If we can find the coordinates for the position of the vertex, we can use that to help us find the values for a and b.

Let's go back to our catapult launch now. In your experimental launches from the floor, where beginning and ending heights are the same, the x-coordinate of your vertex is just half the distance. Your vertex will be reached halfway through your time in the air. From the time your candy reaches the vertex until the time it hits the floor, its height is decreasing at the same rate as an object that has been dropped, so you just use $4.9t^2$ to find how far it dropped, which tells you how high it was.

The vertex form for the equation of a parabola is $y = a(x - h)^2 + k$, where (h,k) represents the vertex, which we just found. If we assume that we launched from the origin, plugging zero in for x and y allows us to find the value for a.[*]

With the values for a, h, and k filled in, we have an equation in x and y. We can simplify it (change it to the form $y = ax^2 + bx + c$), and then modify it for our raised launches by simply changing the value of c from 0 to the height of the launch surface. Now we can use the new equation to figure out where to put a target we want to hit! The target will be on the ground, where the height is 0, so we can plug in $y = 0$, and find x. In real life, the numbers that show up are almost never simple enough for factoring to work, so we'll need the quadratic formula.[†] If we measure the horizontal distance from the floor right below the catapult, to the positive x-value that we get from the quadratic formula, and center the target there, we should be able to hit it. Candy bombing, here we come!

---

[*] If you do your algebra right, you'll get that $a = -k/h^2$.

[†] $x = \dfrac{-b \pm \sqrt{b^2 - 4ac}}{2a}$

Allison and I have never met, and never spoken. Like most of the authors in this section, she blogs about math, and most of us math bloggers read each others' blogs (hers is at infinigons.blogspot.com). She wrote this wonderful story while teaching high school in Chula Vista, California. I'm so glad I found it. —SV

Putting Myself in My Students' Shoes

by Allison Cuttler

I always preach mathematical fearlessness to my kids, my colleagues, and just about anyone who will listen. I go on and on about the importance of being able to sit with a new problem for more than five minutes, or even five days; being able to mull it over, poking around, trying whatever you can to solve it without giving up or losing interest or Googling the answer. I always want my students to try *something* in lieu of just staring, and I am usually stingy with hints.

One thing—quite possibly the only thing—I miss about math grad school is the feeling of sitting down and figuring out a really, really difficult problem. At the time it felt like an empty intellectual exercise because that's all I would do and I felt like I was contributing absolutely nothing to the world, but it definitely helped me develop my mathematical fearlessness.

Since I began teaching it is rare that I actually sit down with a truly challenging problem and force myself to think it through from start to finish. So much of what I do is in a rush. I don't have time to *really* think about a problem because I am trying to plan two lessons for the next day, so instead I think about it for five minutes and then look at how someone *else* did it. Shameful, I know. The question presented itself to me: Can I actually practice what I preach? Am I still mathematically fearless?

My office-mate presented me with this problem about a week ago:

You have a square dartboard. What is the probability that a randomly-thrown dart will land closer to the center of the dartboard than to an edge?

I sat down to solve it and was absolutely stumped. I had no idea where to start besides drawing a little picture. Said office-mate told me that he had banged his head against the wall and couldn't figure it out, which made me a little disheartened because I consider him to be a much cleverer problem solver than me.

Lesson One about how my students feel:

It's difficult for them to actually believe in their abilities when they look around and see classmates who they consider to be "smarter" who are also struggling with the problem.

I took the problem home and presented it to my boyfriend, who really is the smartest math guy I know. He struggled with it for a little bit, went inside the bedroom, and came out about 30 minutes later announcing that he had solved it *and* that he would not tell me how he did it. Fine. Be that way. At that point I was still really struggling; I didn't even feel like I had a solid starting point. I went into the bedroom and I have to admit that I glanced over at his clipboard where he had solved the problem and saw some nasty math that I didn't like. My heart sank even more.

Lesson Two:

When they see another student's solution and don't immediately understand it—and how could you really immediately understand someone else's solution to a problem?—they tend to give up because they think that they could *never* think of that solution. The thought doesn't even cross their mind that maybe they can come up with another way to solve the problem.

So I gave up for a few days, thinking about the problem a little bit here and there but never hard enough so that I'd feel like a failure if I didn't figure it out.

Lesson Three:

Not trying hard is how kids avoid feeling like failures.

This went on until yesterday afternoon. My boyfriend and I spent the afternoon at my favorite neighborhood coffee shop, basking in the San Diego sunshine. I was working on my end-of-year comments when I suddenly remembered the dartboard problem. I asked him to tell me how he had solved it. He looked at me somewhat disappointedly. "Really? But then you'll never keep thinking about it your way."

At that point I still didn't have a way, but a small fire lit inside of me: How could I not have a way? Some idea, some line of reasoning? What would I say to a kid who asked me for help with a problem and didn't have anything of their own to show? So I told him to wait a sec, and I took out a piece of paper and started working. I came up with what seemed like a great solution with a simple answer. Boyfriend checked the work and agreed, but then asked me to look over his solution because he had gotten a completely different answer and had been sure he was correct.

As he was explaining it, he immediately found an error in his reasoning that made his method quite complex to carry out. However, we then went back to my method and found an error, so we worked it through again together. I now have a solution that I'm pretty happy with, that is completely different from his solution, and it feels so good that it is mine. He was right—if I had looked at his solution first, I would never have had the guts or desire to come up with my own.

Lesson Four:

The lengthy process really is worth it! Any human being—teacher, student, adult, kid—feels amazing after coming up with a clever answer to a problem that once seemed insurmountable.

I feel like this was an exercise in my own mathematical fearlessness. I gained a new respect for my students. As I know they do, I felt anxious, inadequate, and angry at various points in this problem-solving process. My new question is: How can I better support them so that they actually want to stick it out until the end?

"I gained a new respect for my students. As I know they do, I felt anxious, inadequate, and angry at various points in this problem-solving process."

What Number am I?

by Jonathan Halabi

There are five true and five false statements about the secret number. Each pair of statements contains one true and one false statement. Find the trues, the falses, and the number.

1a. I have two digits
1b. I am even

2a. I contain the digit 7
2b. I am prime

3a. I am the product of two consecutive odd integers
3b. I am one more than a perfect square

4a. I am divisible by eleven
4b. I am one more than a perfect cube

5a. I am a perfect square
5b. I have three digits

Can you solve this?* Can you use it in your classroom? Can you, or your students, create your own puzzles like this one?

---

* Hints available in back and at: *jd2718.wordpress.com/2009/11/28/puzzle-who-am-i/*

This comes from Math Stories, where Mr. K blogs about his teaching experiences in a Los Angeles middle school. I didn't know Mr. K's first name until he gave me permission to use his post as a chapter. Yay for blogs. And thanks, Friedrich. —SV

An Argument Against the Real World

by Friedrich Knauss

I recently joined a joint lesson planning group. The idea is that we either create a new lesson, or take a previously-developed lesson, and refine the details, hopefully getting more nuanced as the effort is repeated.

The lesson we had yesterday involved analyzing this question:

Sandy has saved up $120 from babysitting. She's going to Tower Records to buy CDs and DVDs. CDs are $12 each, and DVDs are $15 each.

I get that this is supposed to be real world.

Except.

My kids don't get paid to babysit—that's just what older siblings do. Tower Records doesn't exist anymore. They don't buy CDs; they share MP3s. They buy DVDs, but they buy the bootleg ones at the corner for $3. They would spend the whole time telling me how stupid Sandy is.

What if I changed it around a bit:

> Sangemord the Vampire Hunter looted 120 gold pieces in his last raid. He needs to resupply for his next raid. Blessed stakes are 12 gold pieces, and vials of Holy Water are 15.

"By not trying to make the real world fit my numbers, I don't impose a cognitive dissonance."

Exactly the same problem. The graphs will look the same, the tables, the equations, everything math is the same. The difference is that, by not trying to make the real world fit my numbers, I don't impose a cognitive dissonance. The kids won't spend time worrying about whether the story's reality matches with theirs—they realize it's fiction, and will buy into it. The fact that I'm building on an established but unconsolidated mythos (from Buffy through Van Helsing and Vampire$) only makes it easier. They know kind of what the rules

are, but not enough to distract themselves from the problem by arguing with them.

We have a similar lesson that is commonly promoted through the district, of comparing cell phone calling plans. The problems are similar: the kids don't care about what their phones cost—mom and dad pay for them, and even if they did, real world calling plans are intentionally convoluted in order to confuse the customer. They do not translate well to the straight lines we want for our algebra lesson. Once again, you'd be confronted with "That's stupid. My plan has 1500 free minutes. I wouldn't get any of those."

Take that problem, and switch it to leasing a flying broom (which is now thankfully cool for boys to use as well as girls), and those arguments disappear.

When I first started thinking about this, I just thought it might be fun. I'm becoming more and more convinced that if we want to use real world examples, they better be completely real, with realia to back up the premise.* If we are going to create fictional problems to emphasize certain concepts or aspects of a problem, then it is imperative that we eliminate the cognitive dissonance from the students' real world. They are constantly immersed in fiction—they know how to suspend their disbelief for that, and will happily do it in your classroom as well.

---

* Using real data for problems will introduce complications—the world is rarely linear, nor rational. We need to be prepared to deal with that. And there is definitely a place for making our students deal with real world messiness. But, when we are trying to clarify a concept, it seems to me that it is a worthwhile effort to remove distractions until the concepts are cemented, and then provide opportunities to use them in a messy real world situation.

PUZZLE
Octopus Logic
by Tanya Khovanova[*]

Our characters are genetically engineered octopuses. The ones with an even number of arms always tell the truth; the ones with an odd number of arms always lie.

1. Four octopuses had a chat:

    "I have eight arms," the green octopus bragged to the blue one. "You have only six!"

    "It is I who has eight arms," countered the blue octopus. "You have only seven!"

    "The blue one really has eight arms," the red octopus said, confirming the blue one's claim. He went on to boast, "I have nine arms!"

    "None of you have eight arms," interjected the striped octopus. "Only I have eight arms!"

    Who has exactly eight arms?

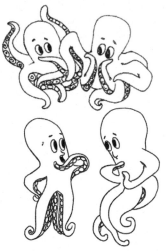

2. Not only do octopuses lie or tell the truth according to the parity of the number of their arms, it turns out that the underwater world is so discriminatory that only octopuses with six, seven, or eight arms are allowed to serve Neptune. Four octopuses who worked as guards at Neptune's palace were conversing:

    The blue one said, "All together we have twenty-eight arms."

    The green one said, "All together we have twenty-seven arms."

    The yellow one said, "All together we have twenty-six arms."

    The red one said, "All together we have twenty-five arms."

    How many arms does each of them have?

---

[*] Tanya Khovanova translated the first two puzzles from the 2009 Moscow Math Olympiad, and made up the next two.

3. The guards from the night shift at Neptune's palace were bored, and they started to argue:

    The magenta one said, "All together we have thirty-one arms."

    The cyan one said, "No, we do not."

    The brown one said, "The beige one has six arms."

    The beige one said, "You, brown, are lying."

    Who is lying and who is telling the truth?

4. The last shift of guards at the palace has nothing better to do than count their arms:

    The pink one said, "Gray and I have fifteen arms together."

    The gray one said, "Lavender and I have fourteen arms together."

    The lavender one said, "Turquoise and I have fourteen arms together."

    The turquoise one said, "Pink and I have fifteen arms together."

    How many arms does each one have?

[Editor's note: After you've solved these, can you make up your own Octopus Logic puzzle?]

Fawn teaches junior high in southern California and blogs at FawnNguyen.com. Her blog is a rich source of ideas and inspiration for me. —SV

Area of a Circle

by Fawn Nguyen

After measuring lots of circles and convincing themselves that the circumference divided by the diameter was always "a little bit more than three," my students had a better grip on the meaning of pi. Now they were ready to explore the area of a circle.

I asked them to draw a circle on notebook paper, any size big enough to measure well. Then I gave each student a centimeter cube and asked them to trace one face onto their paper—to remind themselves how much area one square centimeter covered.

I directed:

1. Give me a guess, only by looking, for the area of your circle in square centimeters. Please write that number on your paper and label it "guess."

2. Now use whatever tools you need to give me a better answer. I know some of you already know the formula for the area of a circle, but you may not use it unless you can tell me where it comes from. (No one even tried.)

I can't tell you how happy I was to see all the different ways the kids tried to approximate area. Their perseverance humbled me. Brenda and Evan divided the circle into eight triangle-ish slices and knew to use "base times height divided by two" to find the area of each triangle, but erroneously used the radius as height. (We saw later how close their miss was.)

After giving them some time to experiment, I pulled them together for the next stage in our exploration,* and had the kids fold their circles like this.

---

* My blog posts about my circumference lessons (*FawnNguyen.com/2012/06/06/20120605 .aspx*) became part of an online conversation with Mimi (*UntilNextStop.blogspot.com/2012/05 /estimation-of-circular-areas.html*) and Sue (in the comments) that led to parts of this area lesson.

"Never once did I answer any of the questions. I just asked them."

They cut out the pieces—turning every other piece 180 degrees—and glued them together. Cristian said, "First we had a circle, then triangles, then a rectangle. That's crazy!"

We talked about how Archimedes had figured out pi by using polygons inside and outside the circle. Now we could see that Brenda and Evan's method would have been correct if they had just drawn their triangles outside the circle. Archimedes' method for finding pi would also have gotten our crazy lumpy shape closer and closer to a real rectangle—especially cool, this "closer and closer" idea is also the basis of calculus.

Never once did I answer any of the questions. I just asked them.

I began with, "What is the area of this rectangle or parallelogram?"

Step by step, as a class, the kids walked this equation—through base of rectangle is half of circumference and height of rectangle is radius—all the way to Area = pi times Radius squared.

This morning, two days after the activity, I did a "My Favorite No"* to see if they remembered: thirty-one out of thirty-three students got the correct circumference formula; twenty-four of thirty-three got the correct area formula. Over half got the bonus for showing me how the rectangle model helped explain the area of a circle.

---

* Shown at *YouTube.com/watch?v=Rulmok_9HVs*, Leah Alcala's "My Favorite No" allows the teacher and class to celebrate mistakes. They first discuss what's right about the wrong answer, and then what went wrong.

EXPLORATION
Coloring Cubes

*by Joshua Zucker**

Julia Robinson
Mathematics Festival

Part 1: Paint, then cut.

We'll take a cube whose edges are *n* units long, paint its surface completely, cut it into unit cubes whose edges are 1 unit long, and then ask how many unit cubes are painted in each way. Clearly, if you start with a one-unit cube, you end up with one unit cube painted on all six sides, and that's it.

1. If you start with a two-unit cube, how many of the resulting unit cubes are completely unpainted? Painted on just one side? Two sides? Three sides?

2. Starting with a three-unit cube, answer the same questions.

3. Repeat for a four-unit cube.

4. Repeat for an *n* unit cube. Can you find the pattern?

Part 2: Cut, then paint.

Now we're going to first cut the cube into unit cubes, paint them, and then put them back together. But there's a little catch! We want to paint with several different colors, in fact as many as possible, so that the pieces can be reassembled to make a cube whose outside is all one color. With a one-unit cube, this problem is a bit too easy. Paint the cube one color, and it's already back together.

5. You can cut a two-unit cube into eight one-unit cubes, and paint them with two colors in such a way that you could put them back together into a two-unit cube of either color. How should you paint them?

---

* See *JuliaRobinsonMathFestival.org* for more information.

6. With a three-unit cube, cut into twenty-seven one-unit cubes, can you paint them with three colors in such a way that they can be put back together into a three-unit cube of any of the three colors? If so, how? If not, why not?

7. Does this generalize? Starting with an n-unit cube, can you cut it into one-unit cubes and paint them with n colors in such a way that they can be reassembled into an n-unit cube of any one of the colors?

I stumbled upon this lovely essay surfing the internet, and then found Chris' site, MathProjects.com. He recently started blogging, which has been a treat. —SV

Textbook-Free: Kicking the Habit

by Chris Shore

I kicked the habit! I am no longer a textbook junkie. I no longer rely on my daily fix of some publisher's bloated curriculum. I am free of my addiction without the help of an arm patch, rehabilitation clinic, or twelve-step program. I quit cold turkey. Here's how.

Several years ago, my school experienced a shortage of geometry books. There was talk of teachers sharing class sets and photocopying pages for students. I decided to try a different strategy. I took this as a professional challenge to see how long I could teach without a textbook. I knew whatever happened would be a growing experience for me as well as my students.

Through no fault of the school library, two or three weeks stretched to seven. By that time, I was well into my "textbook-free" strategy, so I just kept the ball rolling … for the rest of the year. I used only twelve assignments from the textbook in those 180 days. Here is how that unique experience of being textbook-free has changed my teaching forever.

Firstly, I am now much more focused on standards. Rather than leafing through the textbook, I looked at my state and district standards, and established my curriculum from those. After all, shouldn't they be determining what we teach? From there, I grouped the topics into units, and then scheduled individual lessons. This process naturally pared down the number of topics that I taught and allowed me to allocate a full week of instruction to each concept, rather than one day to each section of the textbook.

The second big change that has occurred is in the structure of my lessons. Everything from my homework to my instruction has radically changed. My typical textbook-free lesson was comprised of three to six problems of various difficulty. I often began a lesson with one to three review problems from previously-learned material that applied to the current lesson. This is similar to a traditional warm-up with the exceptions that the problems are very relevant to the new lesson, and not simply arbitrary review.

Sometimes, I began with *the* big problem from the previous night's assignment, and solicited student responses. It is not hard to see that my old practice of dedicating twenty minutes of class time to questions on how to complete the previous homework disappeared. The intent of the class slowly evolved from getting the answers right to understanding the mathematical principles behind the question.

"The intent of the class slowly evolved from getting the answers right to understanding the mathematical principles behind the question."

These introductory problems served as a terrific assessment tool, also. Previously, it was difficult to know how well the students were doing when only a handful of them were asking questions from a truckload of exercises. However, when the whole class was engaged on the same few problems, it was easy to walk the room and evaluate their performance and understanding.

The introductory questions naturally led to the main problem or small set of problems that would drive the lesson. The students were engaged in an investigation, project, or activity relating to the concept. Each day my students came to class to solve problems rather than take notes—a huge change from all the previous "textbook years." This process of problem solving and investigation consumed the full class period. Gone were the days of having the students start homework in class.

The homework assignments were only one to three problems long and were typically extensions of the day's topic, not just practice exercises. I had learned from the international comparisons that America is one of the few countries that pushes the drill-and-kill regime, and that we are near the bottom of the performance pile. So I tried to limit both the number and size of my assignments, and to make them more challenging and contextual.

By doing that I firmly settled the argument regarding the quantity and frequency of homework that students need to be successful. For the skeptics who are still reluctant to abandon their practice of assigning thirty homework problems a night, I have some strong results. My class averages led the district on the district final. And so I'm able to reassure parents that this new homework philosophy is not hurting my students in any way.

Another significant change was my lesson planning. Rather than writing examples of how to complete an algorithm or creating cute acronyms to remember esoteric rules, I actually wrote lesson plans. I started planning each lesson by asking: "What do I want the students to know? What is their common misconception of the topic? How can

I best get them to understand the topic? How can I challenge them within the context of the topic?" I would then try to create a story/context/scenario and a small set of problems that would best develop understanding of that topic. It was so much fun. This change in my approach to lesson planning was actually a reflection of my new attitude toward teaching. My job description truly shifted from covering material to uncovering understanding.

Focused, standards-based curriculum; in-depth, problem-solving instruction; short, conceptually based homework assignments. This experience was so exhilarating that I am now a junkie all over again. I traded my old addiction to the textbook for a new one—creative lesson planning. This is one habit, though, that I never intend to kick.

ACTIVITY
Guess My Dice*

by Kaleb Allinson

I made this up when I taught a low-level Algebra 2 class, and now I use it in all my algebra classes right before we begin factoring polynomials.

I roll two dice that each have eight, ten, or twelve sides, keeping them hidden from view. In the example shown in the photo, I would tell my students that my dice add to 19 and multiply to 88 and ask them to guess my dice.

We play this at the end of class for a week or two before we start factoring polynomials. Then when they discover how to factor polynomials, this dice guessing skill is very helpful. They always realize what I've done and think I'm really tricky.

Variations

Level 1: Two dice. As students get better at it, progress to higher sided dice.

Level 2: One red and one yellow (any colors, really). The red die is negative. (Don't tell them.)

Level 3: Both dice are negative.

Level 4: Mix Levels 1 to 3. Sometimes give fake numbers that would be impossible. When they give up or say it's not possible, ask how they know they have exhausted all possibilities.

Once students have learned how to play, they can get into groups of four and make one person in each group a dice roller and the others the guessers. Then rotate the person who rolls.

---

* Discovered at: *AccumulateARate.wordpress.com/2012/09/07/factoring-with-dice*

The online version of this is—like math—not linear. Check out prezi.com/aww2hjfyil0u/math-is-not-linear/. —SV

Math is Not Linear

by Alison Forster

MATH IS NOT LINEAR.

A background of certain skills can be helpful

before you set out exploring

but as soon as your curiosity says it's time to go…

There are so many directions you can choose!

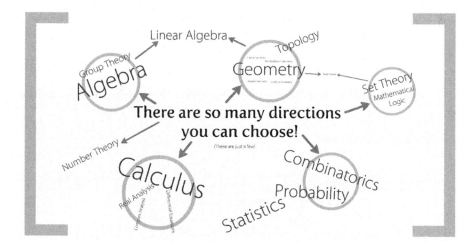

So why do we teach math in hierarchical steps?

1. ARITHMETIC

2. ALGEBRA

3. GEOMETRY (Why, oh why, is geometry sandwiched between algebra classes?)

4. MORE ALGEBRA?? (Trigonometry gets covered somewhere…)

5. PRECALCULUS (What the heck is 'precalculus' anyway? It's not a natural subset of mathematics.)

6. CALCULUS

It seems that to most people, my earlier statement…

(A background of certain skills can be helpful
before you set out exploring . . .)

… is a radical understatement.

Rather, the common opinion holds
that the mastery of one subject is a prerequisite for dabbling in another,
and that,
mathematics is naturally ordered

like a ladder,

it is only correct for students to   take

one

rung

at

a

time.

This is just so …

Wrong!

But why does it matter that math is taught in this order?

It's not motivating.

" Simplicio:
… You need to walk before you can run.

Salvati:

"
No, you need something to run towards!

(from *Lockhart's Lament,* by Paul Lockhart)

Our students spend much of their time studying skills simply because
they will need to use them in a later class. How motivating is it to

say to a ninth grader that he needs to learn about rational expressions because someone may ask about them in two years? Has that ever been a good reason to learn anything?

How much more motivating would it be
to give a student a problem that required rational expressions,
wait for her to discover that she needed more technique,
and then introduce the topic?

Students deserve a better reason to learn something than "this is the next chapter in the textbook."

It prevents students from being exposed to topics they might enjoy.

CONTRARY TO POPULAR BELIEF,
HIGH SCHOOLERS ARE GENERALLY
CAPABLE OF TAKING IN A BIT OF
TOPOLOGY, OR SET THEORY, OR
REAL ANALYSIS HERE AND THERE.

AND THEY LIKE IT.

It fosters anxiety by turning mathematics into a race.

Some students would benefit from a slower pace, or a different route through mathematics, but parents don't want their child to "fall behind."

Seriously, it's not the be all and end all of your mathematics
education that you get to calculus by 12th grade.

I ALSO WORRY ABOUT THE YOUNG PRODIGIES
WHO FLY THROUGH THE STANDARD CURRICULUM,
WITHOUT TAKING ANY SIDE TRIPS, AND THEN
GET MIGHTY SMUG ABOUT IT.

It hinders understanding by obscuring the big picture.

Because our curriculum is so partitioned,
students often don't see
the connections between topics
and miss out on many helpful metaphors.

Things make more sense
when you can mentally "zoom out"...

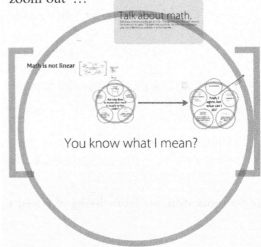

You know what I mean?

It spreads misunderstanding about what mathematics is.

I believe that one of the things high school graduates should learn,
in all the time they spend on mathematics, is what it means
to be a mathematician. It's not particularly useful
information, but I'm sick and tired of
explaining to people I meet
on the bus that I don't
just sit around all day
adding bigger
and bigger
numbers.

[Yeah, I guess this is a selfish one...
But I bet you're sick of it, too.]

Hmm... I agree, but what can I do?

GO ON TANGENTS.

Most teachers do this anyway, to some extent. Embrace it!
Don't be afraid to throw something out there that you think
is way over their heads. You might be surprised.

One of my favorite classes was the day my geometry class
dragged me into talking about infinitely small differences and
a student asked "Is there a number smaller than every other

number, but bigger than zero?" For the next twenty minutes we debated the properties of such a number, and I introduced hyper-real numbers.

> To ninth graders.

>> Yet, I think this was a very natural question, and the student who asked it was no prodigy. The class didn't all understand it, but even those who were mystified felt they had just been let in on a secret: that there was more to math than they had thought. A few students walked out with formal logical symbolism written on their arms as though it were witchcraft.

FORESHADOW.

It's quite common that you need students to do some problem that could be more easily accomplished by methods they haven't learned yet. Let them know! You don't have to teach them the more advanced method, but it will give them a sense of what their future classes will actually be about, and why someone would want to learn them (to save them from the drudgery of their current methods)!

> For instance, try to have students find the area of curvy objects. In time, they'll probably try to fill the areas with polygons that are easier to deal with. At this moment, it's fun to mention that calculus does exactly the same thing, only with a formula that makes it practically automatic.

>> Yeah, I've been known to taunt my classes with "Haha, too bad you guys don't know calculus!"

>> Okay, wow, that sounds seriously sadistic, now that I've typed it out. But the point is, they got an idea of what calculus is, and how it fits into what they already know, and they didn't have to wait until they were in calculus class to get that.

RELATE MATERIAL BACK TO PREVIOUS CLASSES.

Here's a cool question:

Find a rectangle (with integer sides) whose area and perimeter are the same.

Now find another one.

Now find another one.

What, you're stumped? Well, maybe there aren't any more. How could you prove that?

(One solution requires dusting off the quadratic formula. Surprise! Algebra is part of geometry too.)

This is one of my favorite problems for relating algebra and geometry, and I keep learning new ways to approach it!

BE LESS HELPFUL! LET STUDENTS TELL YOU WHAT THEY NEED TO KNOW.

As per the previous rational expressions example, try not to give more technique than students are asking for. Give them problems that require techniques they don't have yet, and make them squirm a bit before helping out. The educational benefits of this go beyond a broader understanding of mathematics, but the reason I'm advocating this practice here is that it demonstrates to students that the structure of mathematics is problem-based and natural, rather than imposed from above.

To be clear, I am not advocating that students get to choose what they study any more than I would let five-year-olds choose what they eat. You still direct the class, but when possible, do it from behind the scenes by providing strategic problems. Math itself often makes it obvious what questions should be asked next. If you've just introduced exponents, what's the opposite of an exponent? Once you've got roots on your hands, what happens if you get a negative number inside of one? Students may make your job easier by asking these questions themselves.

TEACH AN ELECTIVE.

If this is at all possible (and I know it rarely is) I think this is the best way to get students to take seriously the idea that there is not just one path through math, simply because it actually offers them an alternative. Here are some great math elective courses I wish were more common:

DISCRETE MATHEMATICS   *FORMAL LOGIC*   SET THEORY
NUMBER THEORY   *STATISTICS AND/OR PROBABILITY*
HISTORY OF MATH   GREAT PROOFS OF MATHEMATICS
HOW TO MAKE SENSE OF NUMBERS YOU HEAR IN THE NEWS
FERMI PROBLEMS (ESTIMATIONS)

If you don't have time to teach an elective (who does?) you can ask your school to hire another math teacher who can. And if/when they say no, here are more alternatives:

START A MATH CIRCLE OR CLUB.

MAKE A POSTER ILLUSTRATING A COOL MATHEMATICAL QUESTION
AND PUT IT UP WHERE EVERYONE CAN SEE IT.

SET UP A MATH LIBRARY
WHERE STUDENTS CAN READ ABOUT THESE THINGS ON THEIR OWN.
(OKAY, EVEN I KNOW THIS ONE IS FAR-FETCHED.)

I know that there are much larger problems
in math education than this.

And that most teachers don't have the time or
the patience left to take on another crusade.

But if you enjoy math, there is a very simple thing
you can do that would help.

TALK ABOUT MATH.

Talk about anything you like about math. Talk about it
anywhere, with anyone. Tell them why it's great. Tell them
how you think. Tell them how it surprises you, how it
charms you, how it all fits together.
because

MATH IS NOT LINEAR.
You know what I mean?
And whoever sits next to me on the bus is going to understand that.

"Think of a number," I tell the kids (ninth graders, but it would work with younger kids), "and don't tell it to me. Make sure it's not too big, because you need to do some math with it."

"Now square your number. You have a result?" I give them a moment after each step; there's no sense in leaving anyone behind. "Take your whole result, and throw it out, except for the rightmost digit, the units digit. Everyone should have a one digit number."

"Now take that one digit number (everyone has a one digit number?), and square that. Once again, throw it all out, except the rightmost digit. Now, take that last one digit number, and multiply it by your original number." Fussing with paper, a few calculators… And I ask them one by one what their final result is, and tell them one by one what their original number was.

"71."

"Your number was 71."

"72."

"Your number was 12."

"75."

"Your number was 15."

OK, obviously there is a trick, and they knew that one existed just as well as you do. Still, they played this morning three full rounds (and I got one number wrong, and caught two kids who flubbed the arithmetic). And after three rounds, they hadn't broken the "code."

So their assignment (and yours, if you like): Try this game with a bunch of numbers, starting with 1. I suggested that by 20 or 30 they should know the "rules" to teach someone else to be the mathemagician. And I offered a little extra credit.

None of the kids managed to tackle this at home, so one day I wrapped up our lesson fast, divided them into teams, and made them run the trick for every number from 1 through 50. The patterns jumped out, and kids started predicting and testing their predictions.

We did this right after studying Fermat's Little Theorem,[*] which partially explains why the trick works. Only a few kids really understood it, but all of them wanted to, and it made the trick just a bit cooler. I'll keep this in the course.

---

[*] Jonathan must have a little teacher magic in him too. This is a hard nut to crack. Fermat's Little Theorem says that for a prime number p, and a number a not a multiple of p, $a^{p-1} \equiv 1$ (mod p). See the hint on page 355 for more on understanding this trick.

Luyi hosts GeometricDelights.wordpress.com, where she posts pictures of her soda bottle icosahedra, Sierpinski triangle fudge, and more. I asked her to tell me what drew her to her passion for math. —SV

A Young Voice: My Passion for Math

by Luyi Zhang

When I was about four years old I lived in China, and my grandmother would take me out for trips around town. On our walks, she would ask me simple two-digit addition and subtraction problems, and I would do the arithmetic in my head and tell her the answer a few seconds later. Years later my grandmother would tell me how surprised and delighted passersby were to see such a young child solving arithmetic problems so quickly.

About a year later, my parents and I moved to the United States. My grandmother was no longer there to practice math with me, and in her place my mom gave me math problems on a regular basis, but I don't remember those problems being particularly enchanting. I took math classes throughout elementary and early middle school without thinking very much about what I was doing. I was good at math, but my classes never challenged me sufficiently, so I lost interest. I viewed math as easy but boring—just another daily class.

Math Becomes Challenging

When I was in seventh grade, I started at a new school—it was a competitive private school, much more challenging than the urban public school I had attended until then. I was placed into an advanced algebra class, and I felt good about that. Math always came easily to me and I had spent years never missing a single problem, so I showed up to the first class confident. But the teacher walked in and started writing like a madman. Within five minutes I was completely lost. Over the next few weeks, the course continued at that pace, reviewing material that I had never been exposed to before, and introducing new topics that I couldn't even start to comprehend without the fundamentals that the other students seemed to already know. For the first time in my math life, I was struggling.

The class continued on, covering multi-variable linear equations, challenging word problems galore, and graphing sums of absolute value expressions. I was determined to catch up and feel confident with the material—I wasn't going to accept anything less than full understanding from myself. My struggles in the class only fueled my determination. Every night, I would start my math homework eager to devote as much time as necessary to each problem in order to fully understand it. The first problem was usually straightforward enough, but subsequent problems often took me up to 20 minutes.

"I spent many weekend afternoons sprawled out on my bed just thinking about problems and concepts."

I would think about the question, write out equations, review sections in the textbook, and try the problem again. I'd often get stuck. So I would ask in class the next day, and then schedule time with my instructor to review those problems. Sometimes his explanations didn't make sense—but I would think about them at home, over and over again, until they did. I spent many weekend afternoons sprawled out on my bed just thinking about problems and concepts. I had this analogy—each concept that I am learning is like a red brick, and I'm trying to build a stable math house. My first few layers had some holes in them, so when I tried to lay more on top at a fast pace (my advanced algebra class), everything crumbled. I just needed to spend more time picking up the pieces and putting them back together more securely. And that is what I continued to do.

By winter, my class finished up our unit on systems of equations and graphing, and progressed to factoring. This unit was beautiful for me. With the basics of solving linear equations and graphing solidly in my head, I approached factoring with vigor and accuracy, making sure I understood each algebraic manipulation clearly and fully. Just when I had figured out how crucial correctness was to solving problems, my instructor showed us that creativity is also really important. For example, when we worked on the most challenging factoring problems, we often had to take a step—adding a term, subtracting a term, breaking terms then regrouping—that was unexpected and out-of-the-box. As I experimented with lots of strategies, I realized how playful it all was! We were approaching the problems with openness and a willingness to try, try, and try again to understand the core of the problem more deeply, in order to brainstorm creative ways to tackle it.

That breakthrough made math *fun* for me—the exploration was delightful. Of course, this class was not all smooth and effortless after that—there were still topics that, despite a strong concerted effort, did not stick at first—but with some time and distance I came to understand those topics too. That taught me another math learning lesson: that sometimes we need to give ourselves time and space to process the concepts and let them form strongly in our minds. If a concept doesn't make sense, we should loosen our "but I must understand this, or else!" grip, and instead, approach the problem with persistence: come back a week later, two weeks, a month, a few months—and over time, we will understand the topics more strongly.

In my months and months of trying to "fill up the holes in the bricks" of my algebra understanding in seventh grade, I spent a lot of time online, searching on math topics, looking for good explanations. A lot of the strategies we worked on were really challenging and required creative thought (rather than rote memorization), so I often had to search carefully. More than once, the best explanations I found came from solutions to similar problems that showed up in math competitions. Over time, I began to spend more time with these math competition problems because they were plainly so interesting. I enjoyed them because I had to work for them—the work was so rewarding and enjoyable for its own sake. Over time, I began to think that math was really awesome.

Math Competitions

In eighth grade, I participated in a nationally-administered middle-school contest called MathCounts. MathCounts is a challenging test with both an individual and a team component, thus encouraging both individual work and group collaboration. In preparation for the contest, my school held weekly practices. Twice a week, a group of students would meet for an hour to do math problems. The coach would start off each practice with a problem solving strategy, and then we would work through previous contests, going over the problems as a group, highlighting important concepts and ideas along the way. The going over problems was my favorite part—the coach and students would take turns explaining each problem that we didn't see how to solve the first time. All of a sudden it would become so clear and make so much sense! Those moments of clarity, those "Ah-ha!" moments, were rewarding and delightful, even exhilarating.

The coolest thing about these practices is that we were given the freedom to really play with the problems and concepts and discover the solutions ourselves. Instead of learning from a textbook or a lecture, we would give the problems our best effort, and then work as a group to solve the ones that proved too challenging to conquer individually. Working as a team gave us the space to really bond together not only as students, but as friends. I fondly remember the time my teammates and I spent half the period poking fun at our potato-shaped blobs that were supposed to resemble circles. Through all the jokes, we also had an incredible geometry problem-solving session that I still remember vividly and fondly years later. I can't recall a single practice when I didn't leave smiling—even though the problems were hard, the friendships that we forged and the dedication that we shared are unforgettable.

Finding Math Online

Because I enjoyed our in-person problem-solving sessions so much, I wanted to practice online, too. I knew that the national MathCounts website had a forum where people discussed problems and solutions and overall MathCounts events, so I registered and browsed that for a few weeks. One day, I saw a member mentioning the Art of Problem Solving forum, saying that it had a good solution to the problem that they were currently discussing. I clicked on the link and headed over to Art of Problem Solving (affectionately referred to by the acronym AoPS).* I was immediately taken aback—I had never before seen so many problems and so many people discussing them! AoPS had a multitude of forums that varied by difficulty and age level as well as by topic. (Most of the forums are math forums, but there are some music, general discussion, and games forums as well.) I was at once intrigued and inspired, and browsed the forums often in the coming weeks and months.

At first, AoPS was unfamiliar and intimidating—the level of problem-solving and thinking in even the youngest-aged forum (the middle-school forum, my age at the time) was incredibly high, and I had never seen many of the topics that the frequent posters mastered with ease. I found it hard to post at first, because it was hard to find problems that were approachable enough and also because I didn't know anyone there. But over time, both of those difficulties faded away. Even on the math forums of AoPS, there were still non-problem-solving threads, introduction threads by state or threads discussing performances from past years' contests. I began to take part in those discussions, and soon

---

* Art of Problem Solving is an online math school, found at: *ArtOfProblemSolving.com*

I met some other people from my state. Many people exchanged AOL Instant Messaging (AIM) screen names to open chatrooms and hold problem-solving sessions with each other, so I signed up for that, too. At first I only worked with one student from another part of my state. But as the weeks passed, my circle of problem-solving comrades grew, encompassing students from all across the nation. In the process of solving problems and sharing ideas, we became friends, too.

One of the most valuable experiences I had at AoPS was the online geometry course that I took there in eighth grade. The course was structured around really interesting material, presented in an intuitive manner, starting with the basics. The best part is, we were given the freedom to discover concepts by ourselves, with carefully-guided help from the instructor and teaching assistant. We learned through solving problems and seeing the steps and concepts in action. The course focused on rigor and strong mathematical proofs, but at the same time it encouraged playfulness as well. Some of my favorite classes were the super-challenging ones in which we had to draw creatively-placed auxiliary lines, take cross sections, look for obscure similar triangles, and more. It was all so interesting!

In my AoPS geometry course, my classmates were a crucial component to my learning. Every week, we would be assigned ten to fifteen message board problems to work on and then discuss. I would spend hours working through the problems, posting my solutions, and then checking them against others' solutions. This checking not only served as confirmation of my own methods, but it often gave me glimpses of other elegant methods that I may not have found myself otherwise. I owe the strength of my solution-writing to the time I spent practicing on the AoPS class message boards. And I owe my enthusiasm for math largely to the enthusiasm that I saw and shared in this friendly online community.

Over the years, AoPS has continued to mean so, so much to me—it has been an invaluable component to my growth both as a math student and as a person. It has introduced me to a more fascinating and delightful world of math, one that I have grown to genuinely love for its own sake. Through AoPS, I have also formed cherished friendships with other people who are just as passionate about math as I am.

After five years of posting, problem solving, and joy on the forums, I am now on the other side, employed at the company as of February 2011. I write sincere posts on the boards, sharing my advice and experience with the other students around me, hoping that maybe my insight can help them, too. I have graded dozens and dozens of papers through the Art of Problem Solving online school, and I am a teaching assistant for several of their courses this summer.

The work that I have done has been absolutely incredible and has allowed me to fully realize how math is truly amazing and can have such a positive impact on people. I really do want the best for the students, and I try very, very hard to give my very best to them. If my sincere feedback or advice or explanations encourage the students to feel more happy and confident about their math ability and potential, if my words make them smile—even a little—then that would mean the world to me.

My challenging advanced algebra course in seventh grade, preparing for the MathCounts competition, and the AoPS geometry course were what truly ignited my passion for math. Over the years, I have continued to pursue more math, of course with some setbacks along the way but my foundation in basic mathematics and my passion for the subject and its people have remained solid throughout.

Geometric Delights

I do math for many reasons. One of them is because doing math for its own sake brings me an incredible amount of *joy*. I can't begin to describe how much elation and delight geometry has brought me in the past few years. In the fall of my senior year of high school, I began to create 3D geometric inventions out of everyday household materials, just for fun, and to play with a different side of math. Creating a two-foot paper-tube icosahedron has definitely been one of the best decisions of my life. I began to post pictures of my other geometric creations on Facebook, and when they were met with positivity, I started a blog, Geometric Delights,* where I write about my creative geometric inventions and other relevant topics.

Nearly eight months since its inception, Geometric Delights is still going strong, drawing over 20,000 reader views from over fifty countries. But that's not the only way I share my love of math. I have spent the year teaching an after-school algebra class to eighth graders. I help out with local MathCounts teams, watching with delight as their excitement rises when they correctly solve a challenging problem. I volunteer at middle-school math contests, happily handing out pizza, taking pictures, and cheering for the students as they enjoy a memorable day that they have worked so hard for. I make such a concerted effort to give back to the math community because every time I do, I remember how much of an awesome time I had when I participated in math

---

* *GeometricDelights.wordpress.com*

community activities—and I want to inspire that joy and camaraderie in other younger students, too.

Over time, I have realized that what I really like most about math isn't the achievement and self-advancement; rather, it is the process of sharing—of not only creative and insightful problem-solving approaches, but also memorable moments filled with camaraderie, generosity, and incomparable joy.

And that is why I love math.

Community:
Sharing Math

"Orb," designed by George Hart, assembled by all of us!

On Friday, October 3, 2014, the MoSAIC project (Mathematics of Science, Art, Industry, Culture, with website mosaicmathart.org) sponsored a sculpture assembly workshop as part of a weekend-long conference on math and art held at Berkeley City College. The workshop, led by George Hart, provided participants the opportunity to jointly assemble his "Orb" sculpture, made from laser cut wood components, which was then hung in the main gathering area. He has led similar workshops at a number of other MoSAIC events. For more information on the design of "Orb," see gallery.bridgesmathart.org/exhibitions/2015-joint-mathematics-meetings. In the photo, George Hart is at the center. You can see more of his artwork at georgehart.com.

We wanted to open the community section with this photo because this workshop (and others at this conference) built community. Just as an example, I (Sue VanHattum) was able to work with people I greatly admire, and was inspired to try to use a 3D printer soon. (I am standing next to George in the photo, second from the left.)

Introduction and Internet Resources

The Internet is huge. Trying to imagine all the math resources available on it is mind boggling—blogs, videos, interactive tools, games, … with new *kinds* of resources each month. This section tells a few stories and gathers together some useful resources for playing with math. Check them out online, and you'll find others.

The Internet has given us Wikipedia (a user-created encyclopedia), Wolfram Alpha (a math-based encyclopedia that can calculate), You Tube (which spawned many more video sites),* online math games, simulations, and repositories for good lesson plans. There are also many tiny niches that would never make it into a bookstore or theater, but that can blossom online—math poetry† and math comics,‡ anyone? There are lots more, and updates to our recommendations can be found on the *PlayingWithMath.org* website.

"There are many tiny niches that would never make it into a bookstore or theater, but that can blossom online—math poetry and math comics, anyone?"

Most of the time we go online for one of two purposes: finding resources or finding community. When you want to find something, find out about something, or find out how to do something, there are resources and tools online to help you. If you heard someone mention the Platonic solids, and you're curious, Wikipedia can tell you all about them. If you want to find the factors of 123,456,789, you can ask Wolfram Alpha. If you want to see some mathematical origami, you know YouTube will have lots of fascinating videos.

Suppose you want to find a game to help your daughter get better at her times tables. You can Google "times table game" and find lots of stuff, but most of it is mediocre, and now you're stuck. There are way too many; how do you find a good one to show your kid? Now you need a community, so you can ask others who may have used these resources what they think. If you're a homeschool parent interested in learning

---

* See *PlayingWithMath.org/videos* for a wide-ranging list of intriguing videos.

† See: *PoetryWithMathematics.blogspot.com* and *MathPoetry.wikispaces.com*

‡ See: *xkcd.com*, *AbstruseGoose.com*, and *SpikedMath.com* Caution: some of these comics have adult content.

more about how to help your child learn math, you may have joined Living Math Forum, a Yahoo group. (Groups like this are also called email lists.) Blogs and wikis are other ways people create online communities.

Email Groups, Blogs, Wikis, and More

Finding an online community that fits your needs may take a while. The easiest way to find one may be through your real-life communities. If the community you're looking for involves other people doing the same sort of work you do (homeschool parents or math teachers, for instance), there are lots of people blogging, and once you find one blog you like, it will lead you to others. And blog carnivals like Math Teachers at Play,[*] described in Denise Gaskins' chapter, make the discovery process even easier. Eventually, you may want to add your own voice to the conversation by starting a blog yourself. It's free and not much harder to learn than email. Once you know what you want to say, you can get a free blog through Google[†] or Wordpress, and line someone up to mentor you through your first few weeks.

"Reading blogs is like reading magazine articles, but without the advertising and the fluff."

Reading blogs is like reading magazine articles, but without the advertising and the fluff. Once you've decided you like an author, you can follow them using a feed reader.[‡] If they get too repetitive, you drop them. If you'd like to join the conversation, you do.

Math teachers are blogging, having conversations about what works and what doesn't, deepening their professional understanding of their subject and how it's learned. Homeschoolers, tutors, and math enthusiasts are blogging, too. They're all creating a rich brew—exploring intriguing problems, cool ways to get students thinking, and deep ideas about putting it all together.

Conventional uses of the internet for math learning, like homework help and tutoring, are given less attention here than the unexpected delights of a world connected online. One of the many pieces that wouldn't fit in the book, but fits fine on the limitless internet, is Rebecca Zook's informative chapter on the tools she uses in her online tutoring. You can go to *PlayingWithMath.org/moregoodies* to read about the ways Rebecca has found to make a real personal connection with her far-flung students.

---

[*] *LetsPlayMath.net/tag/mtap/*
[†] You can get a blog through Google at *blogger.com*.
[‡] Also called an RSS reader, these allow you to subscribe to blogs and any sites that send out recurring posts. The most popular used to be Google Reader, but Google decided not to support it. *feedly.com* may be a good choice.

Hundreds (possibly thousands) of high school math teachers are blogging these days. Most of their blogs focus on their classrooms, with posts describing their successes and failures, or asking for help improving a lesson. Teachers in this country spend almost all of their workday with students, and get very little chance to talk shop with other professionals. That has suddenly changed. We can sit at home in the evenings, relaxing in front of our computers, and find out what our buddies are doing. We can talk about what works and doesn't. Educators call this a Personal Learning Network (PLN) or a professional learning community. When those are imposed from above by an employer, they aren't likely to be particularly mind-blowing. But when we build our own, our professional learning communities can change our lives.

"Teachers in this country spend almost all of their workday with students, and get very little chance to talk shop with other professionals. That has suddenly changed."

A good example of this sort of professional learning community in action can be seen in the exchange about what makes a good question about logarithms, found on the blog JD2718.* Jonathan wrote a post about two logarithm questions that he didn't like. He wasn't sure what bothered him about the questions, and asked what others thought. Sixteen people got involved in the enlightening discussion that ensued. This detailed conversation is similar in some ways to Japanese Lesson Study.† Their process is lengthier and more formalized, but we are coming up with something on our own that may be just as powerful, and more suited to American sensibilities. Not only are the teachers involved in this discussion learning more (about logarithms and how to teach about them), we are also (re)learning to ask our own questions.

Make Your Own Math

The internet has made me a mathematician. Those of us who like math but are not research mathematicians suddenly have a playground and playmates. I've always enjoyed thinking about math problems more when I could do it in a group situation. Now I get to easily have that. I can forge my own paths, and ask my own questions. I feel more and more like a real mathematician. Learning through our own enthusiasms and our own questions is inborn, but we get out of that habit as we go through our years of schooling. As we relearn question-posing, we will move toward being able to build that value into our classroom cultures.‡

---

* *jd2718.wordpress.com/2010/03/05/why-dont-i-like-these-logarithm-questions*
† Japanese Lesson Study is described in *The Teaching Gap*, by James Stigler.
‡ If you're interested in moving your classroom in this direction, I highly recommend *The Art of Problem Posing*, by Stephen Brown and Marion Walter.

Until I started following the blogs of other math teachers and writing my own, it never occurred to me that I might be able to invent my own math puzzles. In the past few years, I've written a math story called *Eight Fingers* (about the base two and base eight numbers used by the eight-fingered people of another planet), created a puzzle called Holiday Logic, created a truth and lies puzzle like Jonathan Halabi's on page 244, and more. I also made up the little puzzle below for the 21st issue of the Math Teachers at Play blog carnival. I wanted something for the number 21, but I wanted the puzzle to have some other number (or numbers) for its answer. I may be hooked. I don't know if I'll ever come up with enough to put a puzzle book together, but I think I'll keep creating a few each year.

The Numberland News runs personal ads. 21 was looking for a new friend and put an ad in:

Two-digit, semi-prime, triangular, Fibonacci number seeks same. I'm a binary palindrome, what about you?

Will 21 find a friend?

Resources and Tools

Here's a list of some of the interesting free math sites you can find online. A more complete up-to-date list is available at *PlayingWithMath.org*.*

Wolfram Alpha: a "knowledge engine"	*WolframAlpha.com*
Wikipedia: a user-created encyclopedia	*wikipedia.org*
Desmos: a graphing calculator	*desmos.com*
Geogebra: graphing, construction	*geogebra.org*
Scratch: kid-oriented programming	*scratch.mit.edu*
Cut-the-Knot: a math information site	*cut-the-knot.org*
YouTube: video (try searching on math)	*YouTube.com*
TED talks: innovation ideas (search on math)	*ted.com*

---

* By the time you read this book, some of the blogs and websites mentioned here are likely to have moved or disappeared. If you can't find something, just go to *PlayingWithMath.org*, where all the links in this book will be reproduced, by chapter, and will be fixed whenever possible.

Vi Hart videos: wild connections, gone viral	*ViHart.com*
James Tanton: videos of explanations	*JamesTanton.com*
Khan Academy: videos of lessons	*KhanAcademy.org*
MathTV: videos of lessons	*MathTV.com*
Math Playground: games, explorations	*MathPlayground.com*
CoolMath: games	*CoolMath-games.com*
MathCats: games, puzzles, explorations	*MathCats.com*

Although Art of Problem Solving[*] is not free, it's worth mentioning here. It's an online school with lots of challenging math courses.

Movies and TV shows are now available online, too. Donald in Mathmagic Land, a fabulous math movie made by Walt Disney in 1959, is available on YouTube. Three TV shows that might be of interest are Cyberchase, Numb3rs, and Square One.

Technology has been a blessing and a curse in so many ways. I hope you find some of the groundbreaking work described in this section a blessing in your life.

A Note about Online Sites (and a Few More Links)

All of the sites mentioned in the book are correct as of June 2014. If you're reading this book long after that, there's a good chance some of them will have moved or gone defunct. If you go to *PlayingWithMath.org*, you'll find a list of such sites, with new directions when possible.

---

[*] *ArtOfProblemSolving.com*

Math and the
Electronic Commons

Interview with Maria Droujkova, in 2011

Q: *How do you see the internet changing the ways we teach, learn, and play with math?*

A strange word comes to mind—disintermediation. There is no mediation any more between students and creators of knowledge. So anyone can talk to anyone who makes stuff. Just now I was playing with Geogebra because I wanted to describe origami axioms for folding circles, based on the seven Huzita-Hatori origami axioms. I got stuck so I went to talk with Alexander Bogomolny, who created the Cut the Knot website, because we'd happened to be talking recently. He really got me unstuck with it. Now my daughter is getting involved in that project. If she wants, she can talk to Alex and to Brad* who started the circle-folding idea. Both authors have contact forms on their web sites. There's no need to go through any system—like a publisher or a school.

If you want to get new material into classrooms, first you have to get into the curriculum, then train the teachers, and then the teachers have to deliver it to students. That can take years. Now we don't need any of those mediating systems. Students can do it for themselves, directly and instantly. We can skip the publishing company step for any media we want to produce, getting it to people directly as well. You can put content on your blog or Wikipedia or Twitter, and immediately it gets to people. You don't have anyone telling you not to do it.

Q: *What difference does that make in the world? How does that change things?*

It significantly lowers the entry barriers to two things. First it lowers the entry barriers to making your own content. Who's a writer? You're

---

* Bradford Hansens-Smith, the creator of: *WholeMovement.com*

a writer, I'm a writer, my daughter is a writer. Everyone is a creator. You don't have to spend years and years preparing before you publish. You publish right away. My daughter was publishing before she stopped nursing.

The second barrier that is now lower is the barrier to building communities. If you have to go through the hierarchies I just described, the cost of creating a new community is incredibly high. It's like building a new school system. You don't even want to start. You'd have to build the whole hierarchy from scratch. Now you can build communities with anyone is interested in doing it, with no permission and no money, just by pressing a few buttons. So communities are forming every week. A new group springs up for a month to accomplish a project, but if it works well, it may go on. So people just get together and love one another in the context of their mathematics.*

Q: *That makes me think of communities that are not so loving. People are so hostile sometimes in the Math Forum (hosted at Drexel University). Why do you think that is?*

The same reason they're hostile in the Chronicle of Higher Education, and in some bigger blogs. The problem is in the model of authoritative broadcasting from high up in the hierarchy, creating a scarcity mentality. There is this official math forum with official moderators. There's just one of it, and it's connected in mysterious ways to people who make decisions in education. Whenever there is an editorial board of some sort, this territorial response can kick in. But it's always possible to find or to build a smaller community that is loving.

Q: *So you can reach experts and talk to each other on a level playing field, you can make your own things, and you can create community. Anything else?*

You can also find people who will play with you. There are probably only a hundred people in the world who are interested in playing with circle-folding axioms. I don't need a hundred, but I do need three to five of them. I started working on this a few times and stopped. But now I've met a few other people who are interested. Just today, working on Geogebra, I looked up ten different threads on the Geogebra forum. I don't know the people who commented there and they don't know me, but what they wrote helped me with my project. There is this familial

---

* In *Here Comes Everybody: The Power of Organizing Without Organizations*, by Clay Shirky, he mentions "loving one another in the context of Perl." This is Maria's paraphrase.

and tribal effect. I can find this tiny minority for my specific stuff, and I can find this bigger group that can help me with more general questions.

Q: *What would you add to the resource list in the introduction [to this section]?*

One thing that isn't on your resource list is to search for mathematics on particular sites or in specialized ways. For example, you can search blogs; search Twitter and then follow hashtags that crop up; search YouTube for videos or Flickr for photos. There are many curious math communities centered on photography. The problem with any search-based approach is that you need to have general filtering skills. A lot of math online, like anything else, is incorrect or low quality or boring or obsolete. You need to develop filtering skills when you're young and hone them throughout your life.

Q: *How can someone find a community? There are times I want to find a community where I can ask a question, and I don't know where to go. For homeschoolers, I can recommend Living Math Forum. And I can send teachers to my blog to get started. But if someone is not quite in one of those categories, how would they start? How do they find their community?*

There is no easy answer. But there some rules of thumb I can share about how I find communities:

* Find a person who's savvy and ask them
* Find a role model and follow them
* Find one blogger you like and follow them

Following people, you will eventually find communities. You can also ask at "somewhat relevant" forums and blogs that are friendly enough to guide you to the right places.

Q: *I remember a few years ago, you were saying "Where is Math 2.0?" because there weren't a lot of ways to interact around math online. Has that changed?*

In July 2011, we had our one-hundredth online event in the Math Future series, which started with Steve Hargadon interviewing me two years previously, in July 2009, on the lack of Math 2.0—that is, grassroots online mathematical communities. The majority of the projects, blogs, forums, and communities we've reviewed in the series have started up in the last few years. So I can definitely say there is more going on now than five years ago. The ecosystems of online math presence are more robust and the networks are denser. There are also better platforms for

"The online world is becoming more mathematically rich, diverse, and welcoming by the month!"

communication and collaboration, which makes a lot of difference. So yes—the online world is becoming more mathematically rich, diverse, and welcoming by the month!

Q: *What's the most mathematical activity you've used the internet for recently?*

Just yesterday, we had a delightful Math Future event with Gord,[*] who set up a grown-up math club with interactive (and as yet unsolved) visual math problems we could collectively explore on the whiteboard.

Here's another example. Before the webinar started in the evening, I was working on a module for the UMIGO curriculum.[†] A part of this task is making game design chains: from learning objectives to metaphors to game mechanics. For example, adding fractions takes us to addition as putting measures together, which takes us to matching given lengths with several fractional lengths put together, perhaps by building a bridge out of them. I looked at hundreds of sites to collect examples of intrinsic math activities.

Quite a few good ones come from chapter authors in this book: Denise Gaskins' blog, Julia Brodsky's site and notes (soon to be published), Julie Brennan's collections, your salon's descriptions, and so on. The fraction bridge game is Colleen's.[‡] She also leads the online math game design group[§] where we develop ideas such as my metaphor-centered framework. It would be impossible for me to even come up with the framework, let alone to grow it toward its current robust state, without the thousands of open resources we share online, as well as discussions with their creators.

---

[*] Gordon Hamilton, the creator of: *MathPickle.com*
[†] UMIGO stands for You Make It Go: *umigo.info*
[‡] Colleen King of: *MathPlayground.com*
[§] *groups.google.com/group/mathgamedesign/*

Creating Math Teachers at Play

Interview with Denise Gaskins

Denise Gaskins hosts the prolific blog, Let's Play Math. I was curious about what got her started blogging and discovered we had to back up a few more steps.

Q: *How did your math lessons evolve? Did you start out following a curriculum?*

When I first started with my oldest, I did what most homeschoolers do: I bought a bunch of textbooks and did school at home. But I was disgusted with the textbooks. They were boring, and they had no real meat in them. I scrapped those and went to the library. I don't think I did formal math lessons again for my oldest three kids until fourth or fifth grade.

Q: *What sorts of books did you get at the library?*

We read *Family Math*, Peggy Kaye's *Games for Math*, *How Much Is a Million*, books by Claudia Zaslavski, the *I Love Math.* books, and the *Young Math* series. Later we picked up authors like Marilyn Burns, Theoni Pappas, Brian Bolt, and Raymond Smullyan. We also played dice and card games—several of which have made it onto my blog—built block patterns, ran races with a stopwatch, made cookies of course, and more.

We would do oral story problems; I'd make up a problem for one of the kids, and then he or she would make up a problem for me to solve. We live out in the country and have to drive a lot, so we'd do that in the car. Or riddles like "I'm thinking of a number. When you add 2 to my mystery number, you get 5." Of course, the clues got more difficult as the students grew.

And we tried some things that didn't work, too. Timed math drills, for instance, were a complete flop with all my kids. Eventually we went back to using textbooks because it's much easier to have the problems planned out for you. But even then I'd tweak things: work orally and focus on mental math, skip around, do Buddy Math (taking turns, with the teacher working just as many problems as the student does). We did the fourth grade book and then the sixth grade book, because there's so much repetition otherwise. I was much happier when I found the Singapore and Miquon math textbooks.

Q: *I'm impressed that you were comfortable dropping the curriculum like that.*

It helps that I'm comfortable with math; I was a physics major, and of course physics is one story problem after another. Also, I tend to be opinionated and think I can do more than I really can. It helps, too, that we have a very good library. I don't want to give the impression that I dropped traditional math entirely. We would still pick up little workbooks now and then—the kind they sell at grocery stores—especially for my girls, who liked to "play school."

Q: *Most people aren't that comfortable with math.*

Right. My husband brought home a news report that said most people are scared of story problems. My youngest daughter said, "What? Why would anyone be scared of story problems? Story problems are the best." She tends to think of math as being the arithmetic part, so she'll say things like, "I hate math, but algebra is fun." I was the same way myself when I was young.

Q: *Did writing your blog change the way you approach math?*

Well, blogging is more than just writing. It involves reading other people's blogs and commenting, comparing thoughts about mathematics and ideas for teaching it, even getting involved in debates like the "multiplication is or isn't repeated addition" kerfluffle. In a way, the blogging community acts like the Chinese "teaching research groups" mentioned in Liping Ma's book, *Knowing and Teaching Elementary Mathematics*. As for the writing itself, it forces me to sort through and clarify my ideas, so writing my books and my blog has helped me. And I enjoy it.

Q: *Your books?!*

My math books came before the blog; they were similar to it. There's a whole lot more to math than what's in textbooks, and I wanted to help homeschoolers see that. My books started out very simple, fifty pages stapled together. There were four in the series. The first was an introduction to my philosophy of teaching math. The second one covered what I call the math monsters, those topics that mess people up, like fraction division and percents. The third taught a hands-on technique for learning algebra. The fourth is on strategy games, and there's an unpublished fifth one about number games. I sold them for about four or five years, somewhere between one and two thousand copies altogether. They're out of print now.

Q: *I want one! Will you ever republish them?*

After following your blog posts about the progress of your book, I've been inspired to revisit mine. I recently published an ebook version of the first one, *Let's Play Math*, and I'm actively working on several others in the series. Eventually, I hope to see them all in paperback as well.

Q: *What led you to write those books?*

I taught some workshops for new homeschoolers, and my handouts grew into the books, which went through a couple of editions. After finishing the books, I was in a place where I wanted something else to write, and the first Alexandria Jones story kind of came to me. As I thought about that story, the Indiana Jones theme sounded cool, and I knew I could come up with others.

Q: *I love Alexandria Jones. The first time I explored your blog, I read every one of her stories, and wanted more. When did you start your blog?*

I started blogging in a homeschool forum. It was a place where I felt confident. I was hanging out there anyway, and the forum host encouraged me to start writing. When the forum closed down, I was used to writing those posts and needed to keep doing it. I started up my blog, and was delighted at how WordPress* takes care of the technical details.

Q: *The name of your blog—Let's Play Math—makes me wonder how the notion of play has affected your work.*

As far back as I can remember, it's been the playful, puzzle-solving side of math that attracted me. In elementary school, calculations were a tedious chore, but word problems provided the opportunity to try out my deductive powers. Algebra and geometry were exercises in logical reasoning—great fun!

The first article I wrote about math for homeschoolers was "The Case of the Mysterious Story Problem,"† in which I outlined the basic steps of problem solving. But I also tried to communicate that there is pleasure in wrestling with a tough problem, that students can experience a Sherlockian joy when "the game is afoot."

---

* *Wordpress.com* is what Denise uses. She says *Wordpress.org* requires more technical savvy.
† An expanded version of that article is on Denise's blog, at *LetsPlayMath.net/2007/02/26/the-case-of-the-mysterious-story-problem*

When I spoke at homeschool conferences, math games were always my most popular workshop. Parents naturally want their children to enjoy learning, and the people I met were hungry for creative ways to approach math. I started my blog to provide additional resources for my workshop participants, and it seemed natural to focus on the idea of playing with math.

Q: *You've been blogging at WordPress since 2006. What prompted you to create the Math Teachers at Play blog carnival in 2009?*

The Carnival of Mathematics had been going for a while. I enjoyed it, but much of it was over my head. My posts about middle school math felt out of place surrounded by all the high-level mathematics there—like toddlers at a high society cocktail party.

"My posts about middle school math felt out of place surrounded by all the high-level mathematics there—like toddlers at a high society cocktail party."

I already had quite a few readers at my blog, and I didn't feel most of them would be able to go to the Carnival of Mathematics; if it felt over my head it would feel even more over the heads of my readers. I wanted a blog carnival where I felt more comfortable and my readers would find something of interest. There were other education blog carnivals, but those had grown so large that it was nearly impossible to browse all their posts. I wanted something smaller, and just about math. And so, not finding the type of blog carnival I wanted, I selfishly decided to create one. I was worried about splitting the readership, but I think Math Teachers at Play has actually helped the Carnival of Mathematics to grow.

Q: *And how'd you choose the name for that?*

I chose the name "Math Teachers at Play" for several reasons. First, by using the word "teachers," I limited the carnival to school-level math (from preschool to calculus), not the higher-level stuff that tended to dominate the Carnival of Mathematics, and I hoped to attract the growing community of teacher-bloggers. And then, by using the word "play," I hoped to encourage the kind of blog post submissions that I myself prefer.

My favorite blog posts have always been those that captured the playful aspect of learning math, like the video of your math salon or the math circle puzzles you sometimes share. While the MTaP blog carnival accepts almost any post that isn't spam, I like to seek out and highlight writing that reflects the joy of playing with math or that opens a reader's eyes to see a math concept or procedure in a new way.

For example, one of my all-time favorite posts included a comment by Maria Droujkova: "When a kid is feeling bad about being stuck with a problem, or just very anxious, I sometimes ask him to make as many mistakes as he can, and as outrageous as he can." They laugh together at an answer that is clearly ridiculous, and this frees the student's mind to face the problem without fear. That's the sort of playing with math that any parent or teacher can use with a student at any level. I love it!

Q: *Has Math Teachers at Play evolved in any surprising directions?*
Not really. I like it that I'm still discovering new math bloggers. I'm more aware of them, and more consciously looking for them than I was before. But the essence of Math Teachers at Play—the mix of public and home-school teachers and independent learners, the variety of recreational and schooly topics—is there already in the first post. It's been exciting to see other people get involved in it. I never could have kept it going by myself.

Q: *How has the Internet changed your approach to math?*
I've become more aware of other options. For my youngest daughter I can find online drill games, where the older kids would have needed a workbook. There are lots of educational websites out there. It's easy to get overwhelmed.

My daughter and I do use workbooks (currently Math Mammoth, which I found online), but I got tired of hearing her say "I hate math," so we're focusing more on Internet activities this summer. We've explored the Math Cats website,* played SET,† experimented with taxi-cab geometry,‡ found a blog of daily Smullyanesque treasure puzzles,§ and so on. She's written about some of these things on her own blog, Kitten's Purring,¶ which is a major part of her language curriculum.

The Internet has also connected me to the people on the Living Math list. It's a neat way to get to know people. And for my homeschool co-op math classes, I'm more likely to go to the Internet for ideas than to drive to the library thirty minutes away. Or I find books online and order them through inter-library loan.

Q: *Community and resources, that sounds pretty basic. Maybe your blog has changed other people's approaches to math more than it's affected you, Denise. Let's give our readers the basics on Math Teachers at Play, so they can join us there.*
It's published on a different blog each month. You can find old issues, sub-mit blog posts, or offer to host it, at *LetsPlayMath.net/mtap*. See you there!

---

* *MathCats.com*
† *SetGame.com*
‡ *learner.org/teacherslab/math/geometry/shape/taxicab*
§ *4chests.blogspot.com*
¶ *KittensPurring.wordpress.com*

Colleen King, cofounder and director of Math Advantage Learning Center, in Wellesley, Massachusetts, has created the popular site MathPlayground.com. In this chapter, she tells the story of its evolution. —SV

Math Playground: Designing Games for Real Learning

by Colleen King

My fifth graders were engrossed in a game of Decention. The title was a made-up name culled from pieces of the terms decimal, fraction, and percent. The object of the game was to reunite as many number trios as possible based on clues given by teammates.* During the game, and much to my surprise, a rather quiet student shouted, "This is so much fun! I wish everyone could learn this way." It was a sentiment I frequently expressed myself. Was it possible to reproduce online the environment we had created at the math center? Could this level of engagement and depth of learning be recreated on a two-dimensional computer screen and delivered to children everywhere? Finding the answers to these questions would become an enduring and challenging quest for me.

Getting Started

Obstacles I encountered early on seemed insurmountable. It was 2003. I knew nothing at all about creating a web page and even less about programming languages. Our operating budget made no allowance for dream chasing. And I was teaching a full course load. All I had was an idealistic vision and intense determination. But that was enough. I studied everything possible, from pure technology to educational research. I learned html, javascript, Flash, video production, and image editing. I

---

* You can find an online version of Decention at *MathPlayground.com/Decention/Decention .html.*

read the work of Papert, Harel, and Gee.[*] The College of Web 1.0 had supplied me the canvas and all of the necessary tools. I was now ready to bring my vision to life.

My earliest game designs would be classified as drill and practice. While these types of games have their limits, they make memorization more fun, and therefore, more likely to happen. Instant recall of math facts is essential for success in later courses, so making it fun can make a huge difference in a student's success level.

Number Invaders[†] provides an arcade setting for students to practice sums and products. They can focus on a specific addend or factor and practice until they achieve instant recall. Another popular game in this category is Space Racer X.[‡] Students navigate a rocket ship through space while avoiding collisions with asteroids. Multiplication facts are presented in pairs and ultimately control the direction of the rocket. This game is aimed at students who have already learned multiplication but would benefit from further practice.

Deeper Understanding

> "Drill and practice games like these allow kids to have fun while they achieve automaticity with facts. But basic math goes much deeper than this."

Drill and practice games like these allow kids to have fun while they achieve automaticity with facts. But basic math goes much deeper than this. A game design that can support the *understanding* of multiplication as well is much more powerful. I learned this much later in the design process but found it indispensable from that point forward.

What might this look like? Here's a thought experiment: Maybe the object of the game is to build the greatest number of gardens in a specified plot of land. Students are given fencing material. They must make gardens that have the following areas: twelve square feet, twenty square feet, twenty-four square feet, and thirty-six square feet. Students would have to try various factor pairs in order to fit the gardens in the given space. A game such as this not only requires versatility with multiplication facts, it connects abstract concepts of factor and product to more concrete and visual area models. In general, game outcomes should be matched to the student's skill level and goals. Number Invaders is well suited for students who want to develop instant recall of facts. This imagined Garden Game is better suited for students who

---

[*] *Mindstorms*, by Seymour Papert, *Children Designers*, by Idit Harel, and *What Video Games Have to Teach Us About Learning and Literacy*, by James Paul Gee.

[†] *MathPlayground.com/balloon_invaders.html*

[‡] The games mentioned in this chapter are all available to play at *mathplayground.com*. If you can't find one, google math playground along with the game's name.

want to develop understanding. Someday I may manage to program this game, along with the dozens of others I've already enjoyed inventing.

Helping students develop conceptual understanding has influenced much of my current work in game design. An example is Guide the Gecko, a game that asks students to use their knowledge of fractions to solve a recurring problem in the story. Walker, the main character, is trying to get home but encounters gaps in the road that are impassable. Walker has to fill the gaps with boards, represented by unit fractions, and must follow certain rules along the way. At first, the challenges are relatively easy. For example, Walker might be asked to complete a one-meter gap with eight identical pieces.

Once Walker solves that problem, the next challenge would be to complete a gap that is two-meters long, again with eight identical pieces. The width of the gap doubles but the number of pieces the student must use remains constant. Students are asked to make a connection between the doubling of the gap and how the individual fraction pieces need to change. Once students conclude that the pieces must double in size, they then determine the size of the new pieces. Of course, some students will need to discover these relationships through trial and error.

Guide the Gecko encourages exploration so that students can simply test various fraction pieces and still be successful. Further in the game, a tool called the Combinator is introduced. Some of the later challenges require fractions whose numerators are greater than one. The Combinator allows students to build larger fractions by linking smaller unit fractions together. Throughout the game, ideas such as equivalency, relative size, fractional parts, and operations with fractions are emphasized.

My next adventure in game design traded drill and practice for algebraic reasoning puzzles. We had been using balance scale puzzles extensively at the math center and our elementary school students found them both engaging and challenging. In the simplest version, there are two balance scales. One scale has anywhere from two to eight identical objects. The other scale has some number of the first object and introduces a second object that is distinct from the others. For example, the first scale may contain five prisms that have a total weight of thirty. The other scale may have two prisms and three spheres totaling twenty-four. Students have to work out the weight of a single prism and the weight of a single sphere. In more advanced versions, both scales would contain prisms and spheres.

Obtaining the solution to this type of problem requires more complex reasoning. By making interactive versions of these algebraic puzzles, we were able to share an excellent resource and provide access to a seemingly endless supply of problems. Balance scale problems can be found in our Algebraic Reasoning activity. For an even greater challenge, you may try to solve for a trio of variables in the popular Weigh the Wangdoodles game.

Interaction with Videos

While these simple games and puzzles fulfilled a growing need for skills practice, the potential of rich media applications had been untapped. I began to embed both instructional and feedback videos into my activities. The first project to utilize this approach is Thinking Blocks, a math tool* that encourages students to model their math problems. We found that students, when faced with word problems, tended to scan the text for numbers and keywords. While the keyword strategy may work for simple, routine problems, it fails when the wording is more ambiguous. Compare the following problems:

1. Amy has five blocks. Jack has three times as many blocks as Amy. How many blocks does Jack have?

2. Amy has fifteen blocks. She has three times as many blocks as Jack. How many blocks does Jack have?

Students who attempt to solve the first problem could simply isolate the numbers, three and five, and apply the keyword, "times," to find the answer. In contrast, that same strategy would fail when applied to the second problem.

The goal of Thinking Blocks, therefore, is to help students visualize the relationships among the quantities in the problem before working with the actual values. The video support in Thinking Blocks is programmed to recognize the type of problem the student is struggling to solve, and to display a step-by-step video of that particular type of problem.

Who Can Do The Math was my second experiment with integrated video. This activity creates a more personalized interaction between students and characters onscreen. A math problem is presented and animated characters give audio-visual solutions. The characters include a teen boy, a teen girl, and a robot. Students are asked to listen to each solution and then decide which explanation is correct. When I first

---

* Thinking blocks are a way to visually model what's happening in a story problem, first developed within the Singapore math curriculum.

presented it, the students could enter their answers in a poll and had the option to send in their complete solution. The following week, the correct answer was revealed along with a pie graph of the poll results and selected student responses. Twelve of these problems are still available on Math Playground.

Based on the feedback I received, this simple experiment in interaction resulted in some surprising revelations. Girls often selected the male character simply because they thought he seemed smarter. It didn't matter what explanation he provided in the video. Boys, however, tended to choose the robot, stating that it was smarter and would always be correct.

Role-Playing Online

While neither Thinking Blocks nor Who Can Do The Math can be classified as games, these activities represent important steps along the path to more advanced applications. Working on these projects not only broadened my programming skills, it also provided valuable insight about the students who were using the activities. This was the first time I had received extensive feedback from students, the first time I actually met my audience. I thought about how different this online experience was from designing games for students at the math center. The in-person games were always based on the unique interests of my students, all of whom played a role in the development of the games. And, as a result, my students really cared about the games we played. I wanted to design games that connected deeply with my online audience as well.

As I reflected on the successful elements of games at the math center, I began to wonder exactly what the students found so compelling. Why were my students completely absorbed with the algebra adventure game? Sure, they had a desire to win, but that wasn't a strong enough explanation to justify the amount of time the students had invested. I uncovered two important clues as I read through the year-end assessments. In their responses, students shared that they enjoyed the characters they were playing and that they liked working through problems with their teammates. Role playing and collaboration were the dominant driving forces in the games we had played at the math center. Both of these elements were missing from my online activities. I decided to focus my efforts on role play. Could I create simple game environments that would transport students to interesting places and situations?

My first attempt at a role-playing activity was a game called Math at the Mall. Students would visit four different sections of a shopping mall and play the role of a customer. At the toy store, students could

"Why were my students completely absorbed with the algebra adventure game?"

choose games and toys to buy. The toys were on sale so students had to first determine the discount. At the bank, students could request a loan and calculate the interest they would have to pay. The health club gave students the choice of two different membership plans. Students had to decide which one offered the better deal. At the Happy Hamburger, students would order food and figure out how much to tip the waiter. The game elements were rudimentary. At each location, students could earn a gold coin. The goal was to collect all 4 coins. The important part of the game was the experience the simulation provided. It enabled students to apply the math skills they had learned in situations that were part of their everyday lives.

Math at the Mall was successful with students ages ten to twelve, so I decided to develop other role playing activities for that age range. The X Detectives invited students to be secret agents in training. They would obtain skills necessary to find and identify the wayward Agent X. In reality, the activities were an overview of some early algebra concepts. To set the scene, students maneuvered around the X Detectives training facility in an x-mobile. Students transformed shapes, added and subtracted integers, graphed functions, and solved algebraic equations. Students can choose to play in untimed exploration mode or timed game mode. In a follow up to the X Detectives, trainees graduate and become professional agents. In this game, students use the concepts learned in training to actually capture Agent X. This game is currently in development.

Math Apprentice is my most recent attempt to bring real-world applications to my math lessons. In this simulation, students assume the role of apprentices in various math-related careers. As computer animators at Trigon Studios, students manipulate sine and cosine equations to control the characters and action on the movie screen. At Space Logic, students work in the robotics lab, where they explore graphs of distance versus time and program a space rover. Other occupations include roller coaster engineer, bicycle designer, restaurant owner, artist, video game programmer, and home builder.

Games have tremendous potential to transform math education in exciting new ways. Despite the abundance of online games, we have only just begun to explore the possibilities. The two-dimensional role-playing games of today will eventually give way to fully immersive experiences in increasingly-realistic 3D environments. Through these game environments, Papert's concept of Mathland may finally be realized. In Mathland, interaction with mathematical objects becomes the basis for how we learn all mathematics.

Imagine being able to walk along a parabolic curve, view three-dimensional structures from the inside, or see real-time graphs of your avatar's activities. All of that is possible in a 3D environment. During my own work in the 3D world of Second Life, I was able to recreate the functionality of Papert's logo turtle but with the added advantage of a third axis. This tool enabled students to create mathematical art, bridges, towers, and more, all of which could then accept further interaction. In the process of using this tool, students would deepen their understanding of algebra, geometry, and trigonometry.

Games that immerse students in visually-rich settings, encourage exploration, and bring meaning to mathematics will enhance math education in ways we've never imagined. Let's meet in a few years, in Mathland!

If this chapter helps you support any girls in their mathematical journeys, please let me know. I would like to include stories like that on my blog. —SV

Supporting Girls

by Sue VanHattum

Many who have never had occasion to learn what mathematics is confuse it with arithmetic, and consider it a dry and arid science. In reality, however, it is the science which demands the utmost imagination ... It seems to me that the poet must see what others do not see, must look deeper than others look. And the mathematician must do the same thing. As for myself, all my life I have been unable to decide for which I had the greater inclination, mathematics or literature.*

—Sonya Kovalevsky

Sonya Kovalevsky[†] (1850–1891), a Russian mathematician, traveled across Europe in her quest for someone who could help her learn more mathematics. Determined to convince Karl Weierstrass, a world-famous mathematician, to be her mentor, she got him to pose her a set of problems. She worked out solutions to all of them, and he was suitably impressed. Thus began a close working relationship that lasted many years. Weierstrass later wrote to her, saying, "Never have I found anyone who could bring me such understanding of the highest aims of science and such joyful accord with my intentions and basic principles as you." As a woman, she was never allowed to attend his classes at the University of Berlin, so he tutored her privately. Although she could not get a degree from his school, Weierstass knew her work deserved that recognition. Three of the papers she wrote while working with him were so strong they earned her a Ph.D. in 1874 from the University of Gottingen, another college she was never allowed to attend. She thus became the first woman ever to earn a Ph.D. in mathematics.

---

* Perhaps to her regret, her literary efforts have not fared as well over the years as her mathematical achievements have.

† Both her first and last name have many variants when translated into English, Sofia Kovalevskaya is perhaps the next most common way her name is rendered.

Sonya had a daughter shortly after that. It took some years for her to produce more mathematical work, but even with a child, she managed it. In 1880 she presented a paper that helped her to get a faculty position at the University of Stockholm a few years later, making her one of the first women university professors ever. While there she continued to produce new work, and in 1888 she was awarded the prestigious Prix Bordin by the French Academy of Sciences for her solution to a problem in differential equations that had stumped mathematicians for over a hundred years. What else she might have been able to achieve we will never know, for she died three short years later of pneumonia.[*]

Role Models

When I studied the history of mathematics, I was drawn to Sonya Kovalevsky. She was both a mathematician and a writer, and she managed to juggle all that with parenting solo.[†] She lived a passionate and independent life, and I hoped I could be something like her. She reminds me of how important role models are. There are many great women mathematicians you can choose as role models—Hypatia, Sophie Germain, Ada Lovelace, and Emmy Noether are among the most famous.[‡] Perhaps one of them will inspire you or a young woman you know. With their stories of rising above the obstacles in their way and persevering in their passions, they can become role models for girls and women, helping us to see the world of mathematics as our world.

"The best way to make sure your daughter knows the joys of math is to play with it yourself."

You can find more role models in the present and closer to home. One program in the U.S. to help connect girls with role models is Expanding Your Horizons.[§] This is an annual event held on college campuses, introducing junior high girls to women in STEM fields (science, technology, engineering, and math), through a celebratory day full of engaging STEM-related activities. But one day a year isn't enough. How can you make sure the girls in your life meet lots of interesting women who love math?

The best way to make sure your daughter knows the joys of math is to play with it yourself. If you are a math-anxious parent, you can give

---

[*] See *maa.org/pubs/Calc_articles/ma072.pdf* and *AgnesScott.edu/lriddle/women/kova.htm* for more information.

[†] Read her autobiography, *Sonya Kovalevsky: Her Recollections of Childhood*, for a detailed account of her younger years.

[‡] More recent women mathematicians are featured in Claudia Henrion's book, *Women in Mathematics: The Addition of Difference*. She also dispels myths about how mathematics is conducted in chapters like Rugged Individualism and the Mathematical Marlboro Man.

[§] *ExpandingYourHorizons.org*

your daughter a huge gift by facing your fears and discovering ways to enjoy math—show her how to persevere through struggle. (Don't hide the struggle, show it off!) If your goal is to play with it instead of trying to pass a class, you may manage to have an entirely different experience. I created this book for you.* You may already have discovered that re-learning math to help your kids learn it is a lot more fun than what you experienced in school.

To thrive mathematically, we need to see mathematics as something we *can* do, and might *want* to do. But the world gets in the way of girls and people of color doing math. Sexism and racism come in a surprisingly wide variety of packages. You need to know what they look like so you don't think there's something wrong with you. It's not you; it's this messed-up world. This chapter explains many of the subtle ways the world comes between a girl and her math. It also details ways you can get around those obstacles. Some of the mechanisms described apply to both girls and people of color. Knowing someone who looks like me and did amazing things mathematically helps me to believe in myself—role models matter, for both girls and people of color. And stereotype threat (explained below) affects anyone whose people have been put down.

But many of the mechanisms of sexism and racism differ. I am only comfortable writing about what I know deeply, so this chapter is mainly about supporting girls. The research on stereotype threat has focused on both girls and students of color. There are some amazing programs reaching students of color around the country—check out The Algebra Project,† and ask at high schools in your area about other programs emphasizing STEM success for students of color.

> **TIP**
> To support girls, share the stories of women mathematicians, introduce girls to women who do math and enjoy it, and share with them your own enjoyment of math, however basic.

How Math is Taught in Schools

Throughout this book, we've looked at approaches to math that are more playful than what happens in the traditional classroom. But most students learn math in school—in a conventional classroom. Even the most motivated math student could have trouble with that. Math is

---

* My original reason for creating this book was to make some really good writing more available. But as I worked on it, and kept hearing "who is your audience?," I more and more often imagined all the parents and elementary teachers who don't enjoy math, and would like to help their kids have a better experience with it than they've had. I welcome your questions and comments. Email me at mathanthologyeditor@gmail.com to tell me how it's going, or to ask me your math questions.

† Online at *algebra.org* and *typp.org*

typically presented as procedures, without adequate context. And it turns out that this matters more often to girls than to boys.

Math education researcher Jo Boaler spent time in a number of classrooms, some using traditional methods, others using inquiry-based methods.* Her book, *What's Math Got to Do with It?,* describes how girls often have a stronger need than boys do to understand the reasons behind the procedures in math. In classrooms where that need isn't honored, girls are turned off to math—more than boys are. Boys are often more willing to memorize without understanding, leading them to become more successful than girls in conventional high-school math classes. Although memorizing can be useful for the short-term, it is not a good long-term strategy for learning mathematics. So boys and girls are both robbed of meaningful mathematics in these conventional math classrooms.

Boaler's research showed that both girls and boys enjoyed studying math more in inquiry-based classrooms. Girls and boys performed about equally well, the girls showing dramatically better performance than girls in traditional classrooms.

> **TIP**
> To support girls in math classes, approach math holistically, using inquiry-based methods. Ask questions like "Why does that work?" and "How did you know to do that?"

There is almost too much research done on the differences between women and men, girls and boys. Much of it is flawed. For instance, differences have been found between women's and men's brain structures. Often the assumption is made that this is evidence of built-in differences. But brains change, based on what they've been asked to do—experience changes our brains. So the different wiring may be something our amazing brains have done for us in response to the highly gendered world we live in. It seems that there may be differences in the ways women and men learn, and girls seem to respond well to environments in which connections between all the disparate pieces are honored. Whether these differences come from nurture or nature, whether we've trained girls to be this way or they've inherited it, we are unfairly limiting half the population if we do not honor this thinking style in the classroom.

One way to connect things together is to involve a storytelling aspect. I am currently working on learning more of the history of calculus. If my students see the problems scientists were eager to solve in the late 1600s, and how calculus helped solve those, maybe that will help make calculus more real for them.

---

* Inquiry-based learning involves giving students tasks that require them to problem solve, conjecture, experiment, explore, create, and communicate, which is what mathematicians do. Two chapters in the Passionate Teachers section, Dinosaur Math and Area of a Circle, illustrate inquiry-based lessons.

Both boys and girls enjoy math more when it's taught holistically, focusing on the connections among topics and between math and other subjects. Understanding the history behind math can make it feel more human, an important connection for some students. And finding out how it's used in science, art, music, and social studies can also make it more approachable.

Nature versus Nurture

In most parts of the world, women are no longer banned, like Sonya Kovalevsky was, from studying what they choose and entering the profession they choose. Because the laws are superficially equal, many people would like to claim that sexism and racism no longer exist. It's useful to recognize how the mechanisms of sexism and racism have changed, sometimes becoming more subtle rather than disappearing.

Most people have different expectations of girls and of boys. We can see obvious physical differences between men and women, so it's easy to think that our intellects are also different. But so much of who we are comes from the culture we live within that it's almost impossible to tease out what comes from our natures and what comes from the way we're nurtured. Are men better at math than women? I hope my grandchildren will think of that as quaint nonsense, but right now there are still plenty of people who believe it. And no wonder—when we look around us, we see lots more male mathematicians, computer scientists, engineers, statisticians, and accountants. But there is plenty of evidence that this imbalance is in large part a product of our culture.

One way to measure the effect of nurture is to compare different cultures. If the differences between men and women are consistent around the world, then they are probably related to something innate (for example, things like height and muscle mass). But if each culture tells a different story about gender, with the differences between men and women greater in some places and smaller in others, or with women even doing better than men in some countries, or with the disparity changing over time, then we've found evidence that we are teaching our children to play one role or another. That's exactly what a number of studies have found in regard to math performance.

Cultural Variability

Janet Mertz and her colleagues decided to look at international data on high scorers in world championship math competitions. The percentage of girls among those who rank most highly in these competitions varies

"You'd need to consider hundreds of schools to find even half the boys, but the majority of the girls came from just twenty high schools."

widely from one country to another, from below 5% to over 20%. This variability also shows up in the percentage of women among tenured math faculty at elite research institutions in different countries (again, below 5% to over 20%).* This variability can give us a start in understanding how much culture affects girls' and women's achievement in math.

> **TIP**
>
> To support girls, we need economic and political equality for women. Warning: This tip may require activism.

The World Economic Forum has created a measure of the gender gap in each country.† In countries with a smaller gender gap overall, Mertz's group found that there is usually also a smaller gender gap in math performance, or even a reversal. In Iceland, at the top of the list for overall gender equity, girls actually do better than boys in math.‡ Perhaps surprising for those of us from the U.S, our country is not even near the top of the gender equity list.

International comparisons are one way to see that cultural differences have a big effect on achievement, but we can also zoom in and compare schools instead of countries. There's evidence that the culture of individual schools can make a huge difference in young women's math performance. Glenn Ellison, the coach for a middle-school math team, noticed that his team, all girls, didn't look much like the other teams, which were mostly composed of all boys. He checked into the make-up of teams that participate in the American Mathematics Competitions (AMC). Looking at the schools that brought the most teams, you'd need to consider hundreds of schools to find even half the boys, but the majority of the girls came from just twenty high schools.§ Ellison said, "It's significant that the top girls are coming from a very, very small subset of schools with strong math programs. That suggests most of the girls who could be doing well, aren't doing well. The thousands and thousands of other schools in the United States must have a lot of talent, too, but it's not coming out."¶

Dedicated administrators can make a huge difference in the participation rate of girls. At Harvey Mudd College, a new college president helped support an overhaul of the computer science program intended

---

* See: *ams.org/notices/200810/fea-gallian.pdf*

† The measure is based on economic, educational, health, and political equality. A detailed explanation is available at *WEForum.org/issues/global-gender-gap*

‡ See Time article at: *time.com/time/magazine/article/0,9171,1032361,00.html*

§ Ellison clarified this by personal correspondence. He also pointed out that just over 1% of (nonmagnet, noncharter, coed, public) U.S. high schools (i.e., twenty to twenty-five schools) seem to be producing high-scoring girls at more than ten times the rate that you'd expect, given their demographics.

¶ *mit.edu/newsoffice/2009/math-gender.html*

to make it more welcoming to female students. The program has made a big difference.*

Sexism's Many Faces

TIP

To support girls, we need schools with strong math programs that actively welcome girls, making their success a priority.

Sometimes sexism is overt and intentional; other times it is so subtle you need a double-blind study to identify it. And yet it still has powerful damaging effects. We need to know how it works to be able to support girls in their struggles to overcome it. Everything is connected and finding those connections—In this case, knowing how and when we're being oppressed—helps us face it with strength.

It would take a book to detail all the ways our culture derails girls' interest in math and prevents girls from knowing just how powerful they can be mathematically. In the next few pages I'll describe the seven mechanisms listed here, to give some sense of the breadth of this problem.

1. We are told that boys are better at math than girls.

2. Girls and boys are trained to fit in gendered boxes.

3. Parents and teachers can inadvertently act as negative role models.

4. Women are rated lower for the same performance.

5. Teachers give boys better feedback.

6. It's hard to perform well if you worry about confirming stereotypes.

7. Standardized tests under-predict women's abilities.

1. We are told that boys are better at math than girls.

My calculus professor once told me, "Maybe you're just not cut out for this." I will never know whether it was sexism, or his unbiased but wrong evaluation of my capabilities. He probably doesn't know himself which it was. I am lucky that my mathematical capabilities have seldom been questioned. To this day, most women in math have to deal with hearing overtly-sexist comments about their math capabilities.

The president of Harvard, in an address to a conference on the under-representation of women in science and math, claimed that the

---

* *nytimes.com/2012/04/03/science/giving-women-the-access-code.html*

reason there are fewer women in STEM fields was most likely the innate differences in intelligence between men and women. The controversy that erupted may have helped oust him from Harvard, though he committed worse crimes.[*]

One way to provide a protective buffer is with single-sex schooling. The students at women's colleges are more likely than other women to get doctorates. Even though less than 3% of women in college are attending women's colleges, more than 20% of the women in Congress are graduates of women's colleges. It depends completely on the culture of the school whether a single-sex high school will help girls, but one study of girls and boys put randomly into schools, some with a usual mix of about 50–50 girls and boys, others that were close to single sex, found that girls in mostly girls' schools were more likely to enter STEM majors and to succeed in them.[†]

2. Girls and boys are trained to fit in gendered boxes.

There are hundreds of ways in which girls are subtly and not-so-subtly steered toward "feminine" endeavors and away from things like mathematics. From the different responses to pink- and blue-clad babies to gender-segregated aisles in toy stores to TV shows in which teenage girls worry about looking too smart, girls are bombarded by cultural messages that make an interest in mathematics seem unusual. Those twenty high schools mentioned above make a huge difference in the lives of their female students by normalizing their interest in mathematics.

One particular way this gendered socialization affects girls' math skills is that boys are more encouraged to play with blocks and other building toys. This develops spatial visualization skills, in which boys consistently outperform girls. Schools can create projects that encourage girls to play with construction toys and simulated construction on computers.[‡] Even at college level, specific attention to spatial visualization skills can dramatically improve female students' success in calculus.[§]

> **TIP**
>
> To support girls, break the gender conventions in your play— especially by encouraging play with building toys—and in the stories you share through books and movies.

---

[*] Slate wrote a good article on the fiasco, available at: *slate.com/id/2112799* Summers had hypothesized that male intelligence is more variable than women's. Even if this hypothesized greater-male-variability exists, and is not just a product of culture, one would still expect about 15% of math faculty at Harvard to be women, but there were *none*. His other offenses are described at: *MathBabe.org/2012/03/11/why-larry-summers-lost-the-presidency-of-harvard*

[†] *voxeu.org/article/long-run-gains-not-mixing-genders-high-school-classes*

[‡] See: *eScholarShare.drake.edu/bitstream/handle/2092/411/BeisserCIS2006.pdf?sequ* Seymour Papert's book, *Mindstorms*, also has a passage about how changing the project to accommodate typical girls' interests brought girls in.

[§] *aauw.org/2011/09/29/spatial-skills-training-can-improve-stem-retention*

3. Parents and teachers can inadvertently act as negative role models.

One way girls imprint on our cultural expectations is through contact with elementary teachers, who are mostly female. One study found significant effects for girls when their teacher was anxious about math:

> *Early elementary school teachers in the United States are almost exclusively female (more than 90%). These female teachers' anxieties relate to girls' math achievement via girls' beliefs about who is good at math.*
>
> *First- and second-grade female teachers completed measures of math anxiety. The math achievement of the students in these teachers' classrooms was also assessed. There was no relation between a teacher's math anxiety and her students' math achievement at the beginning of the school year. By the school year's end, however, the more anxious teachers were about math, the more likely girls (but not boys) were to endorse the commonly held stereotype that "boys are good at math, and girls are good at reading" and the lower these girls' math achievement.*
>
> *Indeed, by the end of the school year, girls who endorsed this stereotype had significantly worse math achievement than girls who did not and than boys overall.*[*]

A similar dynamic likely operates within the family too, with mothers passing their math discomforts on to their daughters more than their sons. (Do fathers pass on their math discomfort to sons? This research has nothing to say about that.)

4. Women are rated lower for the same performance.

Most U.S. orchestras now conduct "blind auditions," where the applicant plays from behind a screen, so their appearance is not known. This practice has dramatically increased the number of women playing in these orchestras.

It is harder to hide the gender of applicants in other fields. One study found that female postdoctoral applicants either had to publish at least three more papers in prestigious science journals or an additional twenty papers in lesser-known journals to be judged as productive as a

> **TIP**
> To support your daughters, find teachers who are comfortable with math, and find ways to become more comfortable with math yourself (see first tip). To support all girls, we need to help elementary teachers become more comfortable with math.

---

[*] Bellock, Gunderson, Ramirez, Levine. pnas.org/content/early/2010/01/14/0910967107 .abstract

male applicant.* Other studies have found similar gender bias, which is often unconscious.†

5. Teachers give boys better feedback.

Myra and David Sadker spent years observing classrooms, from first grade through college, using a meticulous system they'd worked out for tracking their observations. They found subtle and pervasive differences in the way teachers responded to girls and boys. Their book, *Failing at Fairness*, is eye-opening. When a teacher directs a question at a student, the teacher will wait for nine-tenths of a second, on average, for the student's response. The length of the pause is significantly longer for boys than for girls. If the student has not responded, the teacher may answer the question, ask a related question, give a hint, or give encouragement. With girls, teachers more often simply answered the question themselves. We are so used to this we cannot see the difference unless, stopwatch in hand, we record each "wait-time." Suddenly, it becomes glaring. The teachers who do this do not intend to value the boys more. But the boys still get a better education.

I am an ardent feminist and have been aware of this effect for years. But I think I'm still guilty too. For a number of years, I called on students randomly, using 3×5 cards. Lately, thinking that was too hard on students, I went back to calling on people in a more organic way. But more organic is probably more gendered, with the male students getting more useful interactions with me. Time to pull out those cards again.‡

Is it possible to take a playful approach to overcoming systemic oppression? We can be detectives scouting it out. We can find gentle ways to talk about what we see, making it clear change needs to happen without blaming those who are making mistakes. We can help our girls and our children of color think of themselves as warriors, strong enough to change the world.

---

* Cited in an American Association of University Women (AAUW) report titled *Why So Few? Women in Science, Technology, Engineering, and Mathematics*, on page 41, referencing a 1997 study done by Wenneras and Wold.

† One other study: pnas.org/content/early/2012/09/14/1211286109#aff-1

‡ Writing this chapter made me aware of this. I have just gone back to calling on students randomly, with what I jokingly refer to as my evil cards. I am noticing how big a difference it makes in the participation—quieter students, both female and male, are a more active part of the class.

6. It's hard to perform well if you worry about confirming stereotypes.

There is much recent psychological research on one of the mechanisms involved at the individual level. It's called *stereotype threat*, an odd name. The idea is that stereotypes about us make us feel threatened, afraid that our behavior could confirm the stereotypes, and then we have trouble giving our best performance.

When a group is culturally perceived to be less able in a certain realm, and a test is clearly related to this perceived lack of ability, members of this group will do worse than they would if the test didn't seem to be related to any stereotypes. The reverse can happen for those on the other side of the stereotype, too: men, when reminded that men generally do better in math than women, will do better than they otherwise would on a math test.

One of the things that activates stereotype threat is being reminded of your membership in a group that is stereotyped. One study showed that "simply moving standard demographic inquiries about ethnicity and gender to the end of the test resulted in significantly higher performance for women taking the AP calculus test."*

There can be other interesting twists in the way stereotype threat operates:

The researchers [Catherine Good and Joshua Aronson] asked male and female students enrolled in a fast-paced calculus course at a large public university to take a practice calculus test in preparation for an upcoming exam. The course was the most-rigorous calculus class offered by the university and satisfied requirements for degrees in mathematics, engineering, and many of the natural sciences.

One group of students in the study received the test under normal testing conditions; that is, they were informed that the test was designed to measure their math abilities and knowledge. Among these students, the women performed just as well as the men, reflecting the fact that these were high-performing women.

The surprise came from the second group of students in the class, who took the [same] test under the same instructions but who were additionally informed that the test was free of gender bias. The researchers found that the women in this group outperformed all the other test-takers in this high-level math class.†

---

* *ReducingStereotypeThreat.org/reduce.html*

† (No author listed.) *nyu.edu/about/news-publications/news/2008/01/29/stereotype_threat_affects .html*

TIP

A strong belief in equal capabilities will go far to ameliorate the effects of stereotype threat. Support girls by helping them recognize their own strength.

The site ReducingStereotypeThreat.org has a list of seven researched ways to reduce this effect.* Most of the research is directed at the role of test administrator or teacher. The most accessible finding was this: "It appears that interventions that encourage individuals to consider themselves as complex and multi-faceted can reduce vulnerability to stereotype threat."

Three of the seven strategies listed can be used by individual students. The value of becoming aware of role models was already discussed above, and is one of the ways stereotype threat can be reduced. Another, discussed below, is a recognition of the malleable nature of intelligence. The third, self-affirmation, includes being aware of your values and why they're important to you.

7. Standardized tests under-predict women's abilities.

Men do better on standardized tests than women when the women are just as intellectually capable: "On average, males score 33 points higher on the SAT-Math than females who earn the same grades in the same college math courses."[†]

Researchers have found a number of mechanisms to explain this. Stereotype threat is a big one. Two more that are not obvious are gender differences in risk-taking and speed. On the SAT, wrong answers are penalized just enough so that random guesses will neither help nor harm the total score on average. If you can throw out at least one answer as wrong, then it's helpful to guess. Men are more likely to take that risk.

Timed tests penalize women unfairly. "Numerous studies have found that when the time constraint is lifted from the test, females' scores improve markedly, while males' remain the same or increase slightly."[‡]

Many colleges are willing to forego SAT scores. But the problem isn't only entrance to college; it's also differential selection for scholarships based on these tests.

Talents, Gifts, and Passions

I'm a math teacher. When I mention that to a stranger they are likely to reply by telling me how bad they are at math. And they will often say, "I don't have a math mind." If school were my only experience with singing, I would have been telling people I couldn't sing for most of my

---

* *ReducingStereotypeThreat.org/reduce.html*
† From research dome by Howard Wainer and Linda Steinberg, as reported at: *FairTest.org /gender-bias-college-admissions-tests*
‡ *FairTest.org/gender-bias-college-admissions-tests*

life. I mouthed the words in school choir so as not to embarrass myself. But I have always loved music, and I knew I could sing Christmas carols decently. I am just a slow learner with music. Over the years I have reclaimed my love of music, and I continue to slowly learn more.

Let's bring that to math. Imagine a world in which we play around with math enough that a child recognizes her love of math, even if she's slow at learning new math topics in school. We would recognize that, although it comes more easily to some, we can all find our passion for its beauty, and work at learning it just for joy.

Maybe some day I'll perform some song so beautifully people will flock to youtube to hear my rendition. (Dream on, Sue!) If the learning brings you joy and you work hard, you can go far. U.S. culture often tries to convince us of the opposite—that some people are born with gifts and talents, and the rest of us aren't.

> *U.S. culture instills in students the belief that math talent is innate; if one is not naturally good at math, there is little one can do to become good at it. In some other countries, people more highly value mathematics and view math performance as being largely related to effort.*
>
> —Janet Mertz

In some countries, "I don't have a math brain" would seem like a very odd thing to say. Some cultures are clear that we are good at the things we practice, the things we love.

This relates to a deep problem with the notion of intelligence. Carol Dweck set out to understand how people's ideas about intelligence affect their ability to learn. All the research studies she did on this pointed to the usefulness of believing that our intelligence is flexible and can be developed. She describes this as having a fixed or a growth mindset. Those with a fixed mindset often avoided challenges, apparently because they were concerned about looking bad. Those with a growth mindset didn't mind making mistakes, and relished the experience of a challenging problem.

> **TIP**
> To support girls, remember that joy and passion lead to more learning than duty ever did.

> *Math is a language—as the National Council of Teachers of Mathematics likes to say, "Math is everyone's second language." It is the language of problem solving. Children who grow up in homes where the parents are fluent in mathematics become fluent themselves, in much the same way that children who grow up in other kinds of bilingual households can grow up bilingual—if the parents make the effort to use the language in a pervasive and frequent way in their homes.*
>
> —Mary O'Keeffe

To support a love of math, let people know that they can change their relationship to math.

Losing and Regaining a Love of Math

My story is not as dramatic as Sonya Kovalevsky's, but maybe it's closer to home. I loved math when I was young. I remember playing school with my younger brothers, teaching them math topics I'd just learned myself. My mom took us to the library every week, and I read every children's book on codes and ciphers in that library. So the first "grown-up" book I ever took out of the library was on codes and ciphers. With math, I didn't have to believe what someone *said*, I could know the right answer as well as the teacher did. I liked that.

As I started college, I was placed in the highest-level honors math class at the University of Michigan. The only real evidence of sexism in my math life so far? Before I started that class, I dreamed one night that someone told me a mistake had been made—this class was for boys only. It turned out that only five of the forty students in the class were female. All of the other girls lived at the opposite end of campus, and I never ended up working with them. I worked four hours a night (alone), and ended up with a B−. I was so discouraged by that grade that I put in way less effort during the next semester—and failed the course. I considered switching to another major, but nothing else called to me, and I was able to pass that class when I retook it. So I slogged through a BA in math at U of M, but I left there feeling like I really didn't know much and didn't enjoy doing higher math. That experience gave me a lot of empathy for my students who struggle.

When I began teaching part-time at a community college, I knew I'd found my true calling. To get a full-time position at college level, I'd need a master's degree. At that point I would have preferred a master's in computer science, but the college I'd chosen didn't have that yet. So I took a deep breath and started in on a math master's. I didn't expect to enjoy myself, but I was delightfully surprised to find that I liked almost all of my classes. With better teachers and a slower pace, the math was fun again, and my joy in it returned.

I liked it so much, I thought I'd get a Ph.D. I found my Ph.D. program just as unpleasant as my experience at U of M, and I quit after one year. When I began teaching again, I became immersed in thinking about how to teach math, but rarely did any new math myself. It wasn't until the internet connected me with math circle enthusiasts that I found myself finally becoming a mathematician in my own way.

I had so many interests during college, and I desperately wanted a way to connect my interest in math with my other interests, but I just didn't know how to do that. Decades later, I've finally managed to connect it with my activism and my writing. By some measures the fact that I never got a Ph.D. in math makes me one of the casualties. But that's not the way I look at it. I am doing math, helping others to enjoy doing math, and maybe making a difference in the world this way. My hope is that one day each girl (and boy) of every race will get to play with math in ways that inspire them to work hard at it—each of us loving math in our own way.

This was a group effort, starting out as Rodi Steinig's transcription of Bob Kaplan's commentary as he led math circles at the 2011 Summer Institute, and then evolving with help from Maria and me and a few additions from a blog post by Joy Kogut. —SV

How to Become Invisible

by Bob Kaplan and friends

Students are used to following the teacher, and it's hard to change that dynamic. If you've posed an accessible, intriguing problem, and want to step back so the students can step it up, here are some responses you might try…

Holding Your Cards Close

- I don't know, I'm just the secretary.
- What a good way to put it.
- Why does that work?
- What an interesting idea. Why?
- That's great, but are you really sure about that? Is 19 really less than 18?
- Sounds good, sounds right, it could work, but how could you convince a Martian or a skeptic?
- This may not work, but it might!
- That's a good point.
- That's a good thing you're doing.
- Ah!
- Hey, that's terrific.
- This is great thinking, by the way.
- Your question really clarifies things, thanks.
- I'm in complete doubt—let's work it out.
- Oh, nice idea.
- Why? I'm sure you're right, I just don't see it.
- The numbers 12 and 24 are both in the same family, so they're both good guesses.
- You've found an economical way of thinking about it.

- You can guess—take a risk and be wrong. Sometimes it's fun to be wrong.
- How were we thinking about it?

Thinking Prompts

- What do you think is going on with this?
- Do you see what the previous speaker was saying?
- Can we make this simpler?
- Take a wild guess: 17? 3½?
- What would a harder problem be?
- I have a terrible memory for these things, so I'm going to put them on the board.
- I'm bothered that this is an odd number.
- Wait, can I just check?
- Are these expressions the same? Anyone think no?
- I'm getting confused—we have too many examples up here.
- That's an interesting discovery: you can't have both of these at once, can you?
- I'm not convinced....
- Wait, you're going too fast for me.
- What's a way to be systematic in exploring this?
- Exactly. Give us the argument again—why?
- What stayed the same? What changed?
- Where did we start?
- What seems significant?
- How does this show our thinking?
- Can we generalize?
- How can we capture that thinking in writing?
- Can you come up and explain or walk through your thinking?
- Could we show it another way?

Starting a Math Club or Circle

by Maria Droujkova and Sue VanHattum

You've checked at *MathCircles.org* (hosted by the National Association of Math Circles), you've asked some homeschoolers, and you've investigated at the nearest hands-on science museum. There's no math excitement in your town or close by, and you want to start some.

If you're confident mathematically, the resources you've found throughout this book will be enough to get you started; deciding on content will be your toughest task. If you're less confident, you might want to try to join an adult math circle yourself first, or attend a training session. (Check *TheMathCircle.org* and *MathTeachersCircle.org* for trainings.)

Whatever your level, you'll want support. You can join an email group to ask questions (mathfuture@googlegroups.com might be a good start), and you may want to follow your favorite authors from this book as they blog about their math adventures. Any topic that strikes you as interesting can be researched endlessly online, of course.

Content Resources

Circle In a Box, by Sam Vandervelde, spells out all the details of how to organize and run a math circle. You can buy the book, or download the content for free from *MathCircles.org*, which also provides a collection of math circle videos. Sam makes the assumption that you'll want Ph.D.-level mathematicians, which isn't necessary. There are a lot of people with deep math backgrounds who don't hold Ph.D.'s. *Circle In a Box* has good problems and lots of good advice, but don't be afraid to do it differently.

Out of the Labyrinth: Setting Mathematics Free, by Robert and Ellen Kaplan, is inspiring. There is an extensive list of topics at the end.

Solve This: Math Activities for Students and Clubs by James Tanton. James says, "The activities contained in this book are immediate, catchy and fun, but upon investigation begin to unfold into surprising layers of depth and new perspectives. The necessary mathematics is explained fully along the way."

Moebius Noodles: Adventurous Math for the Playground Crowd, by Yelena McManaman, Maria Droujkova, and Ever Salazar colorfully describes activities that can be done with the very young.

Math from Three to Seven: The Story of a Mathematical Circle for Preschoolers, by Alexander Zvonkin, gives great ideas for circles with the youngest kids. This is part of the Mathematical Circles Library, which includes these other helpful titles: *Mathematical Circle Diaries, Year 1: Complete Curriculum for Grades 5 to 7*, by Anna Burago, *A Moscow Math Circle: Week-by-week Problem Sets*, by Sergey Dorichenko, and *A Decade of the Berkeley Math Circle: The American Experience, Volume I*, edited by Zvezdelina Stankova.

Websites

- Problems created for the Julia Robinson Mathematics Festival: *JuliaRobinsonMathFestival.org/problems.html*
- Rodi Steinig's blog: *TalkingStickLearningCenter.org/math-circle-blog*
- Ideas for the youngest kids: *MoebiusNoodles.com*

Details, Details

This is a quick guide to get you started. *Circle in a Box* also covers all these details and more.

Sign Up or Open Door?

Clubs that have an open-door policy have to plan meaningful activities for one-time attendees. They can have a larger community reach, but are limited in long-term projects and team building. Open-door clubs typically meet once a month, for a longer period of several hours, with multiple activities organized by several leaders, as well as snack and break time. If you choose to have people sign up, you can create a small, tight-knit group with constant membership, usually meeting weekly for shorter periods, that can engage in long-term projects.

Short-term Clubs

We encourage communities that don't have any math clubs at all to start with clubs designed to run for just a few weeks, whether as a mini–camp or as weekly short meetings. Such a club can read a math storybook together, start and finish a unit study, or have a few cycles of problem solving. If members find the experience meaningful, they can decide to continue.

Homes or Institutions?

Many math clubs meet in the living rooms of their organizers, especially if they are targeting a group of friends. This arrangement avoids room booking hassles, provides a relaxed, informal, grassroots atmosphere, saves the club leader travel time, and allows access to the kitchen and other home amenities. On the other hand, meeting on the campus of a famous university or cool software company supplies a certain glamor, gives access to that organization's administrative infrastructure, and can help with recruiting.

Day and Time of the Week

Most young kids do their best math work in the early morning hours. On the other hand, the majority of teens do best in the afternoons or evenings. Most homeschool math clubs meet on weekday mornings or early afternoons, since families can incorporate the club into their regular learning routines. Math clubs for pre-teens that go to school can meet on weekday afternoons or weekends. However, older teens frequently have responsibilities on weekdays. Club leaders can either choose the day and the time according to the audience they want to attract, or get people together first and work jointly on coordinating schedules—which could be the most demanding math problem the club will ever face!

"Snacks are very important for math club success because mathematics burns a lot of blood sugar, and sharing food helps build communities."

Honoring Our Bodies

Snacks are very important for math club success because mathematics burns a lot of blood sugar, and sharing food helps build communities. Fruits and nuts are the best math snacks. Kids typically get hungry after about half an hour of vigorous math activities. When children can fiddle around, clubs go much smoother. Provide modeling clay, small magnetic construction sets, paper for doodling, or wire cleaners to take care of "ants in the pants" and help kids focus on ideas, rather than trying to keep still. For their physical and mental health, kids need relatively frequent opportunities to move around, such as short whole body math games, like Human Knots or Live Mirrors,* that the group can play together every half an hour or so.

---

* Human Knot is described at: *wikihow.com/Play-the-Human-Knot-Game; Live Mirrors is described at moebiusnoodles.com/2011/11/symmetry-game-live-mirrors*

Or Something Else Entirely...

Brainstorm ideas with at least one other person who has committed to making this happen. If the suggestions here don't work for you, throw them out. If you can afford a trip to New York City for your research, visit the Museum of Mathematics. Check out the format of after-school and evening math festivals[*] to see if that's a better starting point. Dream up something new.

Whatever you decide to do, we wish you good luck and much success!

---

[*] Check out: *cmc-math.org/activities/math_festival.html and mathfair.com*

Conclusion

by Sue VanHattum

What conclusions have you come to as you've read through this book? My own conclusions concern parents, schools, and the learning process.

Advice for Parents

Whether you send your child to school, do school at home, or unschool, *you* are their most important role model. If you can enjoy math, that makes it much easier for them to enjoy it and get something valuable out of it. If you are at all uncomfortable with math, changing how you feel about it will make more difference to your child's math future than just about anything else you can do—much of the following advice is written with you in mind.

Make It Fun for Yourself

Start a parents and babies math club, and talk about math ideas while the kids play with blocks.* Write and illustrate math stories for the kids. Start while they're babies so you're not embarrassed about your own math skills. You'll be too tired to be embarrassed. Just go play. You can do it!

Start a math playgroup with other families; take turns leading it. Laugh together about the blind leading the blind. Get a copy of *Moebius Noodles*, by Yelena McManaman, Maria Droujkova, and Ever Salazar, to use as a guide, and follow them online (*MoebiusNoodles.com*) to find even more good ideas. You may also have noticed the wealth of links tucked into the footnotes here, which can start you on endless math journeys. Our website, *PlayingWithMath.org*, will have even more links.

Doing math in a group may seem impossible to you now. If it's too scary to work with other families, find a safer way to address your fears of math. There are lots of good books out there addressing this issue.

---

* Check out *BlockFest.org* for a block festival for kids eight months to eight years old.

Overcoming Math Anxiety, by Sheila Tobias, *Mind Over Math*, by Stanley Kogelman and Joseph Warren, and *Managing the Mean Math Blues*, by Cheryl Ooten, are three good ones. Keep a journal. Write about when math caused you grief. If you can remember back to when it was fun, you'll know you've made progress.

If you can't *do* math in a group, you may want to listen in as other parents discuss math online at the Living Math Forum (go to *groups.yahoo.com/group/LivingMathForum* to join). A daily dose of these conversations among people at all comfort levels, with no judging or shaming happening, may help you to move toward a happier relationship with math.

Learn More Math

If you keep learning, *on your own terms*, it will help you to enjoy math more. Your children will see that you value learning, and value math. You will be more able to offer your children insight.

What does learning math on your own terms mean? It may mean *not* taking a course. It may mean doing KenKen puzzles,[*] and trying to create your own. It may mean playing with origami, and finding out what that has to do with math. (Check out the amazing video, *Between the Folds*.[†]) It may mean approaching math through history. It may mean going back to the first math topic that you had real trouble with, and figuring out what you can do to relearn that material your way. It may mean following one math teacher blog, and trying things out when you're intrigued enough.

Waldorf schools expect their teachers to always be learning a new skill. My friend, Chris, was a Waldorf kindergarten teacher and chose to learn the cello. It wasn't easy for her, but that was ok. Learning something hard keeps us in touch with how hard the learning can be for our students, and how exhilarating it can be at the same time. This is the kind of hard work that feels great!

And learning math on your own will introduce you to the delights of math learned naturally. Wonder why. Play mathy games that get you thinking about "what if." Pursue only the problems you're interested in.

---

[*] KenKen is a number puzzle set in a square grid. In some ways like Sudoku, it uses arithmetic for its clues. Because the name KenKen is trademarked, it also goes by the name calcudoku. You can find daily KenKen puzzles in the New York Times at *nytimes.com/ref/crosswords/kenken.html* and find out more about its history and value at: *MathMamaWrites.blogspot.com/2013/08/kenken-simple-puzzle-that-goes-deep.html*

[†] *greenfusefilms.com*

Enjoy Your Child's Mathematical Discoveries

There are deep ideas even in very elementary math. Just as you thrilled to watch your child's first step (and each new increase in agility) and hear their first word (and each new increase in communication skill), so you can take delight in their mathematical discoveries if you realize how subtle they are. Is 3 + 11 the same as 11 + 3? It seems obvious to us, but it can be an exciting discovery for kids. If a child is at the "counting-on" stage, and has to add 11 more to 3, that's hard work, but counting on to add 3 to 11 is pretty simple. Once a child realizes those two procedures are always going to have the same result, and can therefore be seen as equivalent problems, that child suddenly has a powerful tool for simplifying their problems. And that's what mathematics is really about. Liping Ma's book, *Knowing and Understanding Elementary Mathematics*, is about the deeper understanding Chinese elementary teachers have of math (than do teachers in the U.S.). Whether or not you're interested in that topic, her examples will help you see the depth possible in thinking about arithmetic.

Don't rob your child of the benefits of exploration and discovery by too much explanation, too soon. If you tell them something is so, then they're likely to believe it. That gets in the way of deeper understanding. For example, place value is a complex idea that didn't take root in Europe until a few hundred years ago. As we saw in Pilar Bewley's Trust, Montessori Style chapter, adults are likely to think that the easiest way to multiply by ten is to put a zero at the end of your number. But if you tell a child that, you're hiding all the richness of place value and why this works. The more a child really sees it themselves, the deeper their real understanding of arithmetic will be.

"Measure. Count things out loud. Ask questions about odd and even numbers. Estimate. Wonder aloud. Express curiosity."

Provide a Rich Math Environment for Your Children

Blocks, LEGOs, Polydrons, pentominoes, dice, playing cards, board games ... It's all connected. Make up your own games with the dice or the cards. Explore your own questions with the Polydrons* or pentominoes. Measure. Count things out loud. Ask questions about odd and even numbers. Estimate. Wonder aloud. Express curiosity.

Find a math mentor, or many. Hang out with math lovers. They can be found in math clubs and circles, local universities, robotics clubs, engineering groups, programming communities, science and math Olympiad crowds, and online at blogs and email lists (Living Math Forum is a Yahoo group).

---

* Read Amanda Serenevy's chapter for more on Polydrons.

Good Questions May Not Get Answered Right Away

When you share a history lesson with your kids, you don't expect to know the answers to all their questions. It can be the same way in math. There is no need to have the answer before your student does. Shake out your anxiety and take a fresh look at math. Mathematicians expect to work for years on a good problem; if you take a few weeks, you'll know you're really dedicated.

It is natural for your child to get a superficial understanding of a concept the first time around, and then deepen their understanding gradually over time. If you like reading living math (stories with some math content), it's fine to read them before your child will understand the math. Some children will like a book like *The Man Who Counted*, by Malba Tahan, or *The Number Devil*, by Hans Enzensberger, long before the mathematics in it makes sense to them. As they hear or read the story again and again, the math will gradually take on more meaning. *The Cat In Numberland*, by Ivar Ekeland, is another great story whose mathematical meanings will develop new layers as your child gets older.

It's Okay Not to Write It Down

Mathematics is about thinking; some of that can happen through talking, drawing, and building, so it's okay to let go of written work. Maybe you'll jot down some notes about what your child is learning or take a few photos, but they don't always need to write to learn mathematical ideas. When the math is done on paper, you may want to use graph paper. It helps keep things neat, and it can be inspiring. James Tanton's love affair with math began with counting the square ceiling tiles in his bedroom; graph paper may offer a similar inspiration for your children.

"Your child's growth as a problem-solver is more important than the particular topics you cover."

Trust Yourself (and Your Kids)

Let go of curricula. If you need to start with a curriculum, for the structure and the ideas it gives you, that's fine. Just remember that you're in charge of the learning, and the curriculum is just your assistant. Your child's growth as a problem-solver is more important than the particular topics you cover.[*]

Don't let standards stress you—don't worry about whether the learning happens on the same schedule schools follow. As we saw in

---

[*] Jo Boaler's research, among others, indicate that growth as a problem solver can be more important—even for academic testing—than topic coverage.

Teach Less, Learn More, L.P. Benezet's experiment of waiting until fifth or sixth grade to offer formal arithmetic lessons was very successful.

Games Are to Math as Picture Books Are to Reading— A Delightful Starting Point

Let the kids play games (or make up their own games) instead of "doing math," and they might learn more math. From the book, Denise Gaskins' Math Card War is one place to start, and Pam Sorooshian's suggestion to always carry dice is easy to follow. Learn to play games: Blink, Set, Blokus, Katamino, Chess, Nim, Connect Four, Quarto... Change the rules. Decide which rules make the most interesting play.

Besides games, consider puzzles, cooking, building, science, programming, art, math stories, and math history for ways to bring meaningful math into your lives. Check out the *PlayingWithMath.org* website for lists of good games, puzzles, and toys. If you play around with all those, you can have a pretty math-rich life without ever having a formal math lesson.

Recommendations for Schools

How can schools incorporate the helpful practices discovered by math groups and homeschoolers? These recommendations might help you choose a school for your child, or they might help you advocate along with other parents at your local public school. Perhaps you are lucky enough to have the weighty responsibility of helping to design the programs at a school. Many of the suggestions below are policy recommendations that you can share with policymakers, or use in activist groups to change the schools. A few can be used by individual teachers.

Know Your Students

Part of homeschoolers' ability to work well with their children comes from the obvious advantage of knowing their students well. In Waldorf schools, students stay with the same teacher from first grade through eighth, and Montessori schools have multi-grade classrooms. The Montessori method would be easier for the public schools to implement. If children stayed in the same class for three years, the teacher would get to know them very well, and would benefit from an ongoing group, with fewer new students each year. This sort of transformation would change the nature of the classroom environment, making it much more familial.

"A more sensible assessment process would be based on teachers, as professionals, observing one another, and working together to improve classroom practices. That would also free up billions of dollars for classrooms."

Deborah Meier and others have proved that it's possible to reduce class size (to fifteen students) on a public school budget,[*] and have reaped the rewards of smaller, more intimate groups at their schools. All public schools could do this—if we took away the current expense of endless standardized testing. Public schools in the U.S. are currently spending on the order of $10,000 a year per student, a significant portion of which is going to standardized testing. A more sensible assessment process would be based on teachers, as professionals, observing one another, and working together to improve classroom practices. That would also free up billions of dollars for classrooms.

Include Activity-based Learning

At the elementary levels, math can be approached in so many ways: number talks, games, puzzles, cooking, sewing, construction projects, art, science, computer programming, history, and fun stories. If you think of math-time as a time to enjoy number, measurement, shape, and pattern, it's easy to see how fun it can be.

Students have different math instruction needs at different ages. Elementary students need less instruction and more time to play with mathematically-inspiring materials and questions. Conversations about mathematical topics can clarify their understandings dramatically. The teacher needs a deep understanding of how mathematical topics connect, and why things work the way they do, in order to facilitate these conversations well. Besides discovering the patterns of arithmetic, little kids can learn about infinity, geometry, probability, patterns, symmetry, tiling, map colorings, tangrams, and more. And they can do arithmetic in another base to play with the meaning of place value.

Schools have been pushing academics earlier and earlier. That's not a good idea. If young people learn to read when they're ready for it, they enjoy reading. They read more and more; they get better and better at it; reading serves them well. The same can happen with math. As we saw in Teach Less, Learn More, delaying conventional math instruction until the students were more ready—while still providing opportunities for math-rich exploration—helped both Benezet's and Greenberg's students to learn it more fully. On the other hand, eager students may be ready for more challenge, so math clubs are an important component of an excellent school math program.

Students in the middle-school years still need to play with ideas and math-rich materials. And they need experiences that push them to

---

[*] *The Power of Their Ideas* (1995)

really question their thinking. They also need teachers who can recognize what each student is missing, and what issues each student may have with math. Those who are really solid can explore many questions that do not require algebra, and can take an algebra course in eighth grade. There's no need to push conventional algebra courses any earlier than that, and even eighth grade may be earlier than is wise. (Algebraic thinking, however, can be encouraged at any age. See *Moebius Noodles* for more ideas about that.) Young people's minds are still developing the capacity for formal logical reasoning at this age, and if there is no penalty for doing algebra later (which there does not need to be), it can be valuable to have that added year of development first.

Even at high school level, Jo Boaler's work* has shown the benefits of mixed ability grouping. Students working together on complex problems learn more, and maintain more interest in math, than even students in high-level classes. And even at high-school level, activities can cement the learning. The Candy Launcher catapult activity has given many students a hold on quadratic functions they couldn't have achieved without it.

Math Teachers Must Know and Love Math

Anyone teaching math must enjoy it. Otherwise they will subtly teach their students to join them in not liking math. They also need to understand the math deeply, having questioned why things work the way they do, and seen how different topics connect. Arithmetic is deeper than most people realize.[†] If this requires specialist math teachers in the early grades, then let's do it![‡] Perhaps the classroom teacher can be assisted by a math specialist in Kindergarten through second or third grade, and math class can be conducted by a math specialist in upper elementary. Maybe we can change back after a generation of students has gone through math-friendly schooling. (Teachers: If you don't enjoy math, and you'd like to get over that, make sure to consider the advice for parents above.)

---

[*] *What's Math Got to Do With It?* gives compelling accounts of the excellent classrooms she researched.

[†] To understand the depth of arithmetic one way, read *Knowing and Teaching Elementary Mathematics*, by Liping Ma; for another take on it, play with the Deep Arithmetic puzzles on page 127.

[‡] This is meant for schools only. Homeschoolers have the advantage over classroom teachers of knowing their students intimately, and have more flexibility to change their program to meet their students' needs. Hopefully they also have the time and courage to learn more math.

Textbooks are unhelpful in the long run because most of them try to be too helpful, doing too much of the thinking and giving the student only simple exercises. The one doing the work is the one doing the learning, so give students math problems they really have to chew on. Beginning teachers may need textbooks, for the framework they provide and the activity ideas and developmental advice they can offer. But experienced teachers should look toward moving away from textbooks, both to push themselves to make their own framework for the learning they want to mentor, and so that they can turn that learning over to the students.

Value Concepts Over Procedures

Math is about concepts, connections, and patterns. Facts (like the times tables) and procedures (like long division) are a tiny portion of it, yet they have been given a primary role in elementary school mathematics. My favorite math education quote of all time comes from Marilyn Burns: "The secret key to mathematics is pattern." Mathematicians see our subject as a game, a language, an art form, and more. Everything is connected, often in surprising and beautiful ways.

Classrooms in many countries are way too focused on procedure in math. It's hard for any one teacher to break away from that, because the students come to expect it, and are likely to resist if asked to really think.* My experience has been that offering students something in return for that extra effort, like a more humane way to assess, helps them past that resistance.

Real mathematicians ask "why" and "what if." If you're trying to memorize it, you're probably being pushed to learn something that hasn't built up meaning for you. See Julie Brennan's article on Memorizing Math Facts.† Yes, eventually you want to have the times tables memorized, just like you want to know words by sight. But the path there can be full of delicious entertainment. Learn your multiplication facts as a meditation, as part of a game; see them as part of a connected web of ideas.

"Just like little kids, who ask 'why' a thousand times a day, mathematicians ask 'why.'"

Just like little kids, who ask "why" a thousand times a day, mathematicians ask "why": Why does dividing by a fraction make something bigger? Why are there only five Platonic (regular) solids? Why is the parallel postulate so much more complicated than the four postulates before it? Why does a quadratic ($y = x^2$), which gives a U-shaped parabola as

---

* See *The Teaching Gap*, by James Stigler.
† *LivingMath.net/Articles/MemorizingMathFacts*

its graph, have the same sort of U-shaped graph after you add a straight line equation ($y = 2x + 1$) to it? Why does the anti-derivative in calculus give you area? Mathematicians also ask "what if," with the most famous such question being: What would happen if we exchanged the parallel postulate for something different? The answer surprised them—whole new geometries were born of this question.

Forget the Grades

Grades are really destructive to learning, because they shift the focus from internal motivations to the external motivation of a good grade (or of avoiding a bad grade). Grades may be more destructive in math than in any other subject. People need to feel safe to take the risks that really learning math requires, and being graded makes it hard to feel safe. Grading also focuses students' (and often teachers') attention on particular content instead of on the underlying mathematical thinking skills, which are more important and require deeper intellectual engagement.

The ideal would be no grading, no worrying about when the kids can do a particular procedure. Just play with the ideas. Each teacher can keep a list of the things kids often learn in that age range, and can show parents which things on the list their child has achieved. Portfolios are a way to share what the child is doing without grading.*

In high-school courses, students can be told at the beginning the skills that must be mastered to pass the class. They can keep track, along with the teacher, of what skills they've mastered. They pass when they've mastered all the skills. Still no letter grade, just a pass, or not–yet–passed.

This is the sort of systemic policy change that parent activists and school founders will have to champion. Individual teachers can't throw out grading on their own. (Like other teachers, I am required to give grades in the college courses I teach. So I allow students to take quizzes and tests over with new versions, until they've earned a grade they're satisfied with. That helps, but it's still not enough.) What do you think is the best way to make your classroom a safe place for the risk-taking that goes with real learning?

---

* Deborah Meier's book, *The Power of Their Ideas*, gives evidence for this also. Their students were not graded, had to complete portfolios to graduate, and had much higher college entrance rates than the city at large.

Observations on Learning

During the five years in which I worked on this book, I learned tremendous amounts about math, teaching, learning, writing, and editing. I'm just scratching the surface here with the ideas most related to playing with math.

Build Your Own Understanding

> *What you have been obliged to discover by yourself leaves a path in your mind which you can use again when the need arises.*
>
> —G. C. Lichtenberg*

I first played with Pythagorean triples at the Math Circle Teacher Training Institute in the summer of 2009. I wanted to explore these ideas on my own during December of that year, but couldn't remember how we had proceeded. So I went in my own direction with it. I came up with a process different than the one we followed together during our math circle, and can see every step of my own process in my mind's eye now. I'm still hoping to get a deeper understanding of the more conventional path through this topic, because I think the connections I make will enrich my understanding.

This experience drives home for me how important it is to build your own understanding. No matter how well a topic is *explained*, our understanding is shallow until we've built it up on our own. I knew this in my head, but now I know it more deeply. That still hasn't stopped me from searching for great explanations to use in class. But now I'm trying, harder than ever, to get students to take on the task of building their own understanding.

Here's another pedagogical aspect of my experience with this problem: Algebra hides a key part of the work involved in thinking something through. Algebra distills a problem down to the most essential connections; getting from a problem to an equation is the hard part, and the equation leaves no trace of that work. I can "see" an equation in my mind, once I've worked it out myself a few times. And yet, reading someone else's equations is very slow going for me. In an equation I've worked out myself, I can see how I got there and what I want to do next, as clearly as I see the equation. In the unfamiliar equation, I have to keep reminding myself what I'm trying to do, and what the

---

* Found on the website for the Kaplan's math circles: *TheMathCircle.org*

equation represents.* This relates to a powerful aspect of mathematics—once you've really learned something, it becomes very compressed. But communication can be a struggle if the person explaining their thoughts doesn't understand this dynamic.

I balk at reading unfamiliar equations, and am usually significantly more comfortable reading a verbal explanation of a problem. It's good to remember this when I work with my students—that my brain sees each equation I put on the board as an old friend, while my students' brains are screaming at the alienness of it, along with just not having any familiarity with what it *means*.

The joy of math has just washed over me these past few years. I can pick any problem I want to do, and leave the rest alone with no guilt. There is absolutely no pressure, no obligation, no "should." It's all about interest and fun. And I've learned so much. But learning math is funny—once you really understand something, it's hard to imagine not having known it forever. I put a lot of work into figuring out those Pythagorean triples, but now it seems so easy. ("It's just a simple relationship, really…" she says with a shrug.)

I think I've dramatically improved my three-dimensional visual understanding of shapes by playing with the Polydrons that I bought for my math salon. I've built the five Platonic solids, including a stellated version of the dodecahedron. I've wondered whether I could alternate colors in a symmetric way, and wondered how I might represent a problem like that to think about it on paper. I'm weaker in geometry than in other areas of math, but it's such a fun playground to visit.

Like Jazz, Excellent Instruction Requires Improvisation

During my sabbatical year I got to play with pedagogy, working as teacher or mentor in many different arenas: math classes for young kids at a free school (kids do what they want most of the day), math circles in a few different venues, tutoring two very enthusiastic youngsters, and running my own Richmond Math Salon. Any time I was in front of a group, I reverted to my classroom persona, and wanted to explain. But when I was working one-on-one I was able to let the questions and directions come from the student, and felt my powers of improvisation growing as I nudged my students subtly toward fruitful explorations of their own interests. And when I set up my home to be a celebration of

---

* This particular difficulty is not true of everyone. Some people are more skilled at holding different levels of thought in their head all at once.

mathematics for all ages, it was pretty easy to do the same thing with a dozen or more people at once.

Now I'm more and more often able to find ways to bring the symbiotic energy of a good mathematical conversation into my classrooms. Each class is different, each student's perspective calls me to a new way of connecting a person with the ideas I love, and that is what makes teaching an art form. It is teaching the particular students sitting there in front of you that inspires and requires the improvisation and variation.

We Need Both Autonomy and Guidance

"Building our own understanding requires autonomy, and that requires a guidance both subtle and improvised to fit the moment."

Building our own understanding requires autonomy, and that requires a guidance both subtle and improvised to fit the moment. I have learned how valuable that special kind of guidance is, both to me and to the boy I tutored for three and a half years, from beginning algebra through calculus and number theory.

It is hard to figure out how to provide both autonomy and guidance to kids in school. I used to be focused solely on the autonomy side of this equation, but I see now that kids can get bored if they're at a school and there's no direction. At home, the parent can guide so subtly that autonomy is preserved, but is that possible in a school? Montessori schools guide by the presence of materials that work as thinking tools and call out to the kids to be explored. The less-well-known Reggio Emilia schools highly value children's autonomy, and also provide guidance through a rich environment. You can get a vivid picture of both approaches from Rebeca Wild's book, *Raising Curious, Creative, Confident Kids: The Pestalozzi Experiment in Child-based Education*, which describes her journey to creating an amazing school in Ecuador.

My full-time work is teaching math in a community college. Most of my students will still come to me hating math. I will still have to record grades for them. I will still have to teach a particular set of topics, instead of having the liberty to let students just explore the beauty of math. I will still be teaching classes that students are required to take in order to transfer to a four-year college. I still don't have a perfect way to get them to move past memorizing. But I'm changing the way I grade and getting away from my former dependence on the textbook. I'm creating a richer environment where, over time, more students will decide they want to really "get it." I am happier in my work than I've ever been before.

I hope this book has helped you see your way to a more fulfilling relationship with math. My dream is a world where no one hates math, where people are comfortable using math as citizens and consumers—knowing how to question the numbers and logic in science, statistics, and financial matters—and where people enjoy the hard fun of math. What math delights will you create? I'd love for you to join the conversations at *PlayingWithMath.org*. Hope to see you there.

Resources

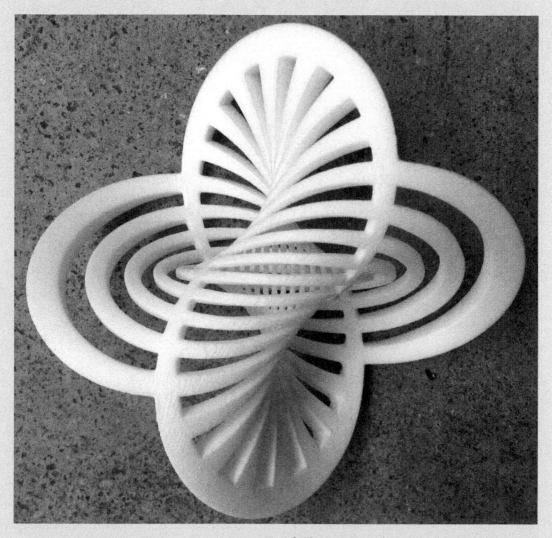

Hopf Fibrations, sculpture by Henry Segerman

This is a sculpture by Henry Segerman based on the Hopf fibration, which is a way in which a sphere in four-dimensional space can be decomposed into circles. It is made using a 3D printer. You can see more of his artwork at *shapeways.com/shops/henryseg*, and a mathematical explanation of this piece and others at *archive.bridgesmathart.org/2012/bridges2012-103.html*. Henry is a professor of mathematics at Oklahoma State University.

Sue's Book Picks

Reading about math was not like this when I was young. From board books to adult fiction, from number pairs to infinity and surreal numbers—there is so much to read, and it's so fun! The list here is very select—I fell in love with each of these books when I discovered it. Julie Brennan and Cindy Chupp have more comprehensive lists at *LivingMath.net* (reader lists tab) and *love2learn2day.blogspot.com* (Math in Children's Literature tab), respectively, both of which are helpfully sorted by topic. I also review my favorite new books on my blog (*MathMamaWrites.blogspot.com*). If there's a book you love, and it's not on this list, please tell us all about it at *PlayingWithMath.org/goodbooks*.

Some of the books included below are biographies of mathematicians, or stories about people interested in math. Although there's not really any math in some of those, they can inspire more interest in math. This guide is divided into four sections—picture books, middle years, older kids and adults, and math education books. The age ranges for the picture books are just my best guess.

Picture Books

The Opposites, by Monique Felix (ages 2 to 6)

One of the earliest math skills, more basic perhaps than counting, is noticing attributes. This book has no words, and yet it tells dozens of stories, each about opposites. Noticing the one attribute that shows opposites in each detail-filled picture is a math game your child will want to play again and again.

Quack and Count, by Keith Baker (ages 2 to 7)

This is a board book—good for the youngest child who will sit and listen to a story. It stays good because it's so luscious—great illustrations, fun rhythm and rhyme, cute story, and good mathematics. Seven ducklings are enjoying themselves in every combination. "Slipping, sliding, having fun, 7 ducklings, 6 plus 1." (And then 5 plus 2, etc.) It would be great to have a book like this showing all the number pairs that make eight, and another for nine, etc. If I ever get to teach math for elementary teachers again, I'd love to get my students to make books like this one.

Anno's Counting House, by Mitsumasa Anno (ages 2 to 7)

Everything I've seen by Mitsumasa Anno is delightful. There is so much to see in his books, many of which have no words. In this book, ten people are moving from one house to another. In each two-page spread you can see one more person who's moved from the left house to the right, along with lots of furniture and other small items. For slightly-older kids, there is *Anno's Mysterious Multiplying Jar*, showing us one island with two counties, which have three mountains each, and so on, until we get to ten jars within each box—a lovely, very visual representation of factorials. In *Anno's Magic Seeds*, the story does need words—we learn of a plant whose seed, when baked, will keep you from being hungry for a full year. The plant grows only two seeds in a year, one of which must be used to grow a new plant. The story explores the conflict this causes. You may also enjoy *Anno's Math Games*. Anno has written over forty books, most available in English.

Two of Everything, by Lily Toy Hong (ages 3 to 7)

A poor old farming couple in China find a mysterious pot. When a hairpin drops in, they scoop two out. The math isn't discussed in the story, but it's pretty easy to add your own thoughts to this delightful tale of doubling.

How Hungry Are You?, by Donna Jo Napoli and Richard Tchen (ages 3 to 12)

There are lots of great of great books on sharing equally. My favorite used to be *The Doorbell Rang*, by Pat Hutchins, but this one is even more delightful. The picnic starts with just two friends; Rabbit is bringing twelve sandwiches and Frog is bringing the bug juice. Monkey wants to come: "My mom just made cookies. I could take a dozen." They figure out how much of each goody each friend will get. In the end, there are thirteen friends at the picnic, and the sharing becomes more complicated. One of the delights of this book is the use of little icons showing who's talking. It would make for a good impromptu play.

I Love Math!, a series by Time-Life (ages 4 to 12)

My son loves these. Each book has a wide variety of stories (fiction and non-fiction), puzzles, games, and more. It's like a very cool math magazine, but hardcover. Titles include our favorites, *Right in Your Own Backyard: Nature Math* and *The Case of the Missing Zebra Stripes: Zoo Math*, along with ten others.

One Grain of Rice, by Demi (ages 5 to 12)

The greedy raja is gently outsmarted by a wise village girl named Rani. This is a very sweet take on the story of grains of rice put on a chessboard. (One grain on the first square, two on the next, then 4, 8, 16, …, until the board is filled. How much rice is that, anyway?)

The Cat in Numberland, by Ivar Ekeland (ages 5 to adult)

The story starts when Zero knocks on the door of the Hotel Infinity. He'd like a room, but they're all full (with the number One in Room One, and so on). It turns out that's no problem—the Hilberts and their number guests are able to make room for zero. The cat who lives in the lobby gets confused—if the hotel is full, how can the numbers make room for Zero just by all moving up one room? Things get worse when the fractions come to visit. This story is charming enough to entertain young children, and deep enough to intrigue anyone. Are you ready to learn about infinity with your five-year-old?

"This story is charming enough to entertain young children, and deep enough to intrigue anyone. Are you ready to learn about infinity with your five-year-old?"

You Can Count on Monsters, by Richard Evan Schwartz (any age)

Each number from one to one hundred is a monster, and each one gets its picture on its own page. All of the numbers (except poor one) are made up from their prime parts. The pictures are amusing, colorful, and packed with intriguing details. The pages in the front and back that explain prime factorization are unassuming, waiting for the reader to decide it's time to find out more. This and *Powers of Ten* would both make great coffee table books, to peruse over and over.

Middle Years

Math for Smarty Pants and *The I Hate Mathematics! Book*, by Marilyn Burns

Full of experiments and puzzles, these two books are part of the Brown Paper Schoolbook series, meant for kids to have fun learning academic subjects on their own.

The Number Devil, by Hans Magnus Enzensberger

The Number Devil visits Robert in his dreams, and gets him thinking about the strangest things! Rutabaga numbers and prima donnas (roots and primes) are just the beginning. Anyone who'd like a gentle introduction to lots of interesting math topics will enjoy this one.

Hannah, Divided, by Adele Griffin

Hannah has a special gift for numbers. This sweet, simple story, set in the 1930's, shows us the world from the point of view of a girl whose eccentricities aren't noticed much, until she goes to the big city to learn more math.

Carry On, Mr. Bowditch, by Jean Lee Latham

This is a fictionalized account of the life of Nathaniel Bowditch, who loved math but had to leave school when his family needed his help. He was indentured to a ship chandlery for nine years. Although that dashed his hopes of someday going to Harvard to study math, it was the right place to learn the mathematics behind navigation. When he finally went to sea, he invented a new way to "do a lunar," and spent endless hours correcting errors in the tables used for navigation. Bowditch's book, *American Practical Navigator*, first published in 1902, is still regularly updated, and is carried on U.S. naval vessels to this day.

Powers of Ten, by Philip and Phylis Morrison

The first photo shows a couple having a picnic. It's shot from one meter above them. The next is from 10 meters, then 100. After we've traveled to the edge of the universe, we come back to the couple and zoom in, down past the sizes of atoms and electrons. Each page has one large photo, and explanatory text about what can be seen at that level.

How to Count Like a Martian, by Glory St. John

A really good way to understand place value is to work with other number bases. This is a detective story in which the history of other number systems plays a starring role. "Out of the depths of the dark and starry night come the first of the faint and mysterious sounds." You have just received a message from Mars. The one kind of language that both Martians and Earthlings would understand is numbers. And so you research the number systems that have been used on Earth, hoping that will help you decipher this message. The book proceeds to explain eight different counting systems, including the abacus and the binary numbers of computers. In the process, the concepts of place value (she just calls it place), base, and zero are explored. By the end of the book, you can see that the beeps and bee-beeps of the message you received are just the counting numbers, Martian style.

The Man Who Counted, by Malba Tahan

Written in Brazil, set in the Middle East, these stories follow the adventures of Beremiz, an accomplished mathematical problem-solver. He uses math to settle disputes, solve riddles and mysteries, and entertain his hosts. I loved how it felt like a mathematical version of *Arabian Nights*.

Math Without Words, by James Tanton

All ages will enjoy the puzzles in this book, which include illustrations of negative numbers, algebra, and more.

Older Kids & Adults

Uncle Petros and Goldbach's Conjecture, by Apostolos Doxiadis

Uncle Petros is a recluse. Our hero, his nephew, is trying to discover his secrets. It seems he was close to proving Goldbach's conjecture, that every even number greater than 2 is the sum of two prime numbers. There is just a tiny bit of math in this, but lots of (slightly twisted) history of math. (Some mature content.)

Journey Through Genius: The Great Theorems of Mathematics, by William Dunham

Each chapter is about both the theorem and the mathematicians who proved it. There is a great chapter on the history behind finding a formula to solve cubic equations, which led to the creation of complex numbers.

In Code, by Sarah Flannery

Sarah Flannery is the daughter of a mathematician. Because she had an interest in math and science, her teacher encouraged her to enter the

Young Scientist Exhibition—a nation-wide competition in Ireland. Her father suggested doing a cryptography project, and she took off with it. After winning the competition in Ireland, she went on to win the corresponding all-Europe competition. She explains her interest in mathematics—with a chalkboard in the kitchen and puzzle discussions over dinner, it came naturally—and the details of her cryptography project.

Mathematical Carnival, by Martin Gardner

There are nineteen short chapters, each from nine to twenty-one pages long. The one on sizes of infinity, a topic I thought I knew well, had a surprising question I hadn't previously thought about. This is one of dozens of puzzle books put together by a master. Check out any of his books to discover a wealth of math and logic puzzles.

Mathematics: A Human Endeavor, by Harold Jacobs

This one is a textbook, and it's delightful. The first chapter, on inductive and deductive reasoning, uses pool tables to get the reader thinking about patterns. Chapters on sequences, graphing, large numbers, symmetry, mathematical curves, counting (permutations and combinations), probability, statistics, and topology round out an introduction to a wide variety of math topics, accessible before algebra.

The Man Who Knew Infinity: A Life of the Genius Ramanujan, by Robert Kanigel

Ramanujan's story would be unbelievable if it were fiction or even slightly fictionalized. Ramanujan was too focused on his own mathematical work to do well in school—he was kicked out of college when he failed exams in his other subjects. It took him years of supporting himself working as a clerk before he managed to catch the attention of a famous mathematician in England, G.H. Hardy, whose interest in him suddenly changed his life. A year later he would sail to England to begin with Hardy the work of making his mathematical results comprehensible to others.

Chances Are: Adventures in Probability, by Michael and Ellen Kaplan

History, philosophy, science, and statistics all come together in this delightful exploration of probability.

Surreal Numbers, by Donald Knuth (requires well-developed math skills)

This book requires lots of work doing the math, and what fun work it can be! Alice and Bill are enjoying their extended vacation on an isolated tropical beach, but are getting a bit bored, when they discover a rock with two "rules" on it. Conway has invented a strange number system through these two rules, and Alice and Bill (along with the reader) are sucked in, trying to figure out how it all works. This is higher math.

Measurement, by Paul Lockhart

Paul Lockhart knows that the joy of math comes from figuring things out for ourselves, so he shows us some of his favorite problems and asks us if we'd like to solve them. (He gives lots of hints, strategies, and techniques, and few answers.) But he went beyond a mere compendium of puzzles, and connected the problems he shows, taking his readers on a delightful journey though size and shape (part one) and time and space (part two). This book is a delight, even if you're not feeling up to solving many of the puzzles. But the more often you put down the book and pick up your pen or pencil and paper, the more fun you'll have.

"The more often you put down the book and pick up your pen or pencil and paper, the more fun you'll have."

Mathsemantics, by Edward MacNeal

This book has one great chapter on estimation that's worth getting the whole book. He talks about having a semantic web in your head that includes a few important numbers, like: the radius of the earth and the populations of the earth, your country, your state, and one very large city. He recommends using these as a basis to estimate often, committing to your estimates somehow, and then finding out the real values of what you estimate. For example, estimate your arrival time when you're in the car, tell the person next to you, and notice the time when you do arrive at your destination. You'll see yourself getting better and better at estimation, along with strengthening your number sense.

Euclid in the Rainforest, by Joseph Mazur

Logic, infinity, and probability are the topics. Adventures in Venezuela, Greece, and New York furnish the background. Mazur has wide-ranging interests, and skillfully brings the math to life.

The World of Mathematics, by James Newman

This four-volume set is a mathematical encyclopedia—perfect for browsing. The articles are approachable and intriguing. My favorite so far is On Being the Right Size, by J.B.S. Haldane (now available online), in which the author explains why giant insects are not possible (at least on Earth), nor people-shaped giants. Why? Because surface area grows as the square of height while volume grows as the cube of height, and systems get out of balance when the ratio of surface area to volume changes dramatically.

How to Solve It, by George Polya

Written in 1945, this book is so good that most math textbooks that discuss problem solving just paraphrase Polya. It has a great summary in front, but the organization of the rest of the book is rather strange—it's alphabetical by the first word of the idea being discussed.

What Is the Name of this Book?, by Raymond Smullyan

Knaves always lie and Knights always tell the truth. Puzzle number 29: *A says, "Either I am a Knave or B is a Knight." What are A and B?* This mysteriously-named book has 271 twisted logic puzzles.

The Joy of X: A Guided Tour of Math, from One to Infinity, by Steven Strogatz

He's not talking down to the reader, and yet this mathematician makes it all clear, from numbers to topology and calculus. He started out writing columns on math in the *New York Times*, and that morphed into this delightful book with thirty short chapters that can each be read independently.

Who Is Fourier?, by Transnational College of LEX

Fourier Series are used to describe sound. Usually an advanced college topic, they are explained in unique, easy-to-understand ways in this charming book, accessible to anyone who has a basic understanding of algebra.

Math Girls and Math Girls 2, by Hiroshi Yuki

The unnamed protagonist is a boy in high school who loves math. He helps Tetra with her math, and is challenged by the problems Miruka poses. In *Math Girls 2*, a few more girls join the gang. The math is challenging in these books, and the storyline makes it all the more fun.

The Art and Craft of Problem-Solving, by Paul Zeitz

How do you go about solving challenging problems? Zeitz discusses tools, tactics, and strategies, and offers a rich storehouse of very challenging problems.

Math Education

Little Kids—Powerful Problem Solvers: Math Stories from a Kindergarten Classroom, **by Angela Andrews and Paul Trafton**

One story for each of the ten months of the school year, from a kindergarten classroom. Here's some of the deep mathematical thinking that young children can do.

The Art of Problem Posing, **by Stephen Brown**

This is a helpful book for rethinking how to approach learning math. The math is at about high-school level.

Math: Facing An American Phobia, **by Marilyn Burns**

I have recommended this book for math-anxious students. What I remember best is her conversation on an airplane with an engineer who adamantly opposed kids using calculators in school. She explained to him how they can be used to explore topics the kids wouldn't be ready for otherwise.

Talking Mathematics: Supporting Children's Voices, **by Rebecca Corwin**

It takes some real skill to get students talking about their mathematical thinking. Watching experts lead the process has helped me move along this path. I think maybe I should read this book every few years, even though I teach college and this is about elementary math classrooms.

Show and Tell, **by Linda Dacy and Rebeka Eston**

Another good book about communicating mathematical thinking in the classroom, this one is focused on Kindergarten to second grade.

Let's Play Math: How Homeschooling Families Can Learn Math Together, and Enjoy It, **by Denise Gaskins**

This is currently an ebook-only edition. I hope her paper edition comes out soon—I don't know how to highlight e-books, and I want to be able to highlight so many things in this great book. Denise tells stories from her years of homeschooling, debunks the many destructive myths about math, helps you learn more about what math really is, and shows you how to do it. She includes problems invented by kids, problems she made up, and classics from mathematical history.

Out of the Labyrinth: Setting Mathematics Free, by Robert and Ellen Kaplan

This is the book that started it all for me. I learned about math circles, fell in love with the Kaplans' sensibilities, and found out how to get involved—participating in math circles, then leading them. They describe circles with young kids. They dispel the myth of talent, convincingly arguing that math is for everyone. And they tell wonderful stories of many people doing lots of challenging mathematics.

Math Power: How to Help Your Child Love Math, Even If You Don't, by Patricia Kenschaft

Recommended for homeschoolers (and other parents) who want to get a better feel for what their children's paths through elementary math education might look like.

Knowing and Teaching Elementary Mathematics, by Liping Ma

Ma changed how we discuss the math needed to teach elementary students. She coined the phrase "profound understanding of fundamental mathematics." In this book she compares the preparation and knowledge of Chinese and U.S. teachers. The Chinese teachers start out with a better grounding in the basics, and then are able to use daily time to work together deepening their understanding even more.

Radical Equations: Civil Rights from Mississippi to the Algebra Project, by Robert Moses and Charles Cobbs

Robert Moses was a civil rights activist in the sixties. When his children were reaching high school age, he realized the schools needed some help providing a math program that would draw students in, and connect with their real-world experiences. He created The Algebra Project, aimed at African-American high school students, as a civil rights organization. This book describes his journey.

Moebius Noodles: Adventurous Math for the Playground Crowd, by Yelena McManaman, Maria Droujkova, and Ever Salazar

I love this book. It came out after my son was past the best age for it, but I hope to share it with friends with babies for a long time to come. Full of playful math activities for babies, toddlers, and big kids, it helps you to provide a rich math environment for your children. [Disclaimer: We share publisher, illustrator, and one author. Lucky us.]

Mindstorms: Children, Computers, and Powerful Ideas, by Seymour Papert

Children can learn to use computers in a masterful way, and learning to use computers can change the way they learn everything else.

How to Enjoy Mathematics With Your Child, by Nancy Rosenberg

The chapters include The Shapes of Numbers, Number Bases and the Game of Nim, Flexagons, Probability and Pascal's Triangle, and A New Approach to Geometry.

Vision in Elementary Mathematics, by W.W. Sawyer

Written in 1964, this book is a delightful reminder that wisdom about how to teach math with meaning is not new. Sawyer suggests starting algebra with problems that involve two variables. These can show the power of algebra, while still being simple problems. This is just one example of his clarity about pedagogy. I may end up reading this book every year before starting classes. Also worth reading are his books *Mathematician's Delight* and *Prelude to Mathematics.*

What's Happening in Math Class? Volumes One and Two, by Deborah Schifter

These books introduced me to good questioning as a method of teaching mathematics. Almost every one of the teacher chapters in these books includes lots of dialogue, both between students and between teacher and students. Between the two volumes, twenty-two teachers tell their stories of working to change their classrooms, and of lessons that engaged their students. Reading these books, like reading teacher blogs, reminds me that the teacher is always learning in a good classroom, right alongside the students. Volume one focuses on what a good mathematics classroom might look like, and volume two focuses more on the struggle the teachers went through as they attempted to change the way they taught.

"Reading these books, like reading teacher blogs, reminds me that the teacher is always learning in a good classroom, right alongside the students."

The Book of Learning and Forgetting, by Frank Smith

Although this book is not about math, the author's insights about learning are very useful for anyone trying to re-conceptualize education, including those of us who would like to help others learn math. Easy to read and thought-provoking.

Math From Three to Seven: The Story of a Mathematical Circle for Preschoolers, by Alexander Zvonkin

Zvonkin conducted a math circle for his pre-school-age kids and some of their friends, and documents his successes and failures with them. He had lots of great ideas for getting very young children to think about deep math. This book is part of the Math Circles Library series, published by the American Mathematical Society in conjunction with the Mathematical Sciences Research Institute.

Hints for Puzzles

by Sue VanHattum

Full solutions are available online at *PlayingWithMath.org/solutions*. (If you can stand the suspense, we advise against looking up answers. The fun comes from the struggle.)

Page 9, Regions in a Circle (from the Introduction)

Play with it first, by drawing circles with 3, 4, 5, and 6 points. Is the number of regions for 6 points surprising? It was to me. You might want to get data for 7 and 8 points. It won't have any obvious patterns, though. What makes new regions form?

   Thinking about that may move you toward a solution. If not, you can try figuring out how many regions get added by each new point. Those numbers are called first differences. The differences between those are second differences. When you find a pattern, you might try to build an equation, but it will be ugly. Go back now to that question about what makes new regions form.

Page 21, Mirror Symmetry

From the footnote on page xxx, "If you don't see what the next shape would be, cover the left half of each shape with your finger, and draw each right half on a piece of paper." If that's not enough, maybe it would help to know that what you just drew are four very common symbols.

Page 25, Imbalance Abundance

Number 2 has three inequalities: the left-hand side, the right-hand side, and the whole thing, reasoning from the upper balance point. In number 4, I got stuck at something that now seems obvious. If the square is heavier than two circles (let's write that as $s>2c$), then it's certainly heavier than one circle. We can always subtract s (or c or t) from both sides of an inequality. Knowing that, and using algebraic notation (things like $s>2c$) will help on some of the problems. On number 12, I needed a hint from the author: "Looking at the lone circle, it hangs down, so a circle must have positive weight."

Page 38, Crossing the River #1

What can stay alone? Leave them and move the others.

Page 38, Crossing the River #2

Since taking an adult or one child across first would do no good (they'd just have to come back), you know the first crossing must be the two kids. Then one kid can bring the boat back. What can you do next? Each step of the way, try things, and see if they get you to a new situation. Once you've gotten one adult across, can you repeat what you did?

Page 44, Foxes and Rabbits

Since the numbers are small, drawing a picture might help. Show the fox who's looking. And show what the fox sees. One of the rabbits seen is also looking; what does the rabbit see?

Page 50, Is This for Real?

Imagine picking this up and pushing the front half down on the left (straightening the cut that goes partway through the middle of the paper) and the back half down on the right (again straightening the cut that goes partway through the middle of the paper, so those two edges will be aligned). Now figure out where the cuts are, and cut your paper the same way.

Page 62, Egyptian Farm Puzzle

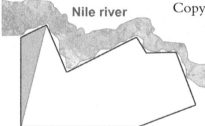

Nile river

Copy the drawing, and make a paper measuring device with 100 units equal to the length of the upper left line. Now draw six lines inside, so there are seven triangles. One way to start is shown to the right. (There are many ways to triangulate, which will all give the same final area.) Now, for each triangle, measure the length of one side (base), and from that use a perpendicular line to the opposite vertex to measure the height. (Or do it the way I did, and use Geogebra to draw in lines and calculate areas.)

Page 74, Vertices, Edges, and Faces

There is a simple equation relating the number of vertices, edges, and faces. Try various combinations of adding and subtracting until one stays constant.

There are five Platonic solids. Can you find a reason why there cannot be any more? How many faces for each one?

Page 81, Honeybee (#1)

Put a number in each cell that describes how many ways to get that far. There is only one way to get to the first cell in the bottom row, so put a 1 there. The first cell after the B in the top row can be arrived at two ways—directly from B, and also from the bottom row, so put a 2 there. How many ways are there to get to the next two cells?

Page 81, Ones and Twos (#2)

First figure out how many ways to get 2.

Page 82, Abeeba (#3)

First figure out how many two-letter words there are, and how many of those end in A. From there, figure out how many three-letter words there are, and how many of those end in A. You may begin to see a pattern.

Page 84, Math Without Words #1

Color in the pieces that you're trying to imagine laying out straight (as if they were string, tied in a loop or not).

Page 89, Math Without Words #2

Can you see a way to organize the 8 different layouts, so they somehow go with what's come before? If you want to cover 5 squares with blocks of width one and two, then the last block is either one or two. If it's one, what comes before it covers four blocks. If it's two, what comes before it covers three blocks.

Page 96, Food for Thought

Algebra will be our superhero here. We're tying to figure out the sum of four numbers. Let's call the numbers A, B, C and D. What have the cows said about the numbers? Can we write that with our variables? (Warning: The phrase, "how big," is sneaky here.)

Page 99, Saint Mary's Math Contest Sampler

- Start with just two colors, and begin a list. What do you notice? I notice that each letter has two possibilities.
- What will the value of an odd digit in the sevens place be? Make a few examples for yourself, and look for patterns.
- How do we find the 100th term in the sequence? Do you know how to add all the numbers from 1 to that number? Can you add pairs of numbers together to get a sum that's always the

same? Once you have that sum, you can subtract the sum of
3 + 6 + ... + last left out number.

* Make a table: first column, numbers 1 to 13; second column,
  their cubes; third column, the running sum. You may notice a
  pattern in this column.

* This one just takes lots of play, experimentation, and persistence.

Page 100, The Candy Conundrum

2. You can have anywhere from 0 to 5 red, along with anywhere from 0
to 4 green, except we don't count it when we have none (0 red, 0 green).

Warning: The higher numbered problems are meant to be hard.
The organizers of the Julia Robinson Mathematics Festival wanted some
questions in each set to be easy enough for everyone, and a few to be
hard enough to be worthy of mathematical research.

Page 127, Deep Arithmetic—Getting to One

To find short and long sequences, use a spreadsheet. Check out 1 to 5
with the new rule to discover some interesting new patterns.

Page 128, Deep Arithmetic—Number Squares

There *are* combinations that will make more than 7 rows, but they may
be hard to find.

Page 155, Self-Referential Puzzle

I think this is the hardest puzzle in the book. It seems impossible at first,
but the bottom row is tangled together in ways we can untangle. How
many times can a particular number appear in the puzzle? This limits the
answers for many of the clues. Clue N is a good place to start.

Page 166, Vedic multiplication...

Use variables instead of 8 and 7. Describe the steps with your variables.

Page 167, To divide by 5...

What does moving the decimal do? What is the effect of doing both that
and doubling?

Page 172, Magic Hexagon

What number does each row and diagonal add up to? To find that we'll
need to know the total for the sum of 1 to 19. (That has come up in
lots of these puzzles!) You can make number pairs all the same to find it:
1 + 19, 2 + 18... Once you know the sum, just keep finding rows and
diagonals that have just one open space.

Page 210, Measuring with Paper

Folding in half divides a measurement by two. What does folding top to side edge do?

Page 223, Alien Math

These seem to be some sort of basic arithmetic problems. How many different digits do you see? It might help to make a list of them.

Page 241, Dartboard Problem (from Putting Myself In My Students' Shoes)

The board has lots of symmetry. How can we take advantage of it? Closer means we're measuring distance. As soon as I start thinking about distances, I want to put in coordinates. (If you find a solution that doesn't use coordinates, please let me know!)

Page 244, What Number Am I?

Experiment. Do any of the clues lead to a contradiction? If you check out the implications of clue 1a, you will get some useful information. Which other clues will this work with? More hints at *jd2718.wordpress.com/2009/11/28/puzzle-who-am-i/*

Page 247, Octopus Logic

Start with one hypothesis, and see if it leads to a contradiction.

Page 251, Coloring Cubes

Where are the ones painted on three sides? …two sides? …one side? …no sides?

Page 264, A Little Math Magic

If you want to *understand* Jonathan's trick, there are three steps:

* figure out the trick (try using a spreadsheet to figure out the results and then to work backward),
* prove Fermat's Little Theorem (a good explanation is at *YouTube.com/watch?v=w0ZQvZLx2KA*), and
* then figure out how the theorem predicts the trick (which uses the fact that $a^4 \equiv 1 \pmod 5$ for all numbers except multiples of 5).

Page 280, Personal Ad for 21

Fibonacci numbers may be the easiest to find. List the two-digit ones, and then see which fit the other criteria.

Meet the Authors and Artists

We are a community of over fifty authors, puzzle- and game-makers, artists, and editors. Just reading our short biographies will give you some idea of the vast diversity of approaches it's possible to take to playing with math and sharing it.

Alison Forster is currently a high school math teacher at the Doane Stuart School in Albany, New York, where she teaches algebra, geometry, precalculus, and an elective of her own design called "Foundations of Mathematics." She got her start having fun with math with homeschoolers at the age of sixteen and never looked back.

Allison Cuttler is originally from New Jersey and fell in love with math at Haverford College, a small liberal arts school outside of Philadelphia. After completing her Masters in Applied Mathematics at the University of California, San Diego, she discovered her true passion for teaching math and programming at High Tech High Chula Vista, a project-based charter school serving San Diego's South Bay community. In the fall of 2011, she moved back to New Jersey and has been teaching at North Star Academy College Preparatory High School in Newark, New Jersey ever since. In her free time she enjoys ultimate frisbee and running, exploring local cuisine, and blogging at *infinigons.blogspot.com*.

Amanda Serenevy is the executive director of the Riverbend Community Math Center, an organization that promotes access to high-quality math education for people of all ages in north-central Indiana. In that capacity, Amanda presents hands-on math activities, leads workshops for teachers, and mentors elementary, high school, and undergraduate students. After teaching in Bob and Ellen Kaplan's Math Circle program in Boston, Amanda became active in the Math Circle movement, connecting mathematicians with young students interested in mathematics. In 2007, Amanda earned a Ph.D. from Boston University with a dissertation on the dynamics of networks of inhibitory neurons. She has published research on mathematical neuroscience and iterated matrix maps, and has additional research interests in geometric topology and mathematical origami.

Avery Pickford is currently a fifth and sixth grade math teacher in the San Francisco Bay Area, California, and the way he teaches math does not equal the way he was taught math. In his fifteen years of teaching he has had the pleasure of teaching math and science to students from third grade to graduate school. He is always eager to discuss progressive teaching, and is especially interested in student-posed problems. In addition to his love of math, he is also an amateur photographer.

Betina Zolkower is an associate professor at Brooklyn College (City University of New York) where she teaches methods and research courses for pre- and in-service middle- and high-school mathematics teachers and conducts research on the functional grammar of whole-group conversations in mathematics classrooms. Betina is the founding co-director of the Grupo Patagónico de Didáctica de la Matemática (*gpdmatematica.org.ar*), a lesson study/instructional design collective of teachers and teacher educators in Southern Argentina whose work is inspired by Hans Freudenthal's realistic mathematics education. Betina is also a photographer (*flickr.com/photos/27519060@N05/*).

Bob Kaplan has worked on mathematics with people from four up, most recently at Harvard University. In 1994, with his wife Ellen, he founded The Math Circle, a program open to all comers, for the enjoyment of pure mathematics. He has also taught philosophy, Greek, German, Sanskrit, and "Inspired Guessing." He is the author (as Robert Kaplan) of *The Nothing That Is: A Natural History of Zero* (Oxford 2000), and with his wife, *The Art of the Infinite: The Pleasures of Mathematics* (Oxford 2003), *Out of the Labyrinth: Setting Mathematics Free* (Oxford 2007), and *Hidden Harmonies: The Lives and Times of the Pythagorean Theorem* (Bloomsbury Press 2010). In the past year, the Kaplans have opened over a thousand Math Circles in Brazil, each aimed at the poorest sections of the country. The program is planned to expand over the next five years. Bob lives with his wife in Massachusetts, but plays cricket for the Grange Club in Scotland, where he first became acquainted with naught.

Carol Cross has worked in education for nearly thirty years. She is a Phi Beta Kappa graduate of the College of William and Mary, and earned a Masters in Education from George Washington University. Carol has taught classes in almost every discipline for students ranging from preschoolers to adults. She worked professionally in curriculum development and technology-assisted education until the birth of her son, when she became a part-time educational consultant and a full-time homeschooling mom. In addition to homeschooling and editing and other freelance educational assignments, Carol teaches classes through Heroic University (*HeroicUniversity.com*).

Chris Evans was trained as a Waldorf teacher and taught Waldorf kindergarten for seven years. She lives in rural northern Michigan, and homeschools her twin daughters. She is always on the lookout for ideas that will help her guide her daughters more effectively, and has been grateful for the chance to try out many of the ideas in this book.

Chris Shore teaches high school algebra, geometry, and an International Baccalaureate math course, effectively engaging adolescents in the mathematics classroom. Chris is the editor and publisher of The Math Projects Journal, a professional newsletter offering innovative math lessons, most of which are published as the book, MPJ's Ultimate Math Lessons. As a leader in implementing instructional change, Chris has made presentations nationwide to teachers and administrators on improving math instruction and raising standardized test scores. He is the department chair at his high school and has led his team to being the highest-performing school in the county. Chris is the 2001 California recipient of the Presidential Award for Excellence in Mathematics and Science Teaching.

Colleen King is the co-founder of a mathematics learning center where she teaches K–12 students the art of problem solving. Colleen's unique approach to math instruction includes computer programming, robotics, science projects, and role-playing games. Each class is an adventure and students enjoy the unpredictable learning experiences. Colleen is probably best known for her work *on MathPlayground.com*, a popular educational site for elementary and middle school students. Colleen's goal is to one day design a game that captures the collaborative problem solving and "hard fun" that takes place at her math center.

Dahlia Evans has always loved to draw and she loves to find cool patterns in math, so she was excited when Sue asked if she wanted to make some of the drawings for *Playing with Math*. Dahlia is an eleven-year-old homeschooler from northern Michigan.

Davide Cervone is a mathematician at Union College, specializing in geometry, who received his Ph.D. under Thomas Banchoff in 1993. Davide has been active in developing methods of communicating mathematics electronically, and is a key contributor to the MathJax and WeBWorK software products. He has also produced a number of mathematical artworks, most of these in collaboration with Thomas Banchoff, including a series exploring the torus in four-dimensional space, featured in the Scientific American Library volume "Beyond the Third Dimension" (1996). To see more, watch the animation: *math .brown.edu/~banchoff/art/PAC9603/tour/torus/torus.html*

Denise Gaskins says, "Math is not just rules and rote memory. It's like ice cream, with more flavors than you can imagine. And if all your children ever do is textbook math, that's like feeding them broccoli-flavored ice cream." As a veteran homeschooling mother of five who loves math, she wants to help other homeschoolers see the variety and richness of the subject. Denise writes the Let's Play Math blog (*LetsPlayMath.net*) and started the Math Teachers at Play blog carnival to share creative ideas for learning, teaching, and understanding math. She's also taught physics, which was just one story problem after another. What fun!

Dor Abrahamson is a professor of education at the University of California, Berkeley. He does research on how students learn mathematical concepts and invents systems for learning mathematics. These two strands of Dor's work come together in an approach called "design-based research," by which researchers can make contributions to both practice and theory. Dor is particularly interested in finding ways of helping children build on their intuition when they learn mathematics. When kids seem to get things "wrong," Dor looks for the grain of "right" in their intuition, and he creates systems that help kids connect these intuitions with formal mathematical ways of describing the world. Most of Dor's work has been on the concepts of proportionality and probability. Recently he has put out a free iPad app called the Mathematics Imagery Trainer for Proportion.

Elisa R. Vanett has been a creative writer for her entire life and is also an artist. She enjoys studying history and anthropology. She is currently going to a community college in South Bend, Indiana, and hopes to transfer to Saint Joseph's College in Rensselaer to study Mass Communication and Creative Writing. She hopes someday to share her story ideas with the world by being a scriptwriter for children's movies and publishing novels, poems, and comics.

Ellen Kaplan was a classical archaeologist through graduate school at Harvard and in Germany, and has also taught biology, Greek, Latin, and the history of many places and times. She began teaching mathematics to integrate an all-male department. But she was so delighted by the breadth and depth of the field that she ended up co-founding the Math Circle with her husband, illustrating his book, *The Nothing That Is* (Oxford 2000), and writing *The Art of the Infinite* (Oxford 2003), *Out of the Labyrinth: Setting Mathematics Free* (Oxford 2007), and *Hidden Harmonies: The Lives and Times of the Pythagorean Theorem* (Bloomsbury Press 2010) with him. With their son, Michael, she has written *Chances Are ... Adventures in Probability* (Viking 2006), and *Bozo Sapiens: Why to Err Is Human* (Bloomsbury 2009). They are at work on their third book. In the past year Ellen and Bob Kaplan have opened over a thousand Math Circles in Brazil, each aimed at the poorest sections of the country. The program is planned to expand over the next five years.

Erik Demaine is a computer scientist and an artist. Since 2001, he has been a professor in computer science at the Massachusetts Institute of Technology. Erik's research interests range throughout algorithms, from data structures for improving web searches to the geometry of understanding how proteins fold to the computational difficulty of playing games. He received a MacArthur Fellowship in 2003. Erik cowrote two books, *Geometric Folding Algorithms* (2007) and *Games, Puzzles, and Computation* (2009). He explores and creates mathematical art together with his father Martin, including curved origami sculptures in the permanent collections of the Museum of Modern Art in New York and the Renwick Gallery in the Smithsonian.

Ever Salazar has been teaching math and physics in Ciudad Guayana, Venezuela for four years. He has always been interested in math, and loves to solve puzzles from math competitions, which were his only source of real math in high school. When he turned nineteen, he discovered Martin Gardner's books, and since then his passion for math has been entangled with the need to show this awesomeness to other people. And when he discovered ViHart, MinutePhysics, CGPGrey, Veritasium and other educational channels on YouTube, he knew that was his place. He is currently teaching Calculus at Universidad Católica Andrés Bello and illustrating for the YouTube channel MinuteEarth.

Fawn Nguyen has been teaching geometry, algebra 1, and sixth-grade math for the last ten years at Mesa Union Junior High in Somis, California. Prior to teaching math, she was a middle-school science teacher for fourteen years. Inspired by her father, who taught math for over thirty years, Fawn has always had a deep love for mathematics, especially problem solving. She is passionate about making math accessible, relevant, and fun for students. She blogs about teaching at *FawnNguyen.com*. Fawn currently is a presenter of the University of California, Santa Barbara's Mathematics Project and is also helping to lead the Thousand Oaks Math Teachers' Circle.

Friedrich Knauss worked for close to two decades as a software engineer, and then decided to reboot his career, switching tracks to the teaching profession. Like most new teachers, he assumed that teaching was mostly a matter of presenting information in a clear and logical fashion, and the eager and hungry young minds would eat it up. It took one year at an inner-city Los Angeles school to realize that subject knowledge was the least part of teaching; he has been using his skills as an engineer and scientist to improve his craft ever since. He blogs at *blog.mathpl.us*.

George Hart is a research professor in the engineering school at Stony Brook University and a freelance mathematical sculptor/designer. He was a co-founder in creating and designing the Museum of Mathematics in New York City (momath.org). You can read more and see images of his artwork at georgehart.com. (Yes, he is related to Vi Hart—she's his daughter.)

Henry Segerman is an assistant professor in the Department of Mathematics at Oklahoma State University. His mathematical research is in three-dimensional geometry and topology. He is also a mathematical artist, working mostly in 3D printed sculpture. Other interests include procedural generation, self-reference, ambigrams, and puzzles.

Holly Rebekah Graff is an unschooling mom and former public school science teacher. She believes that every child deserves the freedom, time, and support necessary to pursue her passions and construct her own rich understanding of the world. She has worked with a diverse group of students, urban and rural, pre-kindergarten through high school, in a variety of settings from crowded urban classrooms to intimate groups of homeschoolers. She currently teaches science classes for homeschoolers at her home in the Catskills of New York. She blogs at Unschool Days (*UnschoolGirls.blogspot.com*) about the school-free lifestyle. Her interests include writing, theater, creating collage, swing dancing, snowboarding, baking, and gardening.

Jack Webster did his undergraduate degree in mathematics at Cambridge University, and is particularly interested in set theory and formal logic. He works in radio communications now as a programmer and mathematician. Jack blogs at *JaxWebster.wordpress.com*, where he has posted a number of other puzzles he has created.

James Tanton has been doing puzzles all his life. He's created *Math Without Words*, a lovely book of puzzles, along with a number of other books and videos taking a playful approach to math. You can find links to all of this and more at *JamesTanton.com*.

Jamylle Carter is a mathematician and a musician. She is a tenured mathematics professor at Diablo Valley College in Pleasant Hill, California. Before landing this position, Jamylle trekked all over the country for mathematics: bachelor's degree from Harvard University; Ph.D. from University of California, Los Angeles; and postdoctoral positions at a large public research university, a science museum, and two National Science Foundation mathematics institutes. She has published research on applied mathematics for image processing. Jamylle has also played piano since the age of five. A finalist in a Los Angeles songwriting competition, she has been a director, arranger, and pianist for choirs nationwide. Jamylle is currently a pianist and choir director for the East Bay Church of Religious Science in Oakland, California.

Jan Nordgreen started writing his blog, think again, in Santa Cruz, Bolivia. Through moves to France, the Cayman Islands, and back to Bolivia, and through hurricane Ivan, France Télécom, and satellite-only connections, he kept the blog going. During his two-year stay in Thailand, he renamed the blog "thnik again" and it shot to the number one Google result for "thnik." He currently resides in Lanzarote, Spain.

Jimmie Lanley is the mom of one creative daughter. After seven years of teaching in public schools, she became a stay-at-home mom when Mel was three years old and the whole family moved to China. She has taught Mel at home ever since. Her research into curricula and homeschooling philosophies led her to a Charlotte Mason style, which she finds very satisfying. Jimmie likes sewing, writing, traveling, and cooking from scratch. She blogs at *JimmiesCollage.com* and *NotebookingFairy.com*.

John Golden is a math teacher educator, elementary and secondary, at Grand Valley State University in West Michigan. He is interested in how people learn math and how to support teachers in the classroom, with particular interest in learning–math–game connections and dynamic geometry. He blogs at *MathHombre.blogspot.com*, tumbls at *MathHombre .tumblr.com*, and tweets from @mathhombre.

Jonathan Halabi lives in the Bronx, where he teaches high school math. He is the founding mathematics teacher at the High School of American Studies at Lehman College (2002) and designed and planned much of that school's curriculum. Jonathan has also taught college math, middle-school enrichment, and methods and content to preservice math teachers. He is a union activist, and is interested in problem solving, numbers, and social justice. He often speaks on mathematical problem solving.

Joshua Zucker is the founding director of the Julia Robinson Mathematics Festival, which brings deep, collaborative problem solving to a wide range of students. He discovered his love for number theory at Dr. Arnold Ross's summer program at Ohio State University over twenty years ago. Joshua taught at Stanford's Education Program for Gifted Youth, community colleges, and public and private high schools, before becoming a freelance math teacher. In 2006, he helped begin the Math Teachers' Circle project at the American Institute of Mathematics. He currently is a part-time instructor for the Art of Problem Solving, as well as a leader at several math circles in the San Francisco area.

Julia Brodsky is a homeschooling mom with three naughty and curious kids. When she is not with her family, she works as a rocket scientist for NASA Goddard, runs a weekly Art of Inquiry math circle for elementary school students (*ArtOfInquiry.net*), organizes the annual Math Kangaroo Olympiad for Montgomery County kids—and still keeps some sanity. She is constantly fascinated by the way children learn and solve problems. Julia grew up in Russia, where she was a mediocre student in one of the best math magnet schools of St. Petersburg. Later, she had a lot of fun working as an International Space Station astronauts' instructor at Johnson Space Center. Julia also enjoys writing poetry, hiking, and watching somebody else working instead of her.

Julie Brennan hosts the Living Math Forum, a five thousand-member Yahoo group engaged in discussion and sharing of math education experience and resources. Her website, *LivingMath.net*, is full of information on teaching and learning math in non-traditional ways. Julie's homeschooling experience is reflected in the site's content and articles, but many parents of schooled children and teachers also benefit from the information. Julie sells Living Math History lesson plans on the site, a fascinating approach to learning math through the study of the masters who discovered it. Julie worked professionally as a CPA and financial consultant prior to staying home with her four children. She currently teaches classes for homeschoolers.

Kaleb Allinson is a high school math teacher and the department head at Lake Stevens High School in Lake Stevens, Washington. He taught middle school during his first four years of teaching and has taught at the high school for eleven years. He currently teaches geometry, advanced algebra and AP calculus. Kaleb has always enjoyed attempting to solve problems that he has never seen before. When he's not teaching he's quite busy with his six energetic kids.

Kate Nowak teaches mathematics at Charlottesville High School in Charlottesville, Virginia. She has loved puzzles, logic, and origami from an early age. In addition to teaching for eight years, Kate has also written real-world lessons at Mathalicious, completed an engineering degree, and fixed airplanes for the U.S. Navy. She is passionate about showing kids that mathematics is fun and fascinating, and improving her craft in collaboration with colleagues around the globe. She has written the popular blog f(t) since 2007.

Lavinia Karl was unschooled. She earned a B.A. in math from Knox College. Now she's in her twenties, exploring life's possibilities.

Linda Palter is a chiropractor in West Michigan. She can also be found square dancing, crafting, and playing fetch and frisbee with a very high-energy dog.

Luyi Zhang is presently an undergraduate math major at the Massachusetts Institute of Technology and an instructor of online math courses at Art of Problem Solving. In middle and high school, she participated in numerous math contests, placing in the top ten statewide in MATHCOUNTS and qualifying for the USA Math Olympiad. She has taught middle-school students through Breakthrough Collaborative and has worked with gifted students at the math camps MathPath and Epsilon. She blogs about her original geometric creations, such as Sierpinski triangle brownies and beaded teddy bears, on her website, Geometric Delights (*GeometricDelights.wordpress.com*).

Malke Rosenfeld is a percussive dance teaching artist, math explorer, curriculum designer, editor, and writer. Her interdisciplinary inquiry focuses on the intersections between percussive dance and mathematics and how to best illustrate these connections for students. In her Math in Your Feet program, percussive dance becomes the platform for a robust choreographic inquiry into mathematical thinking, practices, and topics. You can find out more about Malke's many collaborative math and making projects at *MalkeRosenfeld.com.*

Dr. Maria Droujkova is a curriculum developer and mathematics education consultant. Natural Math, the research and development company Maria founded in 2001, is leading an international community where researchers and developers join parents and teachers in making mathematics their own.

Martin Demaine is an artist and a computer scientist. He started the first private hot glass studio in Canada and has been called the father of Canadian glass. Since 2005, he has been the Angelika and Barton Weller Artist-in-Residence at the Massachusetts Institute of Technology. Martin works together with his son Erik in paper, glass, and other material. They use their exploration in sculpture to help visualize and understand unsolved problems in mathematics, and their scientific abilities to inspire new art forms. Their artistic work includes curved origami sculptures in the permanent collections of the Museum of Modern Art in New York and the Renwick Gallery in the Smithsonian. Their scientific work includes over sixty published joint papers. They recently won a Guggenheim Fellowship (2013) for exploring folding of other materials, such as hot glass.

Mary O'Keeffe is a founding advisor of Albany Area Math Circle, a wonderful community of problem solvers with whom she has been happily making mistakes since 2001. She is also a public policy economist, specializing in public finance and mathematical economics. She teaches economics at Union College in Schenectady, New York, where her students run a free Volunteer Income Tax Assistance (VITA) site for low-income working families, people with disabilities, and senior citizens. She is also the Associate Director of the Math Prize for Girls, which brings together hundreds of young women from across the U.S. and Canada for a celebration of extreme problem solving each year. Her latest initiative is launching the Guerrilla Math Circles movement.

MATHmaniaCS, created by Lenny Pitt, Cinda Heeren, and Tom Magliery, is a project for people exhibiting an excessive passion for MATHematics and Computer Science. The goal of MATHmaniaCS (*MathManiacs.org*) is to bring the fun side of mathematics and computer science to kids of all ages. Their activities include developing engaging educational activities involving discrete math and computer science, and spreading these activities to teachers via workshops and other programs. Lenny and Cinda are educators, researchers, and collaborators at the University of Illinois in the Department of Computer Science. Tom used to play math games with them in person, but departed for the world of commercial software development and now contents himself with participation from afar.

Maurine Starkey is a professional illustrator and game designer. She won the 2012 Hugo award for Best Fan Artist. She shows her artwork at *MyStarkey.deviantart.com/gallery*.

Dr. Melanie Hayes has made it her life's work to help gifted and 2e children find their niche and achieve their goals. She is passionate about creating a world where all children are encouraged to wonder, explore, and think. Melanie holds a doctorate in educational leadership with an emphasis on the intellectual, social, and emotional needs of gifted and talented children. She is also a credentialed teacher and educational consultant with experience in evaluation, assessment, intervention, professional development, teaching, and mentoring. Melanie has gifted twins, so she experiences life with gifted children on a personal level as well, both the joys and the hardships. She writes about her work and family on her blog, Life Among the Gifted, at *MJHayes .wordpress.com*. Melanie homeschools her children and enjoys watching them learn and grow through their daily activities. She loves to travel, paint, sculpt, garden, write, and hike in the wilds.

Michael Hartley, creator of Dr. Mike's Math Games for Kids (*dr-mikes-math-games-for-kids.com*), was raised in Perth, Western Australia. He's loved math since he was a child, so it was natural for him to do a Ph.D. in mathematics, in a branch of geometry. After a ten-year stint teaching in colleges and universities in Malaysia, he returned to Perth to work as a mathematician in the oil and gas industry.

Michelle Martin is a public school teacher at Prairie Creek Community School in Northfield, Minnesota, where she works with a class of fourth and fifth graders. She loves having the opportunity to weave math and other subjects together. Her favorite moments are those when students glimpse the wonder and awe of mathematics. She writes about the work of her class at *PrairieCreek.typepad.com/herons*.

Nancy Blachman strives to make math cool, fun, and engaging, finding her inspiration in the work of Vi Hart and Martin Gardner. Nancy is co-founder of the Nueva Math Circle, and the Julia Robinson Mathematics Festival, and is on the board for the Gathering for Gardner. Nancy has taught after-school math classes and math camp for four years and Mathematica classes for ten years. Nancy earned a B.Sc. in Mathematics from the University of Birmingham, UK, a Masters in Operations Research from the University of California at Berkeley, and a Masters in Computer Science from Stanford University.

Pam Sorooshian has been teaching college-level economics and statistics since 1976. She's also been a homeschooling mom to three now-grown children. Pam is a proponent of unschooling, in which there are no lessons, assignments, tests, or grades, and children learn naturally while following their own interests with the encouragement and strong support of their parents. Pam has been a speaker at many homeschooling conferences and an American Educational Research Association conference, and is on the Boards of Directors of the National Home Education Network and the HomeSchool Association of California.

Paul Salomon is a math nerd.teacher.artist living in Saint Louis. He designed his imbalance problems during his time at Saint Ann's School in Brooklyn, where he taught math to grades five through twelve and helped develop a mathematical art program. Paul shares his own mathematical art through Twitter (@lostinrecursion) and his blog, Lost in Recursion (*LostInRecursion.wordpress.com*). Paul also coauthors Math Munch (*MathMunch.org*), a weekly math blog written with middle schoolers in mind, aimed at helping them dig in to the mathematical world that exists outside of math class.

Pilar Bewley holds two AMI Montessori certifications (ages three to six and six to twelve), as well as a M.Ed. in Montessori Education. A self-professed "math hater" from childhood, she discovered the beauty of mathematics and geometry during her Montessori training courses. She lives with her math geek husband and Montessori baby in San Diego, California.

Ray Droujkov is a self-directed autodidactic learner who routinely wears a wide variety of hats—among them, that of game designer, technical writer, poet, world traveler, editor, and illustrator.

Rodi Steinig is the founder, director, and leader of the Talking Stick Math Circle. Her goal is to awaken the inner mathematician and to shepherd the unfolding of abstract reasoning in every child. Her formal training is in economics and education. Rodi continues to hone her craft of math circle leadership under the gentle guidance of Bob and Ellen Kaplan. Her mathematical interests are logic, history, hydrodynamics, sacred geometry, the misapplication of statistics, and the expression of mathematical concepts via multiple modalities. Rodi blogs at *TalkingStickLearningCenter.org/category/math-circle-blog*.

Sean Sweeney currently teaches high school algebra and calculus just outside of Philadelphia, Pennsylvania at Woodlynde School, a college prep school for students with learning disabilities. He constantly looks for exciting ways to engage students in math who have often had bad experiences with it in the past. More activities, ideas and songs from Sean can be found at *SweeneyMath.blogspot.com*.

Stephen Kennedy first learned the pleasures of mathematics at Stonehill College in Massachusetts and ever since has wondered why nobody told him earlier. He teaches mathematics at Carleton College in Northfield, Minnesota. He co-directs the Carleton College Summer Mathematics Program for Women and served a five-year stint as co-editor of the Mathematical Association of America's magazine for undergraduates, *Math Horizons*.

Sue VanHattum has been teaching math at the community college level for over twenty years, and recently branched out to teach math at her son's freeschool. She created the Richmond Math Salon, a monthly event she hosted at her home, gathering kids and their parents together to play with math. She blogs about math and math education at *MathMamaWrites.blogspot.com*. Sue appreciates both the community-building possibilities inherent in public schools, and the freedom to learn naturally available through homeschooling. Outside of math, teaching, and writing, her interests include gardening, living simply, activism for the rights of all, and children's books. Sue is a single parent, raising one son.

Tanya Khovanova received her Ph.D. in Mathematics from Moscow State University in 1988. At that time her research interests were in representation theory, integrable systems, super-string theory, and quantum groups. Her research was interrupted by a period of employment in industry, where she became interested in algorithms, complexity theory, cryptography, and networks. Several years ago she resigned from industry to return to research. Her current interests lie in combinatorics, number theory, probability theory, and recreational mathematics. Her website is located at *TanyaKhovanova.com*, her highly popular math blog at *blog.TanyaKhovanova.com*, and her Number Gossip website at *NumberGossip.com*.

Thomas Banchoff is a mathematician at Brown University specializing in geometry, who has explored four-dimensional space using the tools of differential geometry. He is also an artist. His joint work with Davide Cervone includes a series exploring the torus in four-dimensional space, featured in the Scientific American Library volume "Beyond the Third Dimension" (1996). To see more, watch the animation: *math.brown .edu/~banchoff/art/PAC-9603/tour/torus/torus.html*

Tiffani Bearup used to be a pretty average, run-of-the-mill, standard-issue mom trying to figure out life in suburbia and her place in it. Then she started unschooling, and things got a little crazy! Crazy good! As this book went to press, she and her three kids were all traveling through South America. She blogs at *FreePlayLife.com*.

Acknowledgements

First, my thanks to all the people doing cool free math stuff online. This book was created through the Internet—I am grateful that it exists. Thanks to Maria Droujkova for being the first to say yes and for patiently guiding the book through its many stages. Thanks to Chris Evans for being my first reader and offering so much great feedback to me and all the authors. Thanks to Contra Costa College for providing me with a sabbatical year—what an amazing privilege!

I am so grateful to each of the authors and artists in this book for coming on this adventure with me—look what we did together! Carol Cross went above and beyond in her role as copyeditor. Most importantly, thanks to my son for putting up with my computer coming between us so much for the past five years—I promise to be with you more for the next five.

Of course there are too many more people to thank. Here's my best attempt…

- People from Living Math Forum, who came through so many times: joining the reader response team and the index team, and individually answering my many questions. My eternal thanks to Julie Brennan for hosting this amazing resource.

- The Reader Response Team, who shaped up the manuscript from a loose collection to a tight, focused book: Basia, Charley, Christie, Cindy, Craig, Danielle, Doug, Dru, Elizabeth, George, Heather, Jack, Jamie, Jason, Jennifer, Julie, Rodi, Shalynn, Steve, and Tammie.

- The Indexers: Christiane, Diane, Dru, Heather, Rachel, and Yee Wah got us started, and Susan Cohen guided me through the process of making a more professional index.

- My family: Ma, Andrew, Alexa, Jeff, Dan, and David offered edits. Ma, Pa, Mary, Jeff, Andrew, Alexa, and David allowed me to go off for a week each summer to the math circle institute. As a single parent I have been quite tied to my son; it made a huge difference in my life to have their help.

- Friends: Linda Palter's artwork was inspiring and showed me how much my friends would add to this book. Melanie Hayes was my sounding board through many months of work, Lani Ka'ahumanu helped me improve my first book proposal. Chris Evans helped me to help the authors improve their work, recruited her daughter into the team of illustrators, and generally held my hand throughout.

- Bloggers: John Golden (now a good friend) helped me think about games and math, and improved a number of my chapters. (Who edits the editor? John does.) Owen Thomas cheered me on from start to finish, Laura Grace Weldon encouraged me to think big. JoAnne Growney helped with the layout of Math Is Not Linear. When I was stuck, Bret Benesh and Angela Vierling-Claassen helped me finish Supporting Girls.

- My student, Jay Selke, helped flesh out the Book Picks section, and accompanied me on a detective hunt at UC Berkeley's graduate library, searching for more information on L.P. Benezet.

- Wildcat Community FreeSchool gave me the opportunity to teach young kids, which is a big part of what started me on this amazing journey.

- Andy Ross answered about a dozen emails, giving me the kind of help an agent gives, even though he didn't want to be my agent.

- Catahoula Coffee and Jimmie Bean's provided wireless access and coffee, along with a friendly community atmosphere for a change of pace from the recliner where I did most of my work.

Where Is the Index?

One of the delights of publishing under the open Creative Commons license (in contrast with copyright) is that we can make a digital version of this book easily available to you, so you can use electronic search facilities. We hope you will enjoy looking up ideas and finding your half-remembered gems this way.

To download a searchable copy of this book, go to: playingwithmath .org/thebook

CPSIA information can be obtained at www.ICGtesting.com
Printed in the USA
BVOW09s1135170315

391977BV00003B/8/P